Emily Ripley Barnes

Narratives, traditions and personal reminiiscences connected with the early history of the Bellows family, and of the village of Walpole

Emily Ripley Barnes

Narratives, traditions and personal reminiscences connected with the early history of the Bellows family, and of the village of Walpole

ISBN/EAN: 9783337086091

Printed in Europe, USA, Canada, Australia, Japan

Cover: Foto ©ninafisch / pixelio.de

More available books at **www.hansebooks.com**

[*Inscription on the south side of the Monument:*]

COL. BENJAMIN BELLOWS,

A WISE, COURAGEOUS, AND HONEST MAN,

BY A LARGE HOSPITALITY,

BY FAITHFULNESS AND ABILITY IN PUBLIC TRUSTS,

BY BRAVELY PROTECTING,

PRUDENTLY COUNSELLING, AND LIBERALLY AIDING

THE FRONTIER SETTLERS,

GAINED

THE RESPECT AND LOVE OF HIS CONTEMPORARIES,

AND MADE HIMSELF A PATTERN

FOR THOSE WHO SEEK TO BE

FATHERS OF COMMUNITIES.

[*Inscription on the north side:*]

TO THE MEMORY OF

BENJAMIN BELLOWS,

THE FOUNDER OF WALPOLE,

WHO DIED 10 JULY, 1777,

AGED SIXTY-TWO YEARS,

THIS MONUMENT WAS ERECTED

IN THE YEAR 1854,

BY HIS NUMEROUS DESCENDANTS.

MEDALLION ON THE WEST SIDE.

ON THE EAST.

ARMS OF THE FAMILY OF BELLOWS OF U.S.N. AMERICA, FROM ENGLISH BELLOWES OF LANCASHIRE, CORRUPTED FROM THE BELLEWS OF DEVONSHIRE AND IRELAND, FROM THE NORMAN DE BELLESEAUX.

Narratives, Traditions

AND

PERSONAL REMINISCENCES

CONNECTED WITH THE EARLY HISTORY OF THE BELLOWS
FAMILY AND OF THE VILLAGE OF WALPOLE,
NEW HAMPSHIRE.

BY

Mrs. EMILY R. BARNES,

THE OLDEST SURVIVING DESCENDANT OF COL. BENJAMIN BELLOWS, THE
FIRST SETTLER OF THE TOWN.

BOSTON:
GEO. H. ELLIS, 141 FRANKLIN STREET.
1888.

PREFACE.

WALPOLE, N.H., November, 1886.

A BRIEF historical sketch of our race was given by Rev. Dr. H. W. Bellows, at the time of the consecration of the monument erected to our common progenitor, Col. Benjamin Bellows, in 1854. A few copies of this were printed, and eagerly purchased, by those who could be served from so limited a number.

Since that time, more than twenty years ago, this book has been widely sought by our kindred wishing to obtain more knowledge of their ancestors; and I have often been urged to supplement that sketch with my own recollections, as I am now the oldest living descendant.

In complying with this request, I have found a pleasant occupation in these last years of my darkened life; and I would say to the kindred who may read these pages, do not criticise too severely the work of one who has attained nearly eighty-six years of age, and who for many years past has been almost totally blind. I may add, that I have drawn almost entirely upon my own recollections, and not upon manuscript records or printed matter, for whatever this book may contain. But, as Dr. Bellows' address at the family gathering, in 1854, garnered up much which properly belongs to this present narrative, I have felt at liberty to make such extracts from the account of the family as seemed of service in carrying out my plan.

Your friend and kinswoman,

EMILY R. BARNES.

[The following note accompanied the circular which was sent to relatives and friends. It is inserted here, as setting forth the character of this volume, as looked at by one of the kindred who was familiar with many of the facts and scenes that are there introduced.]

NOTE.

BY REV. FREDERICK N. KNAPP, OF PLYMOUTH, MASS.

I have read the manuscript which Mrs. Barnes has prepared for publication, entitled "Narratives, Traditions, and Personal Reminiscences connected with the Early History of the Bellows Family, and of the Village of Walpole, N.H."

I commend the book most cordially to all our friends and kindred. It is a book peculiar in its design and treatment. It would be open to all sorts of criticism from a person who should read it for the purpose of reviewing it, either as a history, or as a biography, or as a story; and yet the very features which would thus subject it to criticism are just what give the book its attractiveness and interest to members of the family.

It is nothing more nor less than a rambling talk about the old folks who have gone and the younger ones, now old, when they were children; what they did, and said, and were; where and how they lived; whom they married, and when they died; how they helped themselves, and helped one another, and helped the community around them; how, as a family, spreading wider and wider with each generation, they were still closely knit together by strong family feeling and by marked inherited characteristics; how the emergencies of earlier pioneer life were met, while the refinements and amenities of social life were never lost or forgotten; how the growth and prosperity of the town, which the original settler, Col. Bellows, had founded, were the constant thought of himself and of his descendants; who some of the marked men and women of the town were, outside the family, but helping with them to fill up the picture of those times.

There seems to be nothing to be designated as a regular plan or system in the arrangement or the treatment of topics in this book. It is, as I have said, more like a talk; as if one who had seen and remembered actual events of nearly a century, and had at her command all the traditions which had come down to her quick ears from her great-grandparents,— as if such a one, seated in her easy-chair at a social family gathering, were called upon, first by this one of the kindred, then by another, from all the various branches, without any order of coming, and asked to tell all she knew about their immediate ancestors, especially if she recollected anything about them in childhood, or as youths and maidens, their ways and doings and personal appearance. It is as if, thus surrounded and thus seated, in the quiet dignity of old age and in the sacred and tender confidence of home-life and kindred sympathies,— thus called upon,— she were, in her own free, conversational way, to tell of this person, then of that one, and of the times in which they all lived.

Such seems to me the only "method" which is evident in the writing of this book; namely, absence of all method, excepting such as directs a fireside talk, when the topic is one of common and hearty interest to all who ask the questions and who listen.

Thus written, the same individual may be referred to in perhaps a dozen different places, and at times far apart, as connected with this or that incident; and, too, one who perhaps chronologically ought to have appeared early in the book comes in much later, for the simple and sufficient reason that he was best remembered in connection with some event or story which was just at that moment recalled to the mind of the writer.

One other point I may mention. Prepared in this way, there are innumerable instances in this narrative where the eccentricities of individuals, the home-life, and the more homely phases of life, too, with their embarrassments, failures, and disappointments, are set forth with the simplicity which would mark a free talk among friends,— incidents altogether too trivial in themselves and too personal to be introduced into a book written for the reading public.

I make these statements in regard to what the book is, and also in regard to what it is not (and does not profess to be or wish to be), not so much to forestall criticism as to present to friends and kindred what I hold to be the peculiar feature of attractiveness in this volume, dedicated as it is to those only who cherish the sentiments which gather around the thought of an old family homestead.

It must be fully borne in mind, that these narratives deal almost entirely with those of the kindred who have gone; and that none of the descendants, now living, are named, excepting incidentally in connection with some incident or record of their ancestors. Hence, any individual reading these pages must not be disappointed, or feel overlooked, if he does not find his own name registered, or any mention in detail of his immediate family, however large a place such name or family might rightfully claim in a history brought down to the present date.

And there is another thing that must also be borne in mind; it is this, that the writer, drawing her material chiefly from her own store of personal recollections, will naturally have a great deal more to say in regard to her own particular branch of the family than concerning those with whom she was not in daily contact, although those other branches, perhaps, would furnish equally interesting illustrations of the strongly marked characteristics of the individuals, and of the habits and life of the times in which they lived, provided similar reminiscences could be recorded of their sayings, doings, and familiar social intercourses and home-life.

F. N. KNAPP.

PERSONAL REMINISCENCES.

CHAPTER I.

ACCORDING to the best information we can obtain, the first Bellows of whom any trace can be found in America was John Bellows, who embarked in the "Hopewell," of London, for New England, April 1, 1635. He is entered in the list of passengers as "John Bellows, aged twelve." He married Mary Wood, at Concord, Mass., May 9, 1665, and was the grandfather of Col. Benjamin Bellows, the founder of Walpole, N.H. John Bellows had ten children, the youngest of whom was Benjamin, born 1677. He married, in 1704, Widow Willard, of Lancaster, Mass. Her maiden name was Dorcas Cutler. Their son Benjamin was born May 26, 1712.

The family soon moved to Lunenburg, where the mother died, at an advanced age, in 1747. The town records of Lunenburg furnish abundant evidence of the public spirit and importance of both the father of our founder and of his son. The old homestead occupied by the son Benjamin, and probably by his father before him, is still standing. It is located in the centre of the town, and was connected with a well-tilled farm of eight hundred acres. It was in 1735, October 7, that the son Benjamin married Abigail

Stearns, the sister of the first settled minister of Lunenburg. In 1754, he moved with his family to the valley of the Connecticut, and founded the town of Walpole, N.H.

He seems to have been led to locate at Walpole under the following influences: his father had, in 1736, been one of a committee appointed by the governor of Massachusetts to lay out towns on Connecticut River. Through him the son doubtless learned of the exceeding fertility and beauty of this section. Afterward, prior to 1750, there was a controversy between New Hampshire and Massachusetts as to their boundary line; and a commissioner, with an engineer or surveyor, was appointed by each State to meet together, run out, and settle the division line. Col. Benjamin Bellows, of Lunenburg — for the son had now obtained this military position — was appointed the surveyor on the part of Massachusetts. Thus he made the acquaintance of Benning Wentworth, the governor of New Hampshire, who offered him, if he would settle there, the choice of the unappropriated townships. Thus, in connection with his brother-in-law, Col. Jonathan Blanchard, and Col. Theodore Atkinson, he obtained his charter, removed from Lunenburg in 1753, built a fort, and organized a town government. For several years, during the Indian wars, the family were obliged to live in a garrison. He retained his valuable estate in Lunenburg, which he afterward, by will, bequeathed to his youngest son Joseph. Col. Bellows soon bought up the larger part of the rights of his associates, as named in the charter, and thus virtually controlled the entire township of Walpole. At this time, his family consisted of himself and wife and five children : Abigail, the oldest, seventeen years of age; Peter, fourteen; Benjamin, thirteen; John, eleven; and Joseph, nine years old. The wife died in 1757, and was the first tenant of the burying-ground. She was a woman noted for her force of character, her piety, and her motherly tenderness.

The garrison house or fort, in which the family lived, was built of logs and earth, and surrounded by an outer palisade. Although a private house, it was so important as to be named among the fortresses on the river, and formed one in the regular line of defences. The other fortresses were maintained at the public expense. This garrison house was a hundred feet long and twenty feet wide, with an L of nearly half that size. In 1755, we find that Col. Bellows had within his fort, beside his immediate family, thirty men employed in his service, who went out to their work daily in the fields or at the mill, with their muskets in their hands. I give this picture of the position of Col. Bellows' early dwelling, in order to convey some idea of the sacrifices which were voluntarily made by those who, as pioneers, left a home of comfort and abundance, to plant a new community.

In 1758, Col. Bellows had married, as his second wife, Widow Jennison, whose maiden name was Mary Hubbard, a sister of the wife of Parson Stearns, of Lunenburg. Their children were: Abigail, 2d, Theodore, Thomas, Mary, Josiah; so that at the time of his death, in 1777, Col. Bellows had nine children living, the youngest being ten years old. The Walpole newspaper of February, 1794, contained the following notice : —

"Died in this town, the 21st inst., Madam Mary

Bellows, in the sixty-ninth year of her age, relict of the late Col. Benjamin Bellows. As he had been a father and chief proprietor of the town, so she was a mother in our Israel. She was a woman of exemplary piety, who made it her endeavor to keep a conscience void of offence, both toward God and man; a steady attendant upon the public worship of God, and observer of the institutions of the gospel; an excellent economist, and a charitable friend to the industrious poor. In her death, the town hath lost one who contributed much, in her sphere, to the building it up in its infant state. As a wife, she loved and reverenced her husband, and in her widowhood behaved with wisdom and propriety. She was an indulgent as well as exemplary parent to her numerous descendants, who have cause to rise up and call her blessed. 'Blessed are the dead that die in the Lord!' and their memory is precious. Her funeral was attended by a great concourse of people, from within town and without."

I have felt that these few pages, partly historical, might seem a fit introduction to my somewhat rambling narratives, which are now to follow; which, be it remembered, I do not attempt to present in any chronological order, but merely as, one by one, they come to me.

CHAPTER II.

In recording the memories of so many years, leading back to an early period in my life, I shall put down my recollections of persons and events just as they occur to my mind; and, in gathering these scattered fragments of the records of our race, it can easily be imagined how unsatisfying this banquet of memories may prove to many, who, coming to learn a little, may have a keener appetite awakened for more knowledge of their ancestors. Yet I trust that these homely affairs of every-day life, when viewed from such a distance, may not seem without interest and importance. The stories written on the following pages are the simple narratives of incidents and events, of most of which I have had personal knowledge.

The traditions of our great-grandparents' home-life always held out an especial attraction to me, and I once had a glimpse given me into this ancient abode, which my young imagination had always filled with beings quite unlike other people. My child-mind had taken strange fancies, when listening to the stories that were related of the perils and dangers encountered, while converting a wilderness into this lovely town, which has been the birthplace and home of so many of our kindred.

It was my Uncle Ben, when in a mood to tell stories of his boyhood, who gave me an account of an early visit he once made to these grandparents. "I don't think," he said, "I was ever much of a boy, as I look back upon the time when I should have been one." He was quite young in years when called upon to perform tasks for which much older boys at this time would not be thought competent. He was not twelve years of age when his father sent him from Lunenburg, Mass., to Walpole, N.H., to carry an important business message to his grandfather. It was in November, and the weather cold for such a ride on horseback. There was no other way of travelling at that time. His mother, with some misgivings, prepared him as comfortably as she could for the journey, drawing a pair of his father's long woollen stockings over his legs and shoes, and lining his mittens with fur. With a few other preparations for his comfort, he set out with all a boy's enthusiasm for an unknown country, mostly through the woods. His father directed him to reach a certain place the first day, and there put up for the night. He was very plucky, bravely bearing the cold and fatigue until within a few miles of the desired haven, when he suddenly broke down, and, seeing a comfortable looking farm-house not far distant, on reaching it drew rein, and, with a few tears and some explanations, asked a motherly-looking woman who came to the door if he could have supper, and stay that night. She quickly bade him dismount and give his horse to the little boy, who stood with a look of vague curiosity, examining this young traveller. He followed the woman into the house, when she soon took off his wrappings, and brought him before a huge fireplace, in which was blazing one of those fires of the olden time, such as we never see, but only hear about, in these days. The warmth was very grateful, but still more so was a large pot of boiled corn,—the unfailing supply of those days,—hanging on the crane. It had evidently been cooking through the day for the evening meal. His look in that direction was quickly interpreted; and a bowl of milk, with a generous portion of hulled corn, was placed in his hand; and my uncle said, although so many years had elapsed, he had not lost the sweetness and savor of that delicious repast.

After a good night's rest and a substantial breakfast, he set out again on his weary and lonely journey. He met with no startling adventures, beyond occasionally, though seldom, meeting some one travelling in the same manner as himself, over a long, lonely stretch of road. A pedestrian inquired where he was going. He quietly answered, "To Walpole, N.H."—"Guess so," the man gruffly said. "And what are you going there for?"—"That is my business, and none of yours," he answered, giving his horse a spur, putting some distance between himself and his questioner in a short time.

He reached his grandfather's home at dusk, the second day. The old gentleman received him with much surprise, but great kindness, patting him on the head, with evident pride to find in the boy so much courage and endurance at such an early age. When supper was ready, his grandfather ordered a chair to be placed beside his own for the boy who had come alone from Lunenburg, on horseback, at this inclement season. When he had taken this seat of honor, he became so strongly impressed with the magnitude of the table and the great number of persons surrounding it, that a feeling of shyness took possession of him, and for a few minutes he would have preferred going without his supper. The old gentleman, who kept his eye upon him, observing this, commenced talking merrily, evidently for the purpose of reassuring him; and, loading his plate, at the same time, with a marvellous slice of steak and a potato plentifully covered with gravy, the temptation proved irresistible, and his appetite got the better of his bashfulness. When he had gained courage to look about, he was not surprised at the variety or bountifulness of that hospitable board; for he was accustomed to all that at home,— the only difference, it was not on quite so large a scale. His father didn't kill a beef creature every week, as was done here.

After thanks being given by the chaplain of the family, one of the sons removed his father's chair to its usual place, and he called my uncle to come and sit by him, as he wanted to make some inquiries. He then asked about everybody and everything at his home, and then told him to give all the particulars of his journey, which he did, not omitting the answer he gave the man who inquired what his business might be. His grandfather, patting him, laughingly said, "That was right, my boy; never feel compelled to answer impertinent questions."

The old gentleman then called for his pipe, which his wife filled and brought to him, seemingly as a labor of love on her part, as she sat down quietly by his side with her knitting, and watched the curling smoke as it went upward; and who can tell what thoughts accompanied it?

After one or two naps in a big chair in which my uncle was seated during the process of smoking, he suddenly awoke to the consciousness that the duties of that day were coming to a close. The grandfather was giving some directions to one of his sons, and the grandmother was bustling about with seemingly a good deal of business on her hands. The subject of breakfast was discussed with the girls, and other matters arranged for the morrow, when she turned to her husband, saying, "All is ready," and then seated herself in a chair which she drew close to his side, placing her hand in his, which he tenderly took; then a tall, grave-looking man arose with the younger members of the household, who had all come in to this evening service of prayer.

There were a few last things to be attended to after this. Josiah, then a lad of ten, was called by his mother to unbuckle his father's shoes, and turning to my uncle, she said, "I guess you can hunt the cat and bring her to me, and also the broom." It was her custom, according to an old-time fancy, to examine old puss, to make sure that no stray coal of fire had lighted on her back. And the broom was thoroughly inspected, fearing some latent spark might be concealed somewhere, in readiness to burst into a blaze as soon as they had all retired. It is a tradition that our grandmother daily declared, "They will all be burned up, sometime."

My uncle then, as ever afterward, had a keen sense of the ridiculous; and I have thought his humorous way of telling this story, as no one else could, giving a description of his wonderful activity in catching the poor frightened creature, has done much toward perpetuating the tradition of this particular weakness of Uncle Ben's grandmother.

CHAPTER III.

There were seven sons and two daughters in our great-grandfather's, Col. Benjamin Bellows' family, all of whom I distinctly remember except three, Peter, Benjamin, and Theodore. Although I had no personal knowledge of these three uncles, I learned a great deal about them through other members of the family.

My grandmother would relate the particulars of some of her visits to this parental home, when she and her husband would think they could safely leave home by bringing two of the youngest children with them; and on these occasions it was expected they would visit, in turn, all the brothers also. Peter, the eldest son, who had married into a highly respectable family in Charlestown, N.H., made his residence in that place, having a large farm which his father assigned to him.

I can remember nothing of Uncle Theodore but a few traditional anecdotes. He was a man of mighty proportions and Herculean strength,— a warning to all to beware how they aroused that sleeping lion, which on suitable provocation could bid defiance to a dozen common men. It is a tradition, that he stored many barrels of cider each year for his own use, and would take them into the cellar on his shoulder as easily as most people could a pail of water.

I have only a vague recollection of Uncle Benjamin, better known as "Uncle General." I could not have

been much more than two years old when I made the
attempt to crawl through a very narrow space, under
the gate, that led into his front yard; but it only
proved sufficient to admit head and shoulders, and then
the struggle commenced, as also did the terror in being
caught in such a trap. It was Uncle General who
released and carried me in his arms into the house,
where I was beguiled out of my trouble by a watch
held to my ear, and the bright buttons on his coat-
sleeve held up for my admiration. I suppose these
circumstances, also his kindliness, which children so
quickly recognize, served at that moment to impress
him forever on my memory. He died in that year; but
"Aunt General," as every one called her, lived until
I was sixteen years old. Her maiden name was Phebe
Strong, and she was the sister of Gov. Strong, of
Massachusetts. How well I remember her tall figure
and imposing dignity; but still better the long sermons
I was sent to read to her on Sabbath afternoons. I
think it will not be irreverent to admit that I was more
deeply impressed at that time with the length than the
sentiment they contained, frequently reaching to the
sixthlies and seventhlies; and I can now see the
wearied look on her face as she reverently listened
to the close. She would then say, "Thank you, child.
I think Parson Fessenden gives us pretty lengthy dis-
courses." She was an invalid a long time, and eventually had paralysis, losing the use of one arm entirely
for two or three years before she died. She had an
efficient and devoted attendant in a person by the
name of Maria Smith. I shall never forget the great
happiness we all had in planning for a visit, which was
brought about with some little difficulty. Aunt Louisa,

who had come from Boston to spend the summer with her brother, Mr. Abel Bellows, with whom my grandmother resided, was also deeply interested, knowing what pleasure it would give her mother to receive one more visit from this much beloved sister-in-law, "Aunt General," the widow, too, of that brother whom they had all loved so much. The difficult problem to be solved was, How shall we bring her, helpless as she is? Aunt Louisa disposed of that difficulty very quickly. She was always full of resources for all emergencies, and said at once, "Why not bring her in a sleigh? No matter if it is not sleighing; it is only a short distance."

Very soon a plenty of stout and loving arms were volunteered to draw her over, and a nicely cushioned arm-chair was set in a large sleigh, and she came to the door in great state, and was most enthusiastically received; for it was, indeed, a triumph to get Aunt General out of her room, where she had been so long a prisoner. Each one, old and young, entered into the spirit of the occasion. My grandmother was particularly animated, it was an event so unexpected; and Aunt Louisa, who knew so well how to use her fine powers of conversation, was made, in the excitement, to almost surpass herself. And now this dear old aunt, such a strong-minded woman, and for whom we always had so much reverent respect, was once more a child, and broke entirely down at the expression of so much kindness. There was one little shadow cast over all this cheerfulness; the thought would come that this was in all probability her last outing. Our foreboding proved only too true. When the next springtime came, a little bird would come and sit on the garden gate, and call, in its own plaintive tones, the name of her who had so recently gone away; and my grandmother, tearfully listening, would say, in subdued tones, "Phebe can never come back to us, but we are going to her."

For many years before her death, Aunt General,— it was customary to distinguish these aunts by giving them their husbands' titles,— with only one attendant, occupied this home to which she was brought on coming to Walpole, having known no other since leaving the home of her girlhood. But what a picture of desolation to those who had once shared its hospitalities, who had once sat in that large family circle around the old hearth-stone, made even more inviting by the bright brass fire-dogs and polished hearth! And who knows how many stories of early perils and hair-breadth escapes may have been related, not forgetting old Deacon Foster's humorous anecdotes and sometimes very funny poetry!

I gathered many interesting incidents of this home of our ancestors from my Uncle Abel Bellows, with whom I passed a few years before his marriage. My grandmother, at this time, was considered the honored head of this bachelor home, but was too far advanced in years to assume any domestic duties. His house was directly opposite the house of Aunt General's, across the principal street. He always paid her the most devoted attention, and spoke of her with tender regard. He would never forget her kindness to him while a member of her household, as he had been during several years. His uncle employed him as a clerk in the Register of Deeds office. He used to say, that was the commencement of his business life, except the two days he was a tinman, and worked for Tom Swan.

Aunt General was fond of young people; their attentions always seemed to please her, and she would occasionally invite a few to "come and take tea with her," as the invitation read. At one time, she was employing a seamstress who liked a bit of fun, and proposed to Aunt General to allow her to dress herself for our entertainment in an antique suit she had discovered, which belonged to a very remote generation, and had long been an heirloom in the family. When she entered the room in this quaint costume, I think Aunt General enjoyed the scene quite as much as ourselves. The girl put on the manners of that old time, and she was declared by all present to be quite an actress.

A touching incident occurred the winter following the death of this dear old aunt.

A girl, by the name of Betsey, was a maid-of-all-work in the general's family for more than twenty years. She was a faithful and most efficient person in all the departments of housekeeping, and received for her services fifty cents per week, which was considered ample compensation at this period. She must have commenced her services there when quite young, as she was not yet forty when she was married to the faithful sweetheart who had waited for her so patiently all this time, consoling himself through these lonely years by working steadily to pay for the nice farm he had purchased, so long ago, for "Betsey and I." When these two faithful hearts were at last united in the bonds of matrimony, she brought to his farm such a wealth of stock in cows, oxen, horses, and sheep as could hardly be credited by those who knew what her yearly income must have been. My Uncle Abel, however, could throw a good deal of light upon the matter, by giving a description — often in quite a humorous way — of Betsey's toilet. Her working-dress in winter was a coarse woollen fabric, spun and woven by her own hands, and usually colored with a decoction of butternut bark. One of these dresses was expected to serve her a year, with the protection of a large plaid woollen apron, which she invariably wore. Her shoes were of the most substantial kind, able to go through any amount of hardship with very little damage. It might be supposed that, in such a costume, her appearance could not have been very prepossessing. On the contrary, my uncle said she always looked perfectly neat, with her nicely kept hair; all which must be true, for she served a family that could not have tolerated untidiness. But Betsey's Sunday gown and shoes were the two most important articles in her wardrobe.

Perhaps it will be well to say here, for the benefit of the present generation who may not — in these days of cheap calico — know that a nice print could not be purchased for less than five shillings or one dollar per yard at that period of time; and Betsey's Sunday gown was made of this material, and was worn with as much scrupulous care as would have been a brocade silk. Tradition says, that, when she stood up in it to pledge her vows as a loving and faithful wife to this long patient man, it looked as fresh and bright as on that first Sunday she wore it to church, twenty years before. The calf-skin shoes that always accompanied this dress to church for the same number of years, I am not prepared to vouch for their presence on this important occasion. We can only suppose it to be possible.

The stories I used to hear about Betsey, when I was quite a young girl, were more deeply impressed on my mind by quite a pathetic incident that took place the winter following Aunt General's death. It was a cold, stormy day in December, when, some time in the afternoon, the knocker on the side door was vigorously sounded. My grandmother, who sat knitting in her warm corner, looked up with surprise, saying, "Who can have come in such a terrific storm as this?" I went to the door quickly as possible, and saw standing on the steps a woman, quite advanced in years, who hastily said, "I am told Mr. Abel Bellows lives here." The fine snow was whirling through the open door into my face, and I answered by taking her hand, drawing her into the entry; and then, opening the sitting-room door, I took her in, and placed a chair before the bright, blazing fire, where she seated herself, nearly exhausted. She sat a few moments, looking steadily at my grandmother, and then said: "Nobody knows me! I have come, for the first time in twenty years, to see once more the old home where I lived so long, and the folks I had learned to love so well and can never forget!" Breaking down at this moment, she sobbed out, "They are all dead!" My uncle coming in, and giving one look, exclaimed, "Why, Betsey! this is more than I could ever have dreamed!" and, turning to me, said, "Help her to take off those snowy garments." When grandmother became aware it was she who had served so long in the general's family, she gave her a cordial welcome, while Uncle Abel went to order some refreshment.

Her story was briefly told. She had improved the opportunity to come with a neighbor, who had business here. It was a two days' ride; and, on this last day, she was overtaken by the storm, and with great difficulty they reached here. She said, when they drove into the yard where there was always so much activity and life, the look of utter desolation gave her such a heart-throb as she had never felt before. And, when a stranger came to the door, and informed her those she sought were long since dead and buried, but she would find a Mr. Bellows across the street, she could hardly gather sufficient strength to come to us. My uncle was busily anxious to make the old lady as comfortable as possible, beguiling her out of her trouble as much as possible by talking over the old times, when he was not much more than a boy, and how he had not forgotten the good things she would cook with especial reference to his liking. Although Betsey's dress gave evident signs that she still adhered to the old-time economy, she was treated like a queen. In this, as in other instances, I can remember my uncle showed the Bellows' high ideal of hospitality and politeness. He could understand there were circumstances which could make it not only kind, but noble, to waive all distinctions of caste. This poor woman was detained two days, the drifted roads making it impossible to travel. During these two days, I had the opportunity to listen to several long conversations which this woman entered into with much animation and pathos, especially when calling up old memories of the "gineral," as she persisted in calling him. "Why," she would say, " who could help doing just right who lived there? He never found any fault, only told us to do a thing, and we did it the best we knew how, because it was for him. I shall never forget his picture," she continued, "as he sometimes walked through the kitchen, when he would always have a kind word for us. He was a dreadful handsome man! But I was scared once, when I laughed in prayer time. It was a cold morning, and his brother Theodore, who came pretty often to see him, was there, and came into the sitting-room after prayer was begun, and left the door open. The gineral turned round, and said: 'Shut that door, Theo-dore,' emphasizing the last syllable of his name in such a way as made Mrs. Bellows smile, and I couldn't stand it." As she recalled this circumstance to Uncle Abel's mind, they had a hearty laugh.

I can remember her grateful recollections of Uncle General's care for her pecuniary interest, always telling her when he paid her wages how she had better invest it. It was customary, in those days, for people to put a cow or a sheep out with some farmer to double the stock, in so many years' time. Betsey had done this; and the general had made it a personal business to look after her property; and, when she was at last married, there was such a drove of cattle and sheep left town with her that people turned out to see the sight, and remembered it long afterward!

On the third day, the roads were deemed passable, and the man who had brought Betsey came to take her home again. She left, feeling somewhat consoled for her great disappointment by the kind and tender sympathy given her by these relatives of the family she had come to visit. After preparing a generous basket of lunch, they kindly shook, for the last time, the old hand that had in the long ago done so many things for their comfort, and then saying, not good-by, but the good old Saxon phrase, farewell.

At that time, Uncle General had been dead fifteen years. There is no one living now whose eyes have rested on that majestic form, moving about with so much dignity of manner amidst his fellow-townsmen as to command at once their respect.

At the time of the erection of the monument to the memory of Col. Bellows, the founder, Rev. Dr. Bellows, in his address on that occasion, gave a lengthy sketch of the general's public services both in time of war and of peace, paying a high tribute of praise to his many excellences of character. No one had ever wielded so much and so beneficent an influence in the town, since the days of his father.

CHAPTER IV.

When the general died, in 1802, he left only two children, Col. Caleb Bellows, his only son, and Mrs. Phebe Grant, his only living daughter. Their first child, a daughter, whose name was Mary, died at the age of eighteen. I used to hear her very often spoken of in my early life, and always as one of exceeding loveliness of character and much personal beauty. Her death was a terrible blow, casting a cloud over that household, the shadow of which seemed ever afterward to rest there. Phebe married Maj. Samuel Grant, who for long years, until his death, at a ripe old age, was one of the solid, reliable men of Walpole, marked by his suavity of manner, his sound judgment, his success in business.

Mrs. Grant's home was within a few rods of her father's mansion,— a handsome residence, which her father built for her, and which she occupied as long as she lived. There were six children, four sons and two daughters. The oldest son died at sea. There is but one of the six children now living. The second daughter, Sarah, was nearly my own age, with whom, during our girlhood, I always had pleasant companionship, until marriage caused our paths to widely diverge.

As I now gaze over the wide chasm of nearly seventy years, since I last looked upon that sweet, laughing face, so full of fun, how vividly I can recall every lineament of feature and expression! I can also remember the many serious councils we have held upon questions of dress or etiquette, on receiving invitations to be present where we wished very much to be perfect in both. These two questions were often quite puzzling to our young heads, left without a guide. Our grandmother was so far advanced in years as to take little interest in the conventionalities of society, and Mrs. Grant had one strongly marked peculiarity, which was never explained to her friends, whom she always received cordially at her own home, but she never mingled at all in society after leaving her father's home; therefore Sarah could not consider her as reliable authority on such momentous questions.

At this time, I was fifteen years old, Sarah was a little younger, and, as the distance was short that divided our homes, it can easily be supposed our communications were frequent, especially at this particular period, when we had a dancing school on our hands. There were also many excursions in the spring and summer,— among other things, for wild berries. The early strawberries known at that time were such as we children sought in the fields, which were much more delicious in taste and fragrance than those cultivated now. Our raspberries were also obtained in the same manner; but the way we picked them I think would be worthy of imitation now.

How distinctly I can recall the dancing school we attended, so unlike any other ever taught here! Cotillions were then introduced, and the fancy dances were specially marvellous. But still more so was the teacher himself. Were it possible, one might suppose he was the veritable Mr. Turveydrop that Dickens introduced or brought back to the world some years ago.

Dickens certainly must have borrowed his costume and deportment from our old-time teacher.

As most young people like to dance, we greatly enjoyed this opportunity of learning something new in that department, as well as some other lessons he gave that were quite as important. He was a gentleman, and well-posted in the etiquette of that time. I have reason to remember well the fancy dance that Sarah and myself were to go through with on the last evening of the school. It was necessary that our costume should be especially appropriate. There were no dressmakers and costumers then as now. We had only our own native genius to depend upon; and, where Sarah was interested, I was always sure of success, for she was a born genius in many things. Wholly unlike other girls I had known, she was full of eccentricities, which would crop out in the most unexpected ways. Her wild exuberance would as often surprise as amuse us. I can see her, at this moment, hastily coming across the street into the front yard; and, running up the steps into the hall with her light brown hair hanging about her face and neck, just careless enough to look pretty, she would take a peep through the door which always stood open into the sitting-room, where grandmother, when sewing or knitting, would always be seen in her low-cushioned chair, and, saying good-morning, she would vault out quite three feet in the air, as a bird flies, calling me to come and practise again with her those difficult steps in the fancy dance we were to go through in the evening, which was the close of that long-remembered school.

How clearly I recall the many unsuccessful attempts we made to conquer that wonderful leap, bringing up just at the right place and ending with an indescribable performance of toe and heel. But the most amusing part of all this was at the end of every unsuccessful effort, when Sarah would improvise a gymnastic which only she could perform. Dear old grandmother! How she would try to look grave when we were in the midst of those wild pranks; but she would break down at last, in a convulsion of laughter, for Sarah would always have an extra touch that would compel it.

Perhaps I am lingering too long at this shrine of our girlhood,— that bright and lovely spot in my existence to look back upon, now nothing but a memory, filled with flickering lights and shadows.

A few more years, and young womanhood is attained. At this time, Sarah was married to Dr. Hosmer of Watertown, Mass. Her matrimonial life was of short duration. She was soon called away from her pleasant earthly home, leaving a devoted husband and one of her two daughters, the other having gone before her.

It is of this surviving daughter — this peculiarly gifted one of our race — to whom I wish to call the attention of those of our kindred who may know little or nothing about her, as she has lived abroad the greater portion of her life. But those of us who do know her, how can we speak the name of Harriet Hosmer without a thrill of conscious pride!

I cut from a London paper, some years ago, a beautiful tribute paid her by Lady Erskine, who was then staying in Rome, and was the personal friend of an old and celebrated English sculptor. It was he who introduced to her ladyship Miss Hosmer, who was then at work with him in his studio as a pupil.

Lady Erskine considered it the greatest compliment

that could have been paid her, for she was the first pupil he had ever received. She had many times besought him to become her teacher, but not until he had seen some of the marvellous specimens of her genius would he consent. This great artist had become an invalid from the long years of study and work. He had also acquired many peculiarities, having never married any one but his art, and had wholly excluded himself from society. She, on her part, could bring as many eccentricities to match them, and Lady Erskine said, "It was delightfully entertaining to see these two, so unlike, working together so harmoniously, always yielding with the utmost respect to each other's idiosyncrasies. But," she continued, "what was still more touching, no daughter could give him more tender care, or bestow more devoted attention than she, during the last few painful years of his life."

Now the sad thought comes to my mind,— this noble and gifted woman is the only one living who can tell the story of her childhood's home; but the memory of her sweet mother's girlhood is as fresh and fragrant as in the first hour of our parting.

It is so recently that the last and youngest son of Mrs. Grant — she, the daughter of Gen. Bellows — has passed away, that we have not yet become accustomed to the void he has left.

For many years, of late, he has spent the winter months in the city of New York, taking with him his only surviving daughter, and returning in the early springtime to his home, so long made desolate by the loss of his wife and two lovely children.

Our cousin, George Grant, was one not soon to be forgotten. He had too many characteristics that could not fail to impress his memory upon his friends. He had a fund of quaint humor, and he would often show the kindness of his heart in the most peculiar ways. If he wished to give poor neighbors some of his abundance, they would find it put through a window where he knew it would soon surprise them. I cannot forget the favor with which he regarded cats, animals to which most gentlemen have an antipathy. It was very amusing to see how he could enjoy the frolics of a pair of playful kittens.

At one time, I was first made aware of his return home, when, coming out of church, he laid his hand on my arm, saying he had an important question to ask. After walking a short distance, he said, in a low tone, "Emily, can you tell me where I can find a pair of gilt-edged kittens? I arrived yesterday, and I wish to get them all ready for Nelly when she arrives."

I can recall much in his life showing the originality and brightness of his mind. He left one son and one daughter, to bear his name and honor his memory.

The honored name of her father, Benjamin Bellows, was given by Mrs. Grant to her second son; who, after many years engaged in mercantile life in Boston, retired to a delightful home at Walpole, where he passed his remaining days, interested always in the improvement and adornment of his native village. He married Mary Bellows, daughter of Uncle Si; their two sons, Benjamin Bellows and Edward, both surviving their father and mother. It was to Mr. B. B. Grant that the kindred were very largely indebted for the success of the delightful family gathering at the time of the dedication of the monument, in 1854. He was the efficient chairman of the committee of arrangements, and the presiding officer over the feast. His thorough business methods, joined to his peculiar urbanity of manner, rendered him a fit man to fill both these offices. Another child of Mrs. Grant was Phebe, named for her mother, who married Leonard Stone of Watertown, Mass., where she brought up a family of sons and daughters; one of whom returned to Walpole as the wife of Dr. Kittredge, bringing with her the energy and executive efficiency which have marked so many of the race, and made them always foremost in everything that concerned the best interests of whatever community they might be planted in.

Col. CALEB BELLOWS' HOUSE.

CHAPTER V.

Col. Caleb Bellows, in his early life, was distinguished as the only son of that most honored individual, Gen. Benjamin Bellows; but he soon made a name for himself. How he won his commission, or from whom he received it, I do not know; but, at that period in our history, it seems to have been customary for every gentleman of any force of character or position in society to hold a commission, or have some title appended to his name; and, if we can be allowed to distinguish this class exclusively by their titles, Walpole was highly favored in that line.

I shall never forget the glowing description my mother used to give of an event which took place at this period. It was something in which a large portion of the community seemed to have a deep interest. There had been a long preparation for this event, which was the marriage of Gen. Bellows' only son Caleb to the only daughter of Esquire Hartwell, of New Ipswich. As I was only eight or nine years old, this story had all the charm of a romance; and my young imagination formed a picture that might well compare with some of the marvellous things we read about.

This union of Cousin Caleb, my mother would say, with Miss Polly Hartwell was mutually approved by her and his parents She had the reputation of being one of the best educated young ladies in New England,

and, what was also of great importance, she had a strictly religious training by her parents, who were of the old Puritan type.

Notwithstanding the great difficulty of communicating with foreign parts in those times,— forty miles at that time standing for almost half as many hundred at the present day,— everything that could be known of this celebrated young lady and her antecedents found their way to Walpole. Speculation was rife, and curiosity on tiptoe. How did she look? Did she know anything but Latin and Greek? And, what was of still more importance, would the colonel bring her home on a pillion? Well, these anxiously curious people had not long to wait for an answer to these important questions. The colonel had imparted to two or three of his familiar friends — the names of a few of whom I have already given — the morning of his departure, and the time of his return, when he would bring with him to this lovely home, that was now prepared and awaiting her, the bride he had long sought, and who had now consented to preside over this beautiful establishment.

On the morning of his departure from Walpole, two or three gentlemen stood on the sidewalk awaiting his appearance; and when, on his beautiful black horse, his coat gleaming liked burnished steel in the sun, and elegantly caparisoned, he bounded from his father's door on to the highway, hats were raised, and circled above their heads, he answering with a military salute as he dashed on; and many good wishes were shouted after him until he reached the foot of the hill, when he disappeared from sight.

On the day when he was to return with his bride, all the nearest relatives, with a few invited friends, occupied the spacious parlors of the new mansion, while a group of gentlemen stood in the grounds outside, watching for their approach. A delegation on horseback had gone out to meet the bridal party on their way from Keene; and, as they swept by the old meeting-house, the bell, in more vigorous strokes than ever before, rung out the hour of noon. The distance was now short, and in a few minutes the cavalcade came dashing through the open gateway in gallant style up to the door. She was mounted on her beautiful horse called Sappho, whose splendid trappings nearly threw the colonel into the shade. Her tall figure and dignified bearing, as she alighted, won at once the admiration of all; and she was received outside as gentlemen only know how to honor a lady, and was soon conducted within, where she found hosts of warm hearts and hands to give her greeting.

I have noted down this tradition of our Cousin Caleb's wedding, perhaps not in the same words, but with the incidents the same as my mother related them to me.

There was one important item in which my memory is at fault, or she omitted to say anything about it; but it will be in keeping with the traditions of our race to suppose that there was a banquet prepared worthy of the occasion, such as our grandmothers knew so well how to set before their distinguished guests; and this may have foreshadowed the many hospitable entertainments in the coming years seen at that bountiful board.

And now I have something to say about my own grandfather, Col. Joseph Bellows, youngest son of Col. Benjamin Bellows, the founder. He had always lived in Lunenburg on the old paternal estate, which was his inheritance; and I have heard my uncles say it comprised the greater section and best part of the town; and there was the birthplace of my grandfather's fourteen children. I have heard my grandmother say, with evident pride, that she had ten boys to cut and make for; and she always added, "your grandfather kept me supplied with plenty of material."

I have often painted this dear old home in my imagination as I have heard it described. It must have been more remarkable for its size than elegance. It was one of the first large square houses built in that town, and it was of necessity spacious, to accommodate his own large family and the number of persons he always employed and the guests he always welcomed.

There were several servants regularly employed, and in certain seasons of the year, particularly in spinning time, a large increase of help was necessary; and on this large estate there were also many farm hands constantly at work, making in the total an enormous family.

It may be readily inferred that our grandfather was one of the leading citizens of the town, and he was called to hold some of the most important public offices. His judgment in difficult cases was often sought, and no one who knew him ever doubted his courage and stanch integrity.

A little story, of not much importance in itself, occurs to me here, which grandmother used to relate when there was a sufficient number of us together to listen; for, when she related any adventure, especially if grandfather happened to be the hero, she always liked to have a pretty respectable audience. As I now look through the long vista of intervening years, how vividly I can see that little circle around her chair, each one striving to get the nearest place beside her, but which was usually accorded to our younger cousin Harry,— a frail little fellow then, but who lived to become a vigorous man, and the chief justice of the State of New Hampshire.

She would usually commence her story, by giving a description of the two girls who had been in the family a long time, and not at all given to foolish fears. The sleeping apartments of the girls opened upon a long piazza on one side of the house, and at one end a few steps led down into a large woodshed.

It was in the early part of winter, and a number of men were employed in cutting and drawing wood from the forest, providing thus the yearly supply, and huge piles of logs were lying about in the yard. Our grandmother's domestic affairs were conducted with much system and order; and, at the usual hour for closing the doors for the night, she went into the kitchen to give orders for breakfast, and see to many other things which she made her especial duty to attend to, the most important of which was to see that the fires were all left safe. There were no stoves in use at that time, but large open fireplaces in each room. The kitchen fireplace was a marvel of comfort and convenience, affording ample room for a dozen persons or more at a time to make themselves comfortable before its bright and genial warmth. This winter fire was not permitted to go out from the time it was lighted in the autumn until the warm spring weather made it no longer necessary. Perhaps some of our readers may ask in what these winter fires differed so much from those at other seasons of the year. They were made by placing two huge green logs of six-foot wood in the back part of the fireplace, the lower ones somewhat larger than the top,— often two feet in diameter, and six or eight feet long; and they were kept burning, by piling smaller wood that was dry in front, which was easily kept ablaze, making the room look so bright and cheerful! After she had looked to the safety of things in general, and the fires in particular, she noticed that the girls were gazing anxiously out of the window, and inquired what they saw. They answered, "Not anything;" but, as they still lingered, she became a little impatient, and bade them go to bed. They then told her they were so deeply impressed with a feeling that some one was hanging about the premises, intent on mischief, that they did not dare to cross the piazza. Grandmother then took the candle, and said, "I will go with you, and we will hunt up this mysterious being that so haunts your imagination!" She then looked in every nook, closet, and corner of their room, and then said, "Now, we will go down into the woodshed;" and, giving no time for words, she hastily ran down the steps, bidding them follow her. After looking behind everything that could conceal a burglar, and discovering nothing, the girls were sufficiently reassured to go to bed without any further trouble.

It was the custom, in this house, to retire early to rest, and rise early in the morning. I think it must have been a lifelong habit with our grandmother, as she would almost daily remark that an hour in the morning was worth two in the afternoon. Five o'clock was the hour appointed for rising, in winter, as well as in summer; and, as all were expected promptly to observe this family rule, we can easily imagine the bustle and stir of such a house full of men, women, and children getting ready for breakfast and the duties of the day. On this morning that followed the search for burglars, grandfather was awakened by a great uproar and confusion in the kitchen. His ears were assailed with a strange vocabulary of words, for that house. He was soon in the midst of the confusion, however, and there was no need of inquiring the cause, as it was already apparent. The table showed the remains of a banquet, and his men all stood there, with no clothing but their pantaloons. The weather was severely cold; and, at such times, the workmen were allowed to place their boots, coats, and caps, with other things for comfort, around the huge fireplace, to make them warm for an early departure into the woods; and not a thing could be found to put on their backs or feet. Grandmother was quickly up, and searching for garments; but the greatest trouble was to find something for their feet. It was now sufficiently evident that burglars had really been in the house; and, as soon as breakfast was despatched, grandfather ordered his horse, and was off like the wind. He soon rallied a force, and procured a warrant, finding that his house was not the only one robbed.

There was a family named Scott, living about a mile from the village, who had been harboring some suspicious looking characters, and it was their house he intended to search. The sun had but just risen, when he with his men were at the door; and, placing them so as to prevent any escape, he gave a heavy knock on the door. After waiting a few minutes, a chamber window was raised, and a woman put her head out, inquiring what was wanted. He told her he had come with authority to search her house for a burglar she was suspected of harboring. She declared there was no one but herself and daughter in the house; her husband was away. He then answered that he would be more sure after looking for himself. He told her to open the door, or they would be compelled to open it for themselves. When she saw what a force of men was gathered about the door, she opened it in great agitation, still declaring that no one but herself and daughter were there. The men followed grandfather into the house, when he ordered her to show them every apartment. After looking over the basement, they proceeded up-stairs. After examining several apartments, which she said were all, one of the men pointed to a dark entry-way, at the end of which he discovered a narrow door. When she saw them all going towards that, she threw up her hands, saying, "Now there will be blood-shed!" They soon discovered the door was locked on the inside; and, when admittance was demanded, a voice within answered, "The first one who enters this room is a dead man!" At this, there was a short consultation, which ended by three of the most powerful of their number offering to throw themselves simultaneously against the door with grandfather, thus making their sudden entrance a surprise, which was their only safety. He quickly said he would lead if they would follow; and, giving the signal, with one bound they stood before the wretch, whom they now had entirely in their power. He was armed with a bowie knife, and other weapons they found in his room. He proved to be a notorious burglar, and was arrested. The family also were imprisoned, and when his guilt and theirs was proved, he was sentenced to be hung; and the Scott family, according to the style of that day, to be branded on the forehead as thieves. He made a confession, in which he said it had been his intention to kill the first person who should discover him, on the night that grandmother searched in the woodshed : and, at one time, she was not more than two yards away from the place of his concealment. It was his intention to have taken all the silver he could find. But he had only finished his banquet, finding a goodly supply of dainties, when he heard some one moving, and, knowing there were quite a number of men in the house, he thought a retreat most prudent, and had only time to gather up the men's clothing hanging about the fireplace.

At this period, we were governed by the English code of laws, which still retained some of their mediæval barbarity. They would hang a poor man as soon for stealing a rabbit, or a poor mother for taking a loaf of bread to keep her little children from perishing with hunger, as they would for taking a large sum of money. I hope that they have learned to make more just distinctions.

CHAPTER VI.

I HAVE many times been asked for my Grandmother Bellows' maiden name. I will answer here, it was Lois Whitney,— a name, that of Whitney as well as that of Bellows, that has never been found on a criminal calendar. She was the daughter of Benjamin Whitney, of Littleton, Mass. He had an extensive landed estate, which he inherited, and on which he lived, occupying, perhaps, a house of his ancestor. It was a large and convenient house, giving sunshine and shade to all who dwelt within, and a warm and kindly welcome to the many who liked to visit this rural home.

In some of the sketches grandmother gave of her early life, she would sometimes allude to the struggle her Mother Whitney had in taking care of this place while her father was away, as he, with many others in that vicinity, had been drafted into the English army to fight the French, who were then holding possession of Canada. All the steady help our great-grandmother could obtain was a boy of eighteen years, and who was not remarkable for his courage. There were a few men who were not thought fit for service left behind, and in haying and harvesting time would unite and help each other. At this time, our grandmother was a child of fourteen years of age, and she, with her sister Susan, who was eleven, were the only children of this household.

This little Susan was a fair-haired, pretty child, and

a great pet with her older sister. There is a story our grandmother would tell us, with which we were always greatly entertained; and she seemed to enjoy relating it, for the reason her little sister had such a prominent place in it. It was in haying time, and the neighbors were now aiding in getting the hay from a meadow which could be distinctly seen from the house. To reach this field, it was necessary to cross a strip of swampy land, where a causeway had been made. She would explain this to us as a kind of bridge or driveway, made by filling in a low place until it was solid enough and sufficiently broad to enable the teams to pass over, bringing the produce from the fields to the barn and house. On each side of this bridge, immensely tall grasses and cat-tails were growing in the murky earth. It was on one side of this bridge a battle was fought, which may not have found its way into history, but is none the less worthy to be kept as an incident of the family journal, telling of courage and perseverance. These two qualities, it has been many times proved our great-grandparents possessed in large measure.

As I have already said, it was haying time, and this little Susan was sent every forenoon with refreshments to the men in the field. It was observed that she looked a little pale on returning, one day, and, being questioned as to the cause, said she thought there was a great snake in the swamp, that looked at her when she crossed the bridge. Her mother, thinking it was all imaginary, as she was a timid child, said it must have been a big cat-tail which her imagination had conjured into a snake. On the next day, when she saw her mother preparing the basket for her to take to the field, she refused to go, until her sister coaxed her, by saying she would stand at the door, where she could see her all the way. As she reached the field, giving no sign of alarm, her sister turned from the door to perform some household duty, intending to return to her watch before the child had time to reach the causeway; when she soon heard a piercing scream, and, rushing out to meet her, the child pointed to an object that might intimidate something more than a little child: it was the head of a monster serpent, raised a foot above the tall grasses! Its neck was curved like the nose of a tea-kettle, and, as it rapidly turned its head, which was as large as a person's hand, its eyes seemed to throw out livid streams of fire.

As soon as Grandmother Whitney heard what the children had seen, she at once bade them follow her to the woodshed, where she gave each a long weapon, taking one herself, and ordering her boy to do the same, and follow her quickly as possible. She took no time to calculate the probabilities of victory or defeat; if she had done so, the combat probably would never have taken place. When the boy began to show some reluctance, she told him she would give the first blow, and, at the first sign of cowardice on his part, she would put the blows upon him.

They soon reached the place, and saw the monster who was there, seemingly awaiting them. True to her word, she commenced giving the most vigorous blows; and the boy, seeing it was do or die, followed her example. The monster, in his writhings, seemed to have become entangled in the tall weeds, and not until they were all nearly exhausted could they see any sign of victory. The grass and cat-tails were beaten to the ground a long distance around before it became evident they had conquered him. At this moment, the men, who were in a distant field, saw that the family were in some trouble, and, hastening up to see what was to be done, said it was a miracle they were not all killed. When the dead enemy was dragged out of the swamp, and stretched upon the grass, they said no such horrible serpent was ever seen in this country before. The news of this battle and victory brought a great many persons to see the monster, some living even thirty miles away.

The thought presses upon my mind that I am the only person living who can relate anything of this remarkable woman, Great-grandmother Whitney; and my heart is filled with regret, that I didn't learn more about her when I had the opportunity. My Grandmother Bellows never lost an occasion when she could tell of some remarkable quality her mother possessed, but I was too young to take other interest than that of being entertained. I remember well her description of the struggle she had in taking care of this large estate in the absence of her husband,— for he was gone a long time on business and in military service,— and how she managed to gain something, as she would say, "for a wet day," beside supporting the family; also the high respect in which she was held in her native town, where she had always lived; her perfect system and order in housekeeping, and also taking upon herself the education of her two little girls. Grandmother would say, all they knew of books her mother taught them, and then added, "We were quite as good scholars, if not a little better, than children averaged in those days." The sick, and those in need, were especial objects of her care; and Lois was often sent, sometimes against her own inclinations, to aid in some way the family where a mother or child was ill. Their home was some distance from the village, and the family walked a mile to church. I should think she considered herself responsible for the morals of all that little community in this rural district, as my grandmother said she would frequently rap on some door, as she passed along, and inquire if the family were ready to accompany her.

When Grandfather Whitney returned to his family, after a long campaign of nearly four years, he came with broken health, resulting from the many hardships he endured; and they found the "wet day" she had been preparing for so long; and what she had laid up proved, grandmother would say, to be a great blessing to them, for it took all their time and strength to minister to his varying wants, the few months he lingered with them, when he died, and was buried in the churchyard with his kindred, in Littleton.

Grandmother Whitney lived a widow many years on the old homestead, taking care of herself and daughters, as she had learned to do so well. She made the addition to her family, in the way of help, of a slave girl; her name was Lucy. It was not against the laws of the State, at this period, to employ slave help; but there were only a few families comparatively who availed themselves of this privilege.

This girl, Lucy, proved to be a faithful creature, and became strongly attached to her mistress. Grandmother found great comfort in her when her two daughters were married, and had homes of their own, leaving their mother in the faithful care of old Lucy.

It may be well here to follow the eldest of these daughters, as our lives are so closely connected with hers.

How my Grandfather Bellows became acquainted with, or where he first saw this daughter of Littleton, I cannot say. His own life had been passed in Lunenburg; and, as he was left at an early age with the inheritance of the paternal estate, it is reasonable to suppose he looked about early for a companion to keep him company in this old home, which must have been very lonely after the family had all come here to convert this wilderness into a Walpole. As Lunenburg is not very far from Littleton, as we now calculate distances,— though probably considered quite a journey on horseback at that period,— we can suppose that the personal charms of this country lass, with many other qualities that would serve to recommend her to a sensible young man, might in some way have found their way to my grandfather's ear; and it has certainly been made evident that his suit to this fair dame was not rejected.

It is to be regretted I cannot give any particulars of the wedding that must have taken place, but I am inclined to think it was a very quiet one, as she could never tolerate what would seem like ostentation or display, on any occasion. I also cannot give any assurance to their posterity, that our grandfather did not bring her home on a pillion, but I have more reason to believe she came on her own horse; as I have heard her say more than once her mother didn't let her daughters go from their home empty-handed.

We may readily suppose this dear old home was made very desolate, when no one was left there but the mother with her faithful slave-woman, Lucy, and we cannot be surprised that she improved an opportunity to brighten up her lonely life by accepting old Deacon Foster's offer, "to go the rest of the way with her to heaven." I can recall many anecdotes I have heard related of this old gentleman,— one in particular which grandmother used to tell us. He rode up to the door one morning, seemingly in haste, and told her mother that their neighbor, Mrs. Carter, was in trouble, and in need of help; that she had been violently taken with "a serious and painful breaking out about her mouth." He didn't wait to be questioned, knowing that she would go at once to her neighbor, to see if any assistance could be rendered. When she reached the house, she saw the woman about as usual, and discovered nothing about her face unusual; she then told her of the message Deacon Foster left. "Well," was the response, "I understand pretty well what he meant; for, when he came this morning, I was giving Ben Carter a piece of my mind for his carelessness, and the good Deacon Foster thought my temper made my speech a little unscriptural."

I think this good old deacon, who seemed to have no family of his own, entertained a strong partiality for this Grandmother Whitney during her long widowhood, as I now recall how many times Grandmother Bellows would speak of him as their friend, and her mother finally found him a comforting and pleasant companion during the rest of her walk in life.

After a few years, it was thought best they should pass the rest of their days in Lunenburg, where they were cordially welcomed to the home of their daughter and son-in-law. I have reason to suppose the property they carried with them to Lunenburg was more than sufficient for their continued support.

Grandmother Whitney died not many years after their removal from Littleton. My mother, who was named Sarah Farr for her grandmother, remembered as a child waiting upon her when in bed, and the loving words she would bestow upon her grandchild, when receiving at her hand the cup of drink and other things prepared for her comfort.

Her grave was made in Lunenburg, beside three little graves, where her daughters — the three first children — were laid. Deacon Foster, who came to Walpole with the family, sleeps with our kindred in the old family burying-ground.

CHAPTER VII.

WHEN hearing my Grandmother Bellows describe the home of her childhood, in Littleton,— the large orchard back of the house that filled the world with its fragrance; their many bechives filled with honey, adding not a little to this sweetness; the garden, where a patch was always reserved for herself and sister to plant their hollyhocks, pinks, and caraway; their playhouse made in the old spinning-room, where the music of the wheels was possibly quite as charming as Patti's strains could be to some ears,— my young imagination would paint for me a rare picture of loveliness, and I would resolve to see, sometime, this, to me, incomparable place. Many years had elapsed, when the long waited-for time came at last. It was on a bright and lovely summer's morning, nearly, or quite, fifty years ago, I took my mother and set out for Littleton, about fifteen miles distant from where we then were. As we approached the town, I began to scrutinize every house, as I drove slowly along, but could see nothing that looked familiar,— certainly nothing of that dear old home and its surroundings that in my girlhood I had painted so minutely; but, still going on, we reached a respectable-looking farm-house, where I drove up to the door, and inquired if they knew any one living in town by the name of Whitney. They replied in the negative, but said the name was familiar, as they had often seen it on some old tombstones in the churchyard, about half a mile distant. As they saw we were strangers, they kindly offered to show us in what part of the ground we could find the stones. As we followed on, I began to awaken from this long dream of the past, seeing how futile were the hopes of that bright morning, as we started on our voyage of discovery. Our guide soon brought us to the sacred spot, where a whole family by that name were sleeping, and our great-grandfather was apparently the first one of the family laid there. I never saw my mother so deeply moved, as we silently stood by that sacred mound. Ours were perhaps the first kindred feet that had wandered to this lonely spot for more than a century. The old moss-covered stones were sunken so far below the surface as to leave no part of the inscription visible, excepting the name and date; but "forgotten" was too legibly written upon all around not to feel the full import of that word. After contemplating this forlorn and dreary place sufficiently long to make an indelible impression, we slowly turned away, bidding adieu forever to that narrow strip of earth, hallowed by the dust of one so near of kin to us, and whose life had been so true and strong. Thus ended my lifelong dream of a visit to this ancestral resting-place, fully impressing me with the truth of the old adage, that time is the besom of destruction; for I found no trace of anything I sought,— not even the causeway, made memorable by the great battle of — not Bunker Hill — but the big snake.

CHAPTER VIII.

During the few last years of our grandparents' residence in Lunenburg, there was much in public as well as in private life to make it an eventful period. The struggle had commenced for our independence, and grandfather received from the governor his commission as colonel, which took him from home much of the time, leaving a heavy burden of care upon grandmother. He was detailed to furnish recruits for the Massachusetts regiments, and also furnish supplies for the soldiers from this State. It was on one of these campaigns that grandmother was waited upon by a party of British officers. It was midwinter, and a severely cold time. They coolly informed her they had come into the country in quest of comfortable lodgings, until their army should again commence operations in the spring. It was about this time that orders were received from the mother country that their soldiers should billet themselves upon the inhabitants, here, and make themselves comfortable at their expense. We can well imagine how the loyal women would receive such guests; and grandmother found herself equal to the occasion. She told them she didn't take boarders, whether friends or foes; and her house, large as it was, was certainly not large enough to entertain gentlemen of their cloth! At this, one of their number, who took it upon himself to do the business, said they were obeying the king's orders, and, as she was still considered one of his subjects, any opposition would be useless. They then politely informed her they should return at three o'clock, to dine with her. As the family had their second meal at twelve, she had no idea of submitting to this inconvenience, with her great family to care for; and she made her plan accordingly. At the appointed time, she placed on the table a dish of rather indifferent cold meat, a plate of brown bread, some pickles, and a piece of cheese for desert; she then retired to her sitting-room, awaiting results, but careful to leave the door which opened into the dining-room partially open, so that she could hear the opinions they would probably give of their new boarding-place. They were punctual to the time; and, when the girl showed the way to the dining-room, a volley of oaths soon greeted her ears, and in a moment more the spokesman of the party presented himself at the door, and, in tones of suppressed rage, inquired if she considered what was on the table a dinner fit for gentlemen and officers! Grandmother, not in the least daunted, calmly rose from her chair, confronting him, and replied, if he and his friends were not satisfied, they certainly had her permission to go where they could find better accommodations. He stood for a moment, looking her over, apparently surprised at her courage, and then turned away, saying he should return in the evening for lodging.

When she saw she could not easily starve them out, she decided that she would see what effect freezing would have. There was a large chamber on the north side of the house, with a very small, deep fireplace, in which a fire had seldom or never been made,— for it was wholly inadequate to warm the room at any time, and especially at such a time as this. In the early part of the evening, she had a moderate fire kindled there, and told the girl, when the officers came, to show them to this apartment. It was after the time when the family usually retired that they returned, and, on going into this cold room, they were seemingly, judging from their language, reminded of a warmer place; telling the girl to show them where the fuel was kept. As they were repeatedly heard carrying up wood, grandmother feared some mischief, and did not retire until towards morning, when she called up one of the men to keep watch. It was hardly light when he aroused her, saying he was sure he could smell smoke; and, bursting into the chamber where these men were, it was filled with smoke almost to suffocation, and they were all in a dead, drunken sleep. The household were soon awakened; and the men, after dragging these stupefied creatures out of their beds, commenced tearing up the floor, where they found the large beams under the hearth charred to a coal; and, when the air was admitted, it burst into a blaze, but was soon extinguished. Grandmother said they had hardly recovered from the excitement this had occasioned, before grandfather, to her great joy, most unexpectedly returned home, after several weeks' absence. When he was informed of the outrage, he set out quickly in pursuit of these villains; and, finding them where he expected,— at the tavern,— (as houses for entertainment were then called), he told them if they were not out of town within two hours, he would march them out at the point of the bayonet; and, as they saw he was in command of a military camp where he had soldiers in training ready to be summoned for service, they thought best to hasten their departure.

CHAPTER IX.

It was seventy or seventy-five years ago, that my Uncle Abel Bellows used to enliven his household by gathering five or six of his young nephews and nieces under his roof, during the winter school-term. His residence was such a convenient distance from the old brick school-house that the winter storms afforded us no excuse for non-attendance at school, and the thought of escaping our uncle's vigilance in that respect could not be entertained for a moment. Our grandmother dispensed the honors of this bachelor home. A colored woman and man, Becky and Cyrus, were the servants; and they would hail with great delight the coming of those noisy boys and girls. "Jes' seems like cummin' to life agin, arter bein' dead," they would say. But this sudden awakening was not wholly confined to the kitchen; every part of the house seemed reanimated with just such life as only boys and girls can put into it. I can now vividly recall the merry group that gathered in the large kitchen when games were to be the evening entertainment; but when our grandmother proposed stories, and she had a marvellous treasury of that kind to draw from, how eagerly we sought our places in the sitting-room around the low-cushioned chair, which was placed in the warmest corner, the room all aglow with the bright, blazing fire.

"There is no need to light the candles," she would say; and we were very glad to avoid the interruption occasioned by snuffing them, especially when so unfortunate as to snuff them out.

There was sometimes a little struggle to obtain the nearest place, but that was soon accorded to Harry, our youngest cousin, whom I have named before, and a favorite with all. One glance at that partially useless little hand, which he liked to nestle in grandmother's lap, when sitting beside her, would awaken our sympathies, and win for him any privilege; but his sweet nature would not allow him to take undue advantage of kindness or indulgence.

There were two Indian stories we were never tired of hearing. One, in particular, was a favorite with Harry, for the reason that intended wrong was justly punished; thus showing, in his boyhood, the strong sense of right and justice that qualified him so well for the position he held in after years,— as Chief Justice of the State of New Hampshire.

Looking down upon us, as we had seated ourselves upon the carpet each side of her, she would commence thus: "It was when Burgoyne came sweeping down from Canada, with his horde of Hessians and Indians, threatening death and destruction to all that opposed him, that Gen. Gates issued an order for more troops to help him defend the fort at Ticonderoga; which stood directly in the wake of this advancing army. Your grandfather, with all possible haste, started with the men under his command to join his brother, Gen. Bellows, somewhere, who was already on his way; and their timely aid was highly complimented afterward in a letter from Gen. Gates. They had no pitched battle there, but some pretty lively skirmishes with the Indians, taking a number prisoners; and your grandfather brought three young squaws home to Lunenburg, and one old Indian, who followed them at a distance all the way. Your grandfather would not allow the soldiers to ill-treat this Indian, as they were inclined to do. He said, 'White brother good.'" Perhaps this kindness awoke a kindred spark in the breast of this ignorant child of the forest. He certainly showed his attachment by lingering about grandfather's dwelling, where he was fed and cared for a long time.

A suitable place was provided for the young squaws; they were to be kept as hostages, or to be exchanged for our own people, who were in captivity. They were permitted to go out about the street when they chose; they always showed themselves in full feather, looking quite picturesque in their Indian costume.

Lunenburg was made quite lively at this time by the number of young officers and soldiers that were waiting there to be sent where most needed. Some of these officers had not yet learned to wear their new uniform with becoming dignity, and grossly compromised themselves when riding through the town, one cold, blustering morning. Seeing at quite a distance these untutored children, decked in full Indian regalia, one of the trio turned to his companions, saying, "Now, look out for some fun!" and dashed on at a breakneck speed. On reaching the group, he suddenly drew rein, inquiring if one of them would like a ride; she quickly assented, and he pointed to something near, from which she could mount behind him, intending to start his horse when she gave the leap, and let her fall to the ground. But he had sadly miscalculated Indian agility.

She vaulted into the air, coming down astride upon the officer's nag so suddenly that the affrighted creature started off with such speed that no power of rein could check him. The maiden, however, had secured her safety by winding her arms tightly around her escort; and, as they flew over the road, the wind lifted her long black hair from her shoulders, and kept it streaming out straight behind her, lending no small addition to the novelty of the scene. His brother officers, now understanding the game, started in hot pursuit, and, as they dashed along the street, shouted, "An elopement! an elopement!" bringing the inhabitants to the doors and windows, which were thrown wide open; and pedestrians stood in mute astonishment, gazing after the retreating figures. When the horse had reached his stable, on which he was madly bent, he stopped voluntarily at the Public House, where, as usual, was a crowd of many loungers; soldiers, officers, and idlers were standing and sitting around, discussing the times, and the latest arrivals. Their talk was suddenly arrested, however, by the startling appearance of this couple, followed closely by the other two officers, who still shouted, "An elopement! an elopement!" and for a moment they did not comprehend the situation; but when the young squaw triumphantly leaped to the ground with Indian grace, saying, "Tanky, sir; tanky, sir; had mighty good ride, but did make my hair whirl 'gin!" cheer upon cheer went up, to the great mortification of the gaily decked young officer.

Report said it was long after Independence was achieved when this officer heard the last of his attempt to run away with a young squaw.

CHAPTER X.

Nothing makes more rapid progress than memory on the march; usually leaving many details behind, making it often necessary to retrace our steps to pick up some incident that is better found in its wrong place than not found at all.

On waking in the morning, a new thought or scene will sometimes present itself for contemplation. This morning, to my great surprise, grandmother's wedding dress flashed upon me in all its regal beauty. Where could it have been concealed all this time, never once coming to the light, when I have so recently had the key in my hand to unlock this wonderful hiding place? Well, here it is, just as it was spread out before my admiring eyes one day, years and years ago, when she called me to help her arrange a large trunk full of ancient deposits. She took this out first, and began carefully to remove the many wrappings in which it had been laid away, and then spread out upon the bed a light sky blue damask silk, of such remarkable texture that the skirt would almost stand alone. The bodice was made with a deep point behind, also pointed in front. The sleeves were fitted tight to the arm, reaching only to the elbow; a deep lace fell over the arm. The over-skirt was immensely wide. The silk looked the same on both sides. The flowers were roses, some in full blossom grouped with buds and leaves. I think she enjoyed my enthusiasm over this dress, as she talked a good deal about it, saying it took some thirty yards of that rich material to make it; also, that it was the only silk dress she ever had; that there were only a few people at that period who could afford to purchase more than one dress of such costly material. And when I asked her how she could have kept it looking so perfectly fresh and new, she said she only wore it on great occasions, and had worn it even to church but a few times, and then at grandfather's request; but she took it off as soon as she returned, for she had too many children who would want to put their hands onto it.

She then took out a bombazine dress. This was purchased for her, she said, when she was sixteen years old,—at the time of her father's death. This material was worn only for mourning, and she had kept this all her long life with its sacred associations, having worn it for her father and mother, and then for the three little ones she left sleeping in Lunenburg.

Dear old grandmother! How I like to recall these incidents that seemed of so little importance at the time, but now having gained all that interest that time alone can give to all earthly things. I can see, at this moment, that fair, placid face, encircled in the double border on her cap, which was always so beautifully crimped, and her cap fastened on with a broad black ribbon around her head. How sweet, too, is the memory of that last visit I made to her the summer before she left this earthly abode for the home that had been so long awaiting her! How like a pleased child she would accompany me on my visits to our friends, staying with some of them two or three days! A little scene at Aunt Susan Robeson's — my mother's eldest sister — seems worth relating, as I recall it so vividly. We were to go in the morning, and the distance was so short, that a little walk, she thought, would be more pleasant than a ride; so we set out after breakfast, and as we went slowly along, we met two or three friends who greeted us with much surprise, to see her walking! She replied, "I like to walk, when I have the right company." I didn't let them detain her, knowing that elderly people could better keep going than remain standing. Aunt Susan came down to the gate to meet us, and now I hear her saying, "My heart, mother! this beats all!" The old tone is in my ear, and I can distinctly see the look of pleasure that lighted up her face, which any one, having seen once, cannot easily forget. She was soon seated in the easiest chair, quietly taking out her knitting, which always seemed to rest her after any extra exertion. A few friends dropped in during the day, to congratulate grandmother upon her wonderful activity, at such an advanced age, she being then nearly ninety-one. As the day was closing, Aunt Susan said to me, "Your grandmother looks weary, and we will go up-stairs and sit in my chamber, this evening. The room opening out of it is prepared for you, and she may be induced to retire earlier, if we sit there for company. We had only sat a few minutes, when she rose, saying she was a little tired, and would go to her rest, but would like to have us sit by the window which was near the door, so she could hear our conversation. Hardly five minutes had elapsed before we noticed a strange sound, when Aunt Susan, going hastily to the bed, saw it was grandmother's breathing; and for a moment she thought something serious had happened, as we had no idea she could have had time to go to sleep; but, when I touched her, she opened her eyes, saying, "I am so sleepy," and sunk again into that sweet baby-like sleep that mothers love so well to sit and watch. We both stood over her a few minutes, seemingly occupied with the same thought. How beautiful is this rest, and how lovely this second childhood! She had dropped into bed like a tired little one, and was asleep the moment her head touched the pillow.

Having finished our visit to Aunt Susan, we were to go from there to Aunt Louisa Knapp's, my mother's youngest sister. This name is another key that unlocks memories of nearly a lifetime, and this visit to her with grandmother has ever found a place with my most vivid and cherished recollections. It is pleasant to recall the many little things that were done with reference to her comfort: the food she could most relish without harming her; the comfortable cot bed, brought in and placed beside the one I occupied, as she said, to use her own words, she felt "more at home, when she had company." And how we persuaded her to take a nap after dinner, as she was at first unwilling, saying, she "couldn't spare the time." Our dear Uncle Knapp said, "It seemed so like a child, unwilling to leave its play." After this refreshing rest, she would join the group at the front door, in the wide, long hall that led through the house. This was a favorite place where the family and friends often gathered in a hot summer afternoon. The view from this door was more charming than I can describe! Here I have seen my uncle sit alone for hours, silently contemplating the grandeur and beauty so widely spread out before him!

As I now look through the mist of more than half a century, I can distinctly recall each figure as we sat there on this last afternoon of our visit,— my aunt in her favorite costume, on a hot day, a white dimity wrapper and black silk skirt; the wrapper fastened so snug and trim about her waist with broad strings, tied in a bow at the front, and then her dainty cap, which was always so becoming. Happening to make some allusion to her personal appearance, my uncle quickly replied, "Why, my dear, how can you ever look otherwise than lovely to me!" Perhaps it may not be thought in good taste to repeat that here, but I take a different view of it. Another member of this household, our cousin, Susan Knapp, sits here in this family circle. Who that has ever seen and known her can forget the expression of that face, beaming so full of disinterested kindness to every living creature? Her quaint remarks, this afternoon, about her work were, as usual, very amusing. She was transferring some old embroidery upon a new piece of muslin, making, as she said, a pretty collar for aunt. But the especial charm, this afternoon, was our uncle's conversation, which was always remarkable for its perfect diction. It was delightful to hear him relate an anecdote. No one, I ever heard, could do it so well. On this afternoon, he sought opportunities to say something that would call out a quick repartee from aunt, for which she was always remarkable, and he seemed always to enjoy so much. I think this was more particularly intended for grandmother's benefit, as he would frequently turn to her, saying, "You see, mother, what a debt the world owes you for giving to it such a paragon of wit," and, with the most humorous expression on his face, would say, "I was about to add, beauty!" I must say, here, that he always found her quite equal to the occasion, and no such railery ever went unrequited.

Well, this delightful visit was fast coming to an end; I was to leave, in the morning, for my far-away home. Susan, after tea, gathered one of her lovely bouquets, to take in the morning; and no one ever came or went away without one of these; it was her sweet benediction.

Dear old grandmother! Her eyes were open much earlier than usual that morning; she said she wished to read to me a chapter in the Bible without her spectacles, as it would make a more lasting impression upon my mind; so we sat down, and she read distinctly, without hesitation, one of David's psalms.

After breakfast, she returned with me to our chamber, helping me pick up the few things I had to take away; then going with me to the head of the stairs, she said, "I think I will not go down again, but will take my leave of you here." I can now feel the last loving clasp of her hand, as she then and there bade me farewell forever. The next March she went to the home so long in waiting for her.

This visit was made in the summer of 1833, more than half a century ago. Her death occurred in March, 1834.

CHAPTER XI.

I must now return to Lunenburg; having wandered away from the old ancestral home, leaving much behind that may be of interest to those who read these pages.

The story of our grandfather's misfortunes there has been told in many ways, but none to the letter, as our grandmother's account of the unhappy circumstances that led to his breaking down in health and mind.

In some of the first years of their married life, before his boys were old enough to assist him, he took charge of a lad, thirteen or fourteen years of age, whose parents had died, leaving him a small amount of property, which grandfather was asked to look after; also to take the boy until he was of age, giving him sufficient employment to pay for his support without infringing upon this little property, which, if saved, would help give him a start in life.

This boy was uncommonly faithful, and, as he grew older, he developed a talent for business quite beyond his years. This boy's name was Fowler. Grandfather came to feel that he was so much a part of his family, he did not hesitate to trust him in any department of his business, wherever he was most needed.

When the lad was twenty-one, he expressed a desire to engage in the mercantile business, and the property left him, which had been well taken care of, was put into his possession, with an addition to it by way of compensation for his faithful services. He was also allowed, to a limited extent, to use grandfather's name when purchasing goods in Boston, and for a few years he proved a successful merchant. When the Revolutionary war commenced, he only saw a wider field for his speculations, and he entered still more deeply into his favorite business. It was on one of grandfather's long absences from home, in answer to Gov. Hancock's call for his services, that this young man made heavy purchases to meet an army contract, and used grandfather's name for a large amount, depending upon his bank deposits for safety, and supposing no harm could grow out of this until Col. Bellows should reach home, when it could be made all right; but before my grandfather's foot pressed again his native soil, he was a ruined man, and all of his large possessions were swept away. The tidings met him on the road that the Continental bank was not worth a straw,— not a dollar in it worth more than so much waste paper.

It can easily be imagined how much distress this occasioned. I well remember how my grandmother, in telling this story, would always say, "There was no intentional fraud on the part of this young man, but an unlooked for calamity had fallen upon him as well as ourselves."

It can easily be conceived what a shock this news must have given our grandfather, then far away from home. He hastened to his wife and children, then ten in number, nearly stunned and prostrated by the blow. I have thought how inexpressibly comforting it must have been to know he was coming home to one, who, by her wonderful fortitude and equanimity, would always sooth, rather than aggravate, a great trouble;

for she was never given to complaining under whatever circumstances she might be placed.

As soon as possible after his return, he arranged for all those in his employ, also those with whom he had personal dealings, to come on a certain day, that he might cancel all accounts with them, determined that no poor man should lose a farthing by him. This day made a great draft upon his already nervous condition of mind and body, and he requested grandmother to prepare him something before retiring for the night.

It was soon after midnight when she was awakened by grandfather, calling to her in anxious tones. She quickly aroused some of the family, and sent for their physician. She thought he had been violently taken with fever, or some kind of illness; she thought of brain fever, in consequence of his great fatigue and exciting work on that day. The doctor, who remained with her, looked grave and thoughtful. When the morning that followed that long to be remembered night dawned, and the doctor was preparing to leave, grandmother besought him to tell her the worst, as he seemed unwilling to express any opinion. And as she insisted, he said, "Mrs. Bellows, you compel me to tell you that I fear your husband is hopelessly insane." Alas! how terribly true was that prediction! He never saw a completely sane moment afterward. He was, at this time, forty-three or four years of age. We will pause here for a moment, and, if possible, realize the condition of our grandmother. This was a supreme moment in her life. What will she do? She is fully assured of their pecuniary ruin,— from wealth reduced to poverty in a day. But this is a secondary consideration,— of small importance to her at this moment.

The greater and more terrible thought was the condition of her husband. When she fully realized her situation, she felt that all this was crushing her; but the thought of her ten children came to her rescue, and she said with that thought came strength; and, as she was leaving the room, she met her father-in-law, Deacon Foster, who said, in a tone of sympathy she could never forget, "Lois, my daughter, remember there is an Almighty arm to lean upon, an Almighty hand to guide you; take a fast hold of it, my poor child!"

This dear old gentleman, for many years a member of the family, had reached that period when the infirmity of years was bearing heavily upon him, and he could only be considered as one more added to the number of her children. As all these things were passing through her mind, she was more deeply impressed with the necessity of doing something quickly, and that must depend upon her own decision. She had no one to go to for counsel. She called her oldest sons, although in years they were yet boys, and asked which one of them could best take to their uncle's in Walpole the tidings they must carry from this household, so recently full of happiness and prosperity, but now in deep distress! As we look back upon this misfortune through the long distance of time which has elapsed, how distinctly we can see the different shape it gave to the future of each individual life belonging to that household.

It was during a cold winter that all this, which I have been relating, happened; and a journey from Lunenburg to Walpole, in the way it was usually accomplished, was a matter of serious importance. It was soon decided, however, which one of her boys was to speed away on this errand which was to be taken to Uncle General. Col. John was at Exeter, then the seat of government, and he was notified to meet his brother Benjamin at Lunenburg, the day he should be expected to arrive there. I cannot distinctly recollect if it was Saturday evening or Sunday morning that Uncle General received the news; but I remember it was said that he had started before church commenced in the afternoon, with a sufficient number of teams to bring all the family and their household effects to Walpole. There were ten children, grandmother and grandfather, and Deacon Foster. It gives me a feeling of pride, as well as pleasure, to record the fact that this old gentleman, now too helpless to care for himself, and having no claim but that of marriage with her mother at a late period of her life, was as kindly and tenderly cared for as any other member of the family. This was an act in full accord with the noble-hearted generosity of our race, at that period, in all its branches; and heaven grant that each one of us may see to it that this feature of our ancestors be preserved through all time by their children.

When the colonel joined his brother at Lunenburg, their first work was to arrange matters with the creditors, who were many of them unscrupulous harpies, who demanded that their dues should be paid in hard cash, since paper money had so depreciated, believing that grandfather had large deposits somewhere. It was fortunate that Col. John was there to deal with these heartless scoundrels, who knew under what circumstances our grandfather was made responsible to them, also how utterly impossible it was to obtain specie; and still they refused to receive anything else in payment. But it took the colonel to bring them to terms; and the estates were disposed of at forced sales, realizing not half their actual value; and, when this unfortunate business was cancelled, there was little or nothing left for their family, who had held the first place in society, and also the largest possessions of any of the people in that town, with their wide open doors of hospitality.

When my grandmother related this story, it was never given continuously, as I have been telling it, but those portions of it that seemed pressing most heavily upon her mind at the moment. As I have put all these incidents together, to-day, each one finding its own place, I have thought how reluctantly she seemed to dwell upon any of these scenes, particularly where it was necessary to speak of grandfather's condition. It was from other lips than hers that I learned that, like most other insane people, he had come to think his dearest friends were his bitterest foes. It is impossible for us to conceive how inexpressibly painful it must have been to hear anything like unkindness from lips that had never before spoken to her excepting in terms of tenderest love. Whenever she referred to him, it would be to relate something he had done that was quite remarkable as a public man, or in his important military service, or to give some instance of his tenderness and devotion to his family. I have many times heard her say, "Your grandfather, when at home, never allowed me to get up with a single one of our ten children. If they were restless and needed quieting, it was he who would attend to them; and in the soft, soothing tones of his musical voice, they were quickly lulled again to rest. In all their little ailments, he was a most skilful nurse, always knowing just what to do." It was in these lingering memories of his love and tenderness that she mostly lived, seldom referring to that which was painful.

As soon as our uncles had made the necessary arrangements, they set out with this family for Walpole. The three daughters, who were her youngest children, were nearly babies,— the eldest of them not six years: the youngest son, Thomas, was eight; Abel, ten; with five more older boys. Perhaps it may be well to dwell here, for a moment, upon the manner in which this large family were received by their kindred. Such an example of fraternal sympathy and kindness we seldom have an opportunity of presenting, when we consider all the circumstances: the father of this large family in the condition named, and with him Deacon Foster, an old gentleman, requiring as much care as a child, from the infirmity of years; and then ten children, of various ages from one year to eighteen; but all hearts were brimming over with sympathy and kindness, and there was an abundance of room in every house, which they were made to feel was in waiting for them. Col. John chose to receive my grandfather with his wife and her three youngest children, into his house. The general invited Deacon Foster to become the chaplain in his family, as Mr. Harding, who had long held that office, had died shortly before. The general also received the three youngest boys, Thomas, Abel, and Levi; they were the especial care of Aunt General, and nothing could exceed the motherly tenderness with which she looked to everything necessary for their comfort. The older boys were placed in other homes of the kindred.

As we now pause to look upon the condition of this family, we can fully realize the truth of the old adage, "There is no telling what a day may bring forth." A few short weeks ago, they were enjoying all that a happy and prosperous home could give them; now, homeless. When anything occurred that led grandmother's mind back to this painful period, when the members of her family were all scattered here and there, and not a ray of light to illumine the dark future that lay before her, she said that, in her despair, she would inadvertently drop a word in reference to the additional care so many of her family must be, as Col. John then had a large family of his own; but he would quickly rebuke her, saying, the Lord had filled his house with plenty to overflowing, thus making it incumbent upon him, and a privilege to provide, not only for his own household, but for the needs of those who had a natural claim upon him, especially one so near to him and so dear as his brother Joseph; that he, with the general, would see at the proper time where she could best be situated with all her children together once more; but that, until that time, he and his wife and children were all made happier by the thought, that his roof was large enough to shelter all. She could not recall a moment when she had cause to doubt the sincerity of these expressions of kindness.

How delightful to find these gems with which to brighten the pages of our family traditions! How much of bitterness it must have taken from this cup of sorrow, to find such generous sympathy in her husband's family!

CHAPTER XII.

When the springtime came, true to his promise, Col. John, with the approbation of his brother, Gen. Benjamin, made a proposition to grandmother which she readily accepted; for she could once more gather about her the scattered children, some of whom had sadly pined for the old home, and the mother's wing, although everything had been done to make them comfortable and happy; but they were out of the old family nest for the first time, and their life turned into a different current, and it was hard to get accustomed to this great change.

As Col. John had large landed possessions, he proposed placing grandmother, with her family of boys, upon a farm which he had selected, called the meadow farm, which lay directly on the bank of the Connecticut River, and only about a mile from his own home. There was a pretty and convenient cottage, with barns, and, indeed, all the apparatus that belonged to a nice farm. As he owned the land as far as Westmoreland, the boys could have the privilege of cultivating all they desired to. It was, at first, thought best to have grandfather remain with his brother, but, as he had now become so much more quiet, under the magic influence which the colonel seemed to have over him, she could not think of leaving him to the care of others, who could not know as well as she all his ways and wants; and, even when in his right mind, he was most fastidious in many things.

Well, in due time, grandmother found herself with her little flock and grandfather in this home, so kindly furnished to them, and she was to commence a new life. But oh! how different from the one she was accustomed to! But this was no time for comparisons; her work was all before her, and she must get everything arranged. How well I remember her saying she could do nothing without first laying a plan. She had much system and order, which was carried into every department of life : and now each one of her sons must know what his own particular duties were, and it was her business to assign them. But Uncle John persisted in being dubbed dictator of the potato patch, and he held this office with some distinction; but one day he unfortunately forgot that there was a higher authority than his own, and he undertook some business that was considered not within his jurisdiction.

There was a large amount of work that was to be accomplished on one particular day,— the corn and the potatoes had already been waiting for the hoe too long; each one of the boys had been assigned to their portion of this work, as it was something that all could take part in. I must put in a parenthesis, here, that Uncle Abel, as a boy, always had the reputation of liking gingerbread and stories much better than he did work. Well, he demonstrated the truth of this assertion, on that particular day, by doing nothing at all. His elder brother, the dictator, had long been aware of these shirking propensities, and took upon himself, then and there, to apply the proper remedy, which was nothing less than a regular flogging. This boy, who had never received such retribution before from the hand of any one, could only look upon it as an outrage, and fled swiftly, in much wrath, with this terrible wrong, to his mother. She listened with her usual self-possession to all he had to say. I can now see that look of quiet determination on her face, which her children used to understand so well. She gave no opinion, and made no answer to his tale of woe; but when all her sons, having completed their day's work, came in, and had seated themselves around the supper table, she said, "Boys, I wish you to wait a few moments; I have something to say which I expect you all to give attention to. Since the unhappy condition of your father, I have felt that I stood in a double relation to you, not only as your mother, but with the care and authority of your father devolving upon me; and, so long as you are inmates of my household, I want you to understand that you are to be subject to my authority, no matter if you are fifty years old. And, Jack, I have a special word for you: never again lay your hand in violence upon one of your brothers; when they need discipline, send them to me!"

The incident I have just related came to me many years after it occurred. It was at the time of one of Uncle John's annual visits to his brother Abel, who kept a bachelor's home a number of years before he married, grandmother and myself making a part of the family during this period. Every one expected a time of general festivity during these visits, for Uncle John was always full to overflowing with wit and humor.

His brother was a victim to dyspepsia for more than thirty years, and Uncle John always declared these visits were what saved Abel's life. The truth of this assertion we may never know; but we do know that he survived many years, attaining to a goodly old age. He was over eighty when he died.

It was during one of these visits that a little scene took place, one morning, which presents itself so vividly at this moment, I must give it a place here. At the time grandmother, with her family of boys, was living at this meadow farm, there was a man in the neighborhood by the name of Johnny Martin. He was noted for his eccentricities and originality. It seemed as if nature had provided him with a magic looking-glass, in which he could take his own comical view of the whole world. He could not see anything as other people saw it. He also had a vocabulary of his own,— many words of his own coining,— which he used, in his quaint way, to describe persons and things, to the great amusement of every one who heard him. This man earned his living by performing day's work for his neighbors; and, whenever there was extra work, Johnny was sought, and was always most efficient help, and these days were especially considered as the boys' holidays, for nothing could exceed the mirth and fun that was going on from dawn until dark.

More than thirty years had now elapsed since Johnny was playing his jokes on these boys. He had become comparatively an old man, while Uncle John, who had for many years been a resident of Boston, had accumulated a large fortune in the mercantile business, and was distinguished for his public spirit and financial ability. As I have already said, it was at the time of one of his visits to his brother that the following incident took place. While in the kitchen, one morning, for some purpose, the back door suddenly opened, and a figure presented itself, but kept standing as if transfixed, looking directly at the dignified gentleman, then, putting itself into the most grotesque attitude, burst into an uncontrollable fit of laughter. As soon as he could speak, he vociferated, "Jack, do you remember the flail?" This question brought back, in a flash, the memory of that quaint, original individual he had not seen for more than thirty years. This greeting, so perfectly characteristic, wholly ignoring the lapse of time — picking my uncle up just where he saw him and left him so many years ago — struck an answering chord; and Uncle John, in his merriment, roared for a few minutes as loudly as Johnny Martin. This uproar brought grandmother quickly into the room, to learn what had happened; but, when she questioned her son, he replied, that it must in the future, as it had done in the past, remain an impenetrable mystery. But we came to the conclusion that the story of the flail must have had more of comedy than tragedy in it, as these two individuals seemed to have been the principal actors. It can easily be supposed this opportunity was improved to recall many funny things that took place in that long ago. But more particularly I remember how Johnny revived the memory of that discipline Uncle Abel received at the hands of his brother John, telling all the circumstances in his own quaint way, which brought as many tears as were shed on the former occasion, but of a somewhat different sort. Uncle John, for the moment, laid aside his dignity, and was a boy once more, lending himself wholly to the occasion. Many years were lived over again in that one hour, and whoever saw Uncle John in his moments of inspiration, and heard him relate anecdotes, and describe persons and incidents that had taken place in his life, need not be told of the peals of laughter that followed. And I can recollect how eloquently, at this time, he made grandmother speak to her regiment of boys, when she asserted her authority over them, even after they were fifty years old, if they were under her roof. After reciting her own words, he made the most profound obeisance, and declared he had never since that memorable occasion dared to disobey one of her orders.

CHAPTER XIII.

It was but a few years that grandmother lived at the farm, but it was necessarily a laborious and anxious period. The most happiness she found there was in the thought that she was keeping her children together, and wisely controlling and directing them, until they were sufficiently matured to choose some more congenial occupation than farming proved to be to most of them. There was much that occurred in those few years that helped to shape the lives of these children.

Grandmother's first and greatest trouble in this new home was the change it had wrought in grandfather. Away from the control and the soothing influence of his brother John, that peculiar influence which always seems to result from the recognition of the presence of quiet authority, his malady increased, bringing great additional care and anxiety to the family. It was then that Col. John brought this brother back to his house again, and received him in such a kind and sympathetic manner that his malady seemed at once greatly allayed. He assured him that no harm could come to himself or to his family, and it was his wish that he should stay with him permanently, so that he could give his personal attention to him. "But you must be very quiet here," he said, "as Si and Roswell are at home studying for college, and must not be disturbed." And here grandfather remained until the time of the colonel's death, which was quite a number of years afterward.

The colonel died in 1812, and grandfather's death occurred in 1815.

It was a common remark, what a wonderful influence Col. John always had over his brother, who would listen to his persuasions as to no other one; but he could never be reasoned out of some idiosyncrasies, which he carried to his grave. Before my grandfather's reason was dethroned, he was widely known as a gentleman of most courtly manners, strong intellect, broad humanity, executive ability, and also unusually interesting and pleasing in conversation. This last was due, I presume, in some measure, to the rich, clear, musical, tones of his voice, so full of sweet cadences, such as an individual seldom meets with more than once in a lifetime. How I wish it were possible for me to catch sound once more of the words, oh! and ah! spoken with the sweet pathos in which my grandfather could utter them!

During the last fifteen or twenty years of his life, a stranger could hold long conversations with my grandfather without a suspicion that he was not all right; and such opportunities frequently occurred, for Col. John, as well as his brother the general, kept open house, following the example of their father. The colonel was in the way of entertaining many celebrities, who were in the habit of visiting this town at that period. Perhaps some of them were attracted by Col. John's daughters, who were known far and wide as belles in society, brilliant in person and in conversation. As I now look through the mist of nearly seventy years, I distinctly recall four of them in their youthful beauty; and there is no reason to doubt that many admirers might have come to Col. John's with such high hopes as only to make their disappointment more severe. It was well known that Col. John was very proud of his daughters, and he naturally demanded much for them.

Somewhere in the last years of Uncle Colonel's life, I remember, as a little child, running away from my home, and the great scramble I had to reach his house, which stood on the top of the hill. I was in search of my grandfather, who, on seeing me, came quickly and picked me up in his arms, expressing surprise and great pleasure that I should have run away in order to find him. It must have been in fruit time, for, as I recollect, he took me into the garden, and held me up high, so that I could pick the cherries from the tree for myself, and then carried me home to my mother. I have heard her say many times, and grandmother also, that nothing could exceed his tenderness for little children! If he saw them too far away from home, or in any place of danger, no trouble was too great for him to place them in safety.

His brother, thinking at one time if he could persuade him to take more exercise it would benefit his health, proposed to work an hour with him every morning in the garden. To this proposal, grandfather quietly remarked, "John, have you not learned that my work was completed long ago in this world? If the Almighty has anything more for me to do, it will be in a country where the devil don't take the proceeds."

He employed a large portion of each day in reading the scriptures, which were perfectly familiar to him. The Psalms of David he would often repeat, and the Book of Proverbs was entirely at his command. His conversation was usually upon religious themes, with those who wished to talk upon such subjects; and great surprise would sometimes be expressed at the clearness of his reasoning upon such topics, when his mind was so clouded upon others.

I can well remember his daily visits to my mother. Her quiet, gentle ways were always a balm to his troubled spirit. I could not have been more than three or four years old, for he often took me to school, and would sometimes carry me a part of the way in his arms.

At the time of his brother's death, he was taken to the home of his oldest son, Mr. Salmon Bellows, who lived about four miles distant.

The death of this favorite brother was a terrible blow to his tottering mind, and made it still harder for him to bear, from the necessity it brought of changing his residence. My grandfather did not long survive his brother; I was about sixteen years old when he died.

It always fills my heart with sadness, when I think of my grandparents, with the cloud upon them,— they whose early life gave promise of so much happiness; they were happy in each other,— happy and proud of the large number of children that blessed their sunny home, making it, as grandmother would say, so bright and full of life; especially, she would add, when your grandfather and I returned from a few days' visit to our friends, taking perhaps one or two of the youngest children,— the little girls. There was always such a tumult of joy, as only a dozen boys of all ages can make; and my father would say, "Boys, if you devour these children, and your mother also, you will never have an opportunity to be so glad again."

CHAPTER XIV.

I THINK I have already stated, that there were ten sons in this family before there were any daughters; and each of the big boys had his own pet kitten, as these girls were called. Sally, the second daughter, always found a stanch friend in her brother John, both in childhood and also in her more mature years. There were so many half-grown boys, that the two or three eldest, who had nearly reached manhood, were distinguished as the big brothers. I have heard my mother, who was that little Sally, often relate instances of his loving-kindness. One, in particular, occurs to me at the present time.

At that period, it was customary in many country places to have a shoemaker come to the house and make the shoes, especially where there was a large family; and one pair was generally expected to do duty for a year. Should they happen to give out, it was not uncommon to see the children about home barefooted, or on their way to school looking and feeling quite as happy, if not a little more so, when wading through the warm sand with their naked toes, or perfectly free to ford a brook or mud puddle, should such an irresistible attraction lay in their path; but when the nipping frost was a good deal in advance of the shoemaker, tears would express the general feeling better than smiles.

It was on one of these occasions, when the shoemaker had been engaged in his rounds to come to the house, and finding many more feet to be shod than he anticipated, he was obliged to leave before quite finishing his work. There was one more pair to be made, and those were for little Sally; and he faithfully promised to bring them the next Saturday night. Although it was only three or four days that intervened, to her child-mind, that far-away time seemed to belong somewhere at the end of the world; but, when at length the day came all right, the shoes did not come, and little Sally went to bed, bitterly sobbing out her disappointment. This man lived nearly opposite them, across the Connecticut River, at Westminster, Vt., in a little cottage which could be seen from the river bank.

The next morning, her big brother, wrapping her up warm, carried her in his arms to the bank of the river, where he said he was going to have a talk with that man, and see if he had not left the shoes at the wrong house; so he commenced calling in a loud tone, and went on talking as if he were answered, telling her that, when she woke up, the next morning, she would find her shoes close by her little bed, waiting for her to put them on; and sure enough, he had managed in some way to get her a pair of boughten shoes, which she found in the morning, just as he had said. It was many years afterward that she learned what an effort her big brother had made to procure those shoes; for he had walked many miles that Sunday, not reaching home, on his return, till late in the evening. Shoe shops were few and far between in those days, in those frontier settlements.

Our grandmother used to say she never knew how

she struggled through these years on the meadow farm; the weight of her responsibilities seemed, at times, greater than she could bear, though her oldest sons were always ready to aid her in every possible way. A good and faithful girl, too, was found to assist her in the house. At that time, every kind of cloth that was used was spun and woven at home, and the wool and flax from which it was made was raised on the farm, and it took no small quantity of cloth for all the inside and outside garments for a family of fifteen.

This family was not unlike all others, save for the greater number of them, in variety of temperament; and it has been a puzzle to me how such a flock were all kept together so long; and it could only have been through the strong influence of that mother. They certainly did not leave the home-nest until sufficiently matured wisely to choose for themselves their different pursuits; and now we have come to what proved to be a turning point in the lives of some of this family.

There was an opportunity given for a new landlord in the public house, by the death of Asa Bullard, who had made that place famous for many years. Uncles John and Joseph, though very young men, hardly more than boys, became successors to Mr. Bullard; and, as neither one of them was married, there was no one in their estimation who could do the honors of the establishment so well as their mother. She did not discourage her sons in this new enterprise, yet it took no small amount of persuasion to obtain her consent to this personal charge in a new and somewhat distasteful field of duty. She soon found herself in the new establishment, leaving her two youngest boys, Abel and Thomas, at the farm, in the care of Lydia, to whom the little boys were attached; for she then, as ever afterward, had a peculiar charm for children.

How long my uncles remained in this new business, I do not know, but probably long enough to secure means for commencing a more congenial employment, as one of my earliest recollections is of my Uncle Joseph's dry goods store, where Uncle Thomas, his youngest brother, was employed as a clerk. From the many anecdotes I have heard, I think he must have been quite an attraction. He was a remarkably fine-looking young man, with a grace of manner that made him quite charming, especially to the ladies. It was then, as it is now, customary for the farmers to come from over the hills that surround Walpole village, every Saturday afternoon, to purchase their weekly supplies, which generally included a jug of whiskey. There were no laws at that time against selling liquors, nor was public sentiment what it now is.

As the farmers made Saturday afternoon and evening a special time for recreating themselves generally, the conviviality would occasionally last until a late hour at night, particularly if Sam Drury and Sam Gilchrist appeared in the street: for that was the signal for a fight, unless Tom Bellows was there to interfere. He could prevent it, when no other person could. He held a kind of magic influence over these turbulent spirits, which was due in some measure to his entire fearlessness of them and his own self-control. He would not hesitate a moment to interfere; and spectators were astonished to see how quickly these men recognized his authority. He was, then, quite a young man,— not much more than twenty; and his brother, Maj. Jo, as he was always called, when speaking of him would say, "I have a host in Tom; were he not present, my store, on Saturday nights, when these men come in after they have been drinking, would be a pretty fair representation of pandemonium." By a stroke of his ready wit, he would turn a threatened quarrel into a roar of laughter, and he could hasten their departure by saying, "Gentlemen, I am waiting to sing our favorite song," which consisted of quite a number of very comical verses; but the last verse ended with a chorus, the words of which were, "For I'm going, going, going, going home!" They were not only expected to join in this with their voices, but to represent the sentiment by their action; and they knew he would not sing it unless they performed their part to the letter. It meant go. He had a charming voice, and would sing this particular song with great gusto, as I can bear witness, having heard him many times after I became old enough to remember it. It was in this happy way he would get rid of these revellers and brawlers, without incurring their ill-will, but rather making himself a favorite; and this was the secret of his power over them, especially over old Sam Gilchrist, who always held Tom Bellows in the highest veneration.

This Sam Gilchrist was, in his palmy days, quite a man, belonging to a company who were in among the first settlers in Walpole; and he had for his wife a near relative of Gen. Allen, whom I remember as a distinguished citizen of this town, and whose residence was the next door to my Uncle Abel Bellows, and of whom I must say a word, as he was a figure in the town. Gen. Allen must have left an indelible impression upon every one living within the sound of his voice. He was the most active and bustling man I ever knew. In summer, when we slept with our windows open, at my uncle's, we were usually awakened as early as half-past four by the thunder tones in which the old general would be giving orders to the servants in the house as also to the out-of-door men. He had a great farming business to see to, mostly on farms at quite a distance down the river, and breakfast for all hands must be ready at an early hour, and his own carriage ready at a particular moment; and when we heard the wheels roll out of his door yard, with a sigh of relief we would finish our morning nap.

Well, to turn again to Sam, as showing what sort of men these times had to deal with. Sam's connection with this family of Gen. Allen was all I ever knew of anything respectable that belonged to him. His long habits of intemperance had made a brute of him, and the many hand to hand fights he and Sam Drury had engaged in had nearly obliterated every human semblance from his face. This face was horrible enough to our childhood; but still more terrible was old Sam's cry, peculiar to himself! He would always continue his potations, if allowed to do so, until he reached a state of insensibility; but, when about half-way there, he would commence pacing up and down the street, roaring, his voice sounding like some wild animal's, and tears streaming down his face like rain. When at this pitch, it was always dangerous for any one to interfere except Tom Bellows, as Sam always persisted in calling him, declaring, at the same time, he was the only friend he had on earth.

My Uncle Joseph had a few very valuable sheep,

which he wished to remove from one pasture to another, which was two or three miles distant; and Uncle Thomas was sent to do it. He was successful in driving the sheep a part of the way, when all at once they scattered in every direction, and for a few minutes there was no visible cause for alarm; but, on going a little farther, he saw old Sam Gilchrist lying in the middle of the road dead drunk. The sheep, in their fright, had all turned back; and, as it would be impossible to get them past him, the only thing to do was to get him out of the way. That, however, was no easy task; every effort to rouse him proved fruitless, and my uncle began naturally to feel very angry, and seeing a suitable long pole in the fence, he drew it out, and made such an application of it to Sam as brought him to his senses sufficiently to enable him to get on to his feet. But he had sense enough to know that Tom, his best earthly friend, had beat him with a bean-pole, as he persisted in calling it; and, for many weeks after this occurrence, he made a point of coming into the store on the usual day of their high carnival, and telling the story of the terrible outrage his best friend had perpetrated upon him. Uncle Thomas at last told him, if he would never repeat that story, or in any way refer to it again, he would give him a new pair of shoes; and Sam accepted the terms with a solemn pledge.

On the next Saturday, he was seen in the street, but, as the afternoon was coming to a close, and Sam had not appeared in the store, Uncle Tom was congratulating himself on thus getting rid of such a scourge, when his attention was attracted toward the door, and the object of his thought was standing there with two or three of his old comrades looking directly at him. His first words were, "Oh, Tom!" Here he broke down. When he had gained a little composure, he cried out, "I haven't forgot, Tom, that air promise, but oh, Tom! Them was an awful good pair of shoes, but I can't forget that d —— bean-polling!" and here he commenced his roaring cry again, which was the terror of all women and children within hearing.

I have given this lengthy description of one of the miserable creatures of that olden time more particularly to show the tact and wise discretion with which Uncle Thomas would manage better than any other one that portion of the degraded population such as in that day was to be found in every settlement. As I have more to say of Uncle Tom, by and by, I will only add here, that a few years later, when twenty-four or five, he developed quite a military taste, receiving several promotions. I am reminded of this by a very perfect likeness of him lying upon the table before me now. It was painted on ivory, and he is in his military costume, which was so very different from that of the present day that I will describe it. Here is the broad shirt collar, with a corresponding width to the collar of his coat; a white neckerchief, filled out with what was called a padding, perhaps to make his neck look large. The wide collar with its square ends comes up around his face, revealing only a small portion of the chin and nose. The hair is combed up on the top of his head, and turned over, looking like hay when raked in a windrow; and a long lock is made to stand up straight from the centre of the forehead, and a profusion of powder, I should think, was indicated. This was painted nearly one hundred years ago, by a celebrated artist in Boston.

After the lapse of more than seventy years, how vividly I can recall the joyous circle of young cousins, as we sat on the doorstep that warm, summer evening, listening and laughing so merrily at Uncle Tom's funny stories; and now, of all that happy group, there is nothing left but a memory,— save myself to tell the story!

CHAPTER XV.

As I have but briefly spoken of Col. John Bellows and his household, when telling the story of my grandfather, I am aware that there are yet many of his descendants living, who will perhaps read with interest the further recollections I have brought with me from childhood of that distinguished branch of the family. He received what in those days was a princely inheritance from his father, consisting of lands and all kinds of stock, as well as money. His land spread itself from the river bank up on to the broad hillsides, reaching a number of miles in extent. His residence was located upon an eminence, which overlooked the whole village, commanding also a wide reach westward in Vermont, and a splendid view of the river as far as Bellows Falls, named for his father, and four miles off. He was eminently fitted by nature as well as education to preside over such an estate, by his rare business ability, also his dignity and courtly manners, representing the true gentleman that he was.

My first recollection of him is when I was between three and four years old. He was on his way to the post-office, where he went every morning on horseback; as he passed our door, he saw I was just leaving on my way to school, which was at the other end of the village. He called my mother to reach me up to him; and this delightful ride as far as the schoolhouse I have never forgotten.

Col. John's house was the one since owned and occupied during the summer months by Rev. Dr. Bellows, with the wonderfully beautiful view from its broad piazzas, overlooking the rich valley of the Connecticut.

I also distinctly remember the garden which was situated where the lawn is now. I can still see in imagination those gorgeous flower beds, separated from the large vegetable portion of the garden by a long line of hollyhocks in every shade of color; also the great variety of rosebushes that decorated the edge of the terrace. On each side of the steps, which led from this into the garden, there was a large bunch of crimson peonies, which were my especial admiration; and when my grandfather put one of these into the handful of flowers I sometimes took home, my little cup of bliss was running over.

This beautiful home had an irresistible attraction for my childhood. I somehow felt that wherever my grandfather and Uncle Colonel were, I had a right to be; and there my feet would often stray, feeling sure of that welcoming smile from Aunt Colonel, also, even while she was questioning me if I had not run away. At this time, she had been an invalid several years, greatly suffering from rheumatism. I can now recall that sweet, pale face, and the fine blue and white striped linen dress she usually wore, and which was made from cloth manufactured in her own house, so celebrated for the fineness of its texture. Her large easy chair was placed in the sitting-room where she could look, when the doors were opened, through a dark pantry, which communicated with the kitchen; and thus she could sit here when she couldn't walk, and direct her domestic affairs. Dinah, the colored woman, who received her instructions at headquarters, was the one to transmit her mistress' orders, and insure their proper execution by the other domestics.

This colored woman had lived many years in the family, and was highly valued for her faithful and efficient service. When Aunt Colonel was not able to direct affairs of the household, old Dinah swayed the domestic sceptre; and woe to all within her jurisdiction who were not prompt to fulfil every duty that belonged to them! She bore the marks of age as I can first remember her, and was very arbitrary in her way of giving orders. This impression was stamped upon my memory by the tone of her voice, when bidding me go right to my aunt, and keep there; as I was sometimes compelled to go in at the kitchen door, when the front gate was fastened so that I could not open it. But I cannot think I was very much daunted by this reception, for the toes of my shoes would always turn in the direction of that house whenever I could escape from the vigilance of my mother.

At the time of these memories of my childhood, Uncle and Aunt Colonel were past the meridian of life, and only three children remained at home,— Hubbard, their youngest son; and the two youngest daughters, Maria and Harriet. There were nine children, six daughters and three sons; all of whom, except Fanny and Sophia, I distinctly remember. Those two daughters died before I was born. Fanny, named for the child that died, married David Stone, an enterprising merchant, at the time, in Walpole. She was the second daughter, and lived but little more than a year after her marriage. She was the first whom death had called away from that large and happy circle of brothers and sisters. Sophia, the beautiful, as she was often called,— how can I speak that name with the reverence I feel at this moment, having heard it so often from my mother's lips? There were only a few days' difference between her age and my mother's; and the lives of these loving cousins were singularly interwoven, as from babyhood they were almost inseparable companions. Both were sweet and gentle by nature, and I have heard my mother say she could never recall a word or look of unkindness that passed between them. It was not very long before my mother's death that she was relating to me some incidents of their early life, and I think the memory of this sweet cousin had not lost a particle of its freshness or fragrance for her when she was ninety-six years old.

I recall, at the present moment, one or two incidents I have heard my mother relate. Ever after she was old enough to leave her own mother, she made her home most of the time in the family of her cousin, Caleb Bellows, with whom she had always been a favorite, and by whom she had been greatly petted from her earliest childhood. The distance from his charming home to her Uncle John's was made very short by crossing a deep ravine, which separated the two hills upon which their houses stood; and these two children found very little to prevent their passing much of their time together. During the warm weather, it was a frequent occurrence for them to bring their porringers of bread and milk, at the close of the day, and take this delicious repast together under the shadowing branches of the great elm which was their trysting-place. This magnificent tree is still standing in all its primitive glory and majesty at the bottom of the ravine, making in itself a forest, its long and leafy branches casting their shadows over my own home, where I now sit writing these random recollections, and which by a singular coincidence is situated within hearing of the babbling brook that has watered its roots for at least two hundred years. And in that long ago, before my eyes were darkened, and all that is lovely was hidden from my view, I used often to stand upon the edge of this same ravine, looking down upon its wild beauty; and it required no great stretch of imagination to convert the rippling of this merry flowing brook into the chatter of those children over their porringers of bread and milk.

Another incident which may be worth jotting down, as telling something of young life in those old days, occurred when these children were not quite old enough to be called young ladies. Mrs. Caleb Bellows went to visit her parents at New Ipswich, and requested my mother, at the age of fourteen, to do the honors of the house during her absence. At this time, there was a young student who hailed from New Ipswich; he was therefore received by the family as a guest for a few weeks. He was remarkably tall, and exceedingly stiff in manners, putting on an air of dignity that was much beyond his years, and quite terrifying to such very young ladies as Sally and Sophia Bellows, who had always been treated as children; but this young gentleman had seemingly magnified them into something quite different from what they chose to consider themselves, for they utterly refused to receive his gallantries.

It unfortunately happened, on the first day after Mrs. Bellows' departure, that the colonel was called away on business, and detained until a late hour in the evening; consequently he was not at home, to take his tea with this young trio, where he was so much needed, to give a little assurance to the presiding genius of this repast; who finding herself in an entirely new position, her timidity got the better of her discretion; and at the outset she made one or two blunders in what was the precise etiquette of the tea-table at that period. This did not help to reassure her, and her situation was becoming more painful, as she was making a desperate struggle to conceal her merriment, and knew her Cousin Sophia was in full sympathy with her. It took only a moment more to bring things to a crisis. This precise young gentleman made an unfortunate remark, which caused her to look up at her cousin, and they both burst into an uncontrollable fit of laughter; leaving the table, they rushed from the room up-stairs, and locked themselves in their chamber, as much frightened at their rudeness as though they had committed a crime. In the morning, they came to the conclusion it was best to tell the colonel all about it; and, to this end, they sought an interview with him at the earliest moment, and related to him all that had happened. He listened to what they had to say with a very comical expression on his face, and when they begged him to excuse them from appearing at the breakfast-table, he gave his arm to each of them, saying, "Now, girls, you can have no fear; and, if that young scapegrace puts on any more of his ridiculous airs, it will be he who will run away, and not you."

This little episode I have heard my mother relate many times, as it afforded an opportunity to show how tenderly and kindly her cousin Col. Caleb would always shield her from everything that could wound or disturb her feelings in these early years of her life, when she was so shy and timid ; and how he, perfectly understanding her nature, would always, when present, come to her rescue. My mother, during her long life of ninety-six years, cherished the most grateful memory of this friend of her childhood.

Her lovely cousin Sophia — I can almost hear the tender tone with which my mother always pronounced that name — was too sweet and fragile a flower to bloom long upon earth. She was called home in all her beauty and young loveliness at the age of eighteen, leaving a void in her home here that nothing could ever fill, and a desolation and wound in the hearts of her family that time had no power to heal.

Her early death seemed foreshadowed to herself, as she said to my mother, many times, she should not live very long. Once, as they stood watching from their front windows a funeral procession moving slowly up the hill leading to the burying-ground, she turned, saying, "Sally, I shall very soon be carried up that hill in just that way, and I wish you to be prepared for it." Her prediction proved only too true.

CHAPTER XVI.

I MUST now go back to an earlier period, to the history of one branch of the family. Many traditions of that earlier time came to me through my grandmother's conversation; whose grateful remembrance of the kindness of her husband's brother, Col. John, in the time of her great sorrow, would prompt her to speak of them often.

When she first became acquainted with her sister-in-law, they were both at the best period of life,— between forty and fifty years of age. Both were intensely practical women, having superintended large households, and reared large families of children; and my grandmother would say, the only thing in which I surpassed my sister Rebecca, she had only nine children, while I had five more than that number. At this period, it will be remembered it was decreed that nothing should be used in the colonies but what could be grown and manufactured by our people; and in almost every household, whether rich or poor, might be found the spinning-wheel and quill-wheel and loom, and all the apparatus necessary for making cloth, both cotton and linen; and every man, woman, and child was clad throughout in what was called, at that time, homespun. Ambition was stimulated, and there was great competition, especially in the linen fabrics; as these were used for all kinds of purposes,— undergarments, dresses, aprons, pocket handkerchiefs, and neckerchiefs. Whatever could not be made by themselves, from flax and sheep's wool, people learned to do without. Col. John had too much of the Bellows spirit and patriotism to purchase a single article from a foreign power that was continually heaping insults upon his country; and his wife deeply sympathized in this sentiment. His daughters had always been elegantly dressed, for his great pride was centred in his family, and everything that fancy or fashion suggested was provided with a liberal hand. Under the new law of the colonies, as has been said, a change became necessary; all these foreign luxuries must be laid aside. As his family was the leading one, their example would be followed by the rest of the community, at least by all loyal citizens. It was this state of public affairs that aroused Aunt Colonel's ambition; and she turned her attention particularly to this department of the household economics. The finest wool and beautiful flax were raised upon this great estate, and in sufficient quantity to make cloth for an army, if need had been; and it was not only the quantity but, the quality, that was the more remarkable. It was said, that some of her white linen would equal in fineness of texture the imported Holland that was used in those days for gentlemen's shirts, not used for the bosoms alone, as at this day, but for the whole garment, long, large, and wide, as I can bear testimony; for how can I ever forget the long stretches of hemming, every stitch taken with my then little fingers, and the long side seams sewed over and over, and then felled down? But more especially do I remember the stitching of wristbands and collars. A thread was drawn out, and two threads were taken at each stitch.

The linen fabric that was made for dresses was

famed for its beauty. It was blue and white narrow stripe, colored in the yarn, and the texture was as delicate as the imported muslin. The fine checked linen made for aprons was beautiful.

When I was five years old, Harriet, the youngest of Col. John's family, was ten; we attended the same school, and, as she passed our door, she would often call to take me with her. I remember perfectly her slight, trim figure, and pale, sweet face, like her mother's. There was a small, round scar on her temple, near the left eye, about as large as a five-cent piece. It was made by a burn, when she was a baby. This scar was, in my estimation, a great addition to her beauty. But I more especially remember the glossy, striped dress and the lovely blue plaid apron, always shining, and without a wrinkle in it. I think this daughter must have resembled her sister Sophia. She was always noted for her kind and gentle manner, loving and tender to all her friends during her short life. I shall never forget a most painful illness, produced by a very slight accident, when she was about twenty-two years old: she ran the head of a needle under her finger-nail, which she did not mind much at the time, but it soon commenced paining her until it amounted to agony. Her hand and arm were frightfully swollen, and nothing could relieve the pain. Old Dr. Twitchell, of Keene, was sent for; and the first thing he did was to lay the finger and hand open to the bone, which probably saved her life. I recollect the trouble and excitement this occasioned in the whole community of friends, and it was a long time before she recovered. It was a number of months she tended her hand upon a pillow. It was the impression of many that she never fully recovered from that illness. I think she was twenty-five or six when she died. How perfectly I recall the deep sympathy that was expressed during this painful and long illness, and the solemn hush that pervaded the street on the day of her funeral, many of the leading business men being her near kindred!

At that time, she, with her sister Maria, had, since their father's death, been making their home with their sister Hannah, Mrs. David Stone. This was his second marriage, he having previously married Fanny, the sister next older than Maria, whose death we recorded. They occupied what is now called the Elmwood house, Mr. Stone having built this residence in 1812; and, at the time, it was considered the handsomest dwelling-house in the village. He had previously occupied, and I think built, the house Mr. William Buffum and family have since owned.

But to return to Aunt Colonel and her manufacture of cloth. Her success had become widely known, probably reported by the people, who came from towns quite a long distance off to get spinning to do of both wool and flax. As the only way of travelling was on horseback, they often made a most ludicrous appearance when bringing home the product of several weeks' labor. The piles of yarn would be tied upon the horse behind them and before them, often wholly concealing the rider, especially when seen approaching from a distance; and a lively imagination could easily convert this moving mass into some huge animal belonging to some unknown species. There was one woman in particular that belonged to Aunt Colonel's troop of spinners, and who lived nearly twenty miles away. She was always spoken of as "old Mother Barnard." No disrespect was really intended. It only seemed the most fitting way to specify her quaint individuality. She was especially noted for the huge piles of yarn she would bring on the smallest specimen of a horse. Old Dinah would sometimes say, unless one had a near view, it would be hard to tell which was the yarn or which was the horse. The woman herself was physically very diminutive; but those who belonged to that household soon learned that that was not the way to measure her, particularly the colonel's boys, Josiah and Roswell, who at first considered her only a target for their sharp shooting. They quickly found that their arrows would invariably recoil upon themselves, often giving them much the worst of the game; for they had nothing to match the keen wit of this woman, and, to the surprise of all, they were forced to make an ignominious retreat, to the great satisfaction of my grandfather, who could never tolerate even the semblance of rudeness to the poorest creature. Col. John's sons were strictly trained by him in the observance of good manners; but we can suppose they were, like all boys, overflowing with exuberance of spirits, as Josiah in particular was prone to be. He was so full of mischief that he was constantly getting himself in little scrapes, which annoyed his father so much that on one occasion he told him that he deserved the greatest punishment he could inflict, and so he had fully determined to send him to college, and now nothing remained but for him to prepare himself for it. This bit of information came to me from hearing Cousin Si, as he was always called, relate the story when making one of his evening visits to my Uncle Abel. I was then fifteen or sixteen years old. His conversation was always very interesting to me. There was no better talker in the Bellows race,— perhaps not one who had more general knowledge, or could impart what he knew in a more interesting manner or better choice of words. He said, at this time, his father would have succeeded in carrying out his threat of putting him through college if the boy had not succeeded in running away. He came to the conclusion he would obtain his knowledge in his own way, and that was by observation. It used to be said of him, "What Si Bellows don't see and hear is not worth seeing or hearing." He was fine-looking, having the culture of a gentleman; but tradition says he did not wholly lose the love of mischief that was born in him. Well, this Mother Barnard made herself invaluable to Aunt Colonel; for, while she could spin such quantities of yarn, nearly as fine as a spider's web, Aunt Colonel could make such cloth as no one else attempted to imitate; and this branch of industry was carried on on such a large scale, wholly superintended by Aunt Colonel, that it required a large number of operatives. There was a Scotch woman employed for more than twenty years: she did no other work but weave. There was a large basement room in the house fitted up for this special purpose, and here Mrs. Sally Lathwood reigned a queen at the great loom; and war to any invaders of this precinct!

In some of the earlier years of her labor in this family, when the colonel's boys were between manhood and boyhood, there was an occasional skrimmage between them and Mrs. Lathwood. I think, at some period, she had been greatly troubled by their depredations in her room, through the spirit of mischief that seemed to possess them, and the colonel then and there ordered them never to set foot on her premises again. When the colonel gave a command, his military experience led him to expect it would be obeyed. Some time had elapsed, and order reigned in Warsaw; but this queen of the loom was none the less regarded as an enemy to the peace of these juveniles; and no opportunity was lost to annoy her in some way whenever she was discovered outside of her premises. Her Scotch nature would not allow her to receive an insult tamely. She believed thoroughly in the old Mosaic law, a tooth for a tooth, and an eye for an eye; and it happened, sometimes, that these young culprits got the worst of it.

The colonel left home, one morning, with the expectation of being detained through the day. Roswell and Si could not lose the opportunity to pay off, at least in part, some of this old debt. They had bided their time already too long. They had plotted to make what they termed a military attack upon the enemy's camp. To this end, they busily employed themselves with the necessary preparations. Some of the help, who were friendly to the old woman, informed her what was going on. She fortified herself at once with the means she had, barricading her doors, and arming herself with a long birch rod, saying there was nothing that contained so much virtue in it for boys as that, when well applied. After making these preparations, she awaited the foe; she had not long to wait before their approach was announced by the tooting of a tin horn and the beating upon a tin pan. This music was performed by a couple of boys, recruited in the neighborhood for this occasion. Her door was soon assailed, which at first resisted their battering ram; but it soon flew open, leaving a free entrance to these wild-cats. Captain Si's first order was to seize the booty, which she stoutly defended; but, being overcome at last, they took possession of her quill-wheel and swifts, and commenced marching off in great triumph with these trophies of war, when they were unexpectedly met on the war-path by an ally of the enemy not put down in the programme. The colonel, unbeknown to them, had returned sooner than he himself expected, and, hearing the uproar below, was on his way to see what the trouble was, when he met Si and Roswell, bearing off the quill-wheel and swifts which they had so ruthlessly captured. Cousin Si said he knew, by the twinkle in the old gentleman's eye, they would not get the thrashing they deserved; but the colonel, taking in at once the situation, shouted in a tone of thunder, "Halt!" He then ordered them to return at once their booty, and to report themselves to their mother, where he should investigate their proceedings. The result was, that they were ordered to go respectfully and humbly, and ask the old woman's pardon. This was a terrible humiliation, and, rather than submit to it, they begged their father earnestly to give them the thrashing they had expected; but no, a respectfully worded and courteous apology had to be made.

I have already said Cousin Si was in the way of passing an evening, not unfrequently, at my Uncle Abel's house, bringing with him his great exuberance of spirits, and the house usually became a scene of great merriment while he remained; and sometimes his stories would make it a little uproarious. When he told that story of his father's intention to send him to college, and the manner of his escape, Mr. Dickinson was present. He was the minister of this place, and had a standing invitation to take tea at my uncle's on a given evening each week. He was also a bachelor. His keen sense of the ridiculous and brilliant wit, he would sometimes indulge in, especially when he came in contact with those as keen as himself. It can easily be imagined there was some pretty lively joking. Mr. Dickinson, on this occasion, told the story of some one saying, "If a Bellows should happen to be shut up in a room with a book, if there was no other possible means of escape, he would go through the window;" and he thought Cousin Si was a pretty fair specimen of that particular class who belonged to the race.

As I present these home incidents, I am led to suggest that if there is not as much enthusiasm over them as over the excavations of Nineveh and Troy, I hope it will be borne in mind, these persons and things have not been buried from all knowledge of the world quite as many years as those ancient cities.

CHAPTER XVII.

AT the time I was about six years of age, Maria, who was not very far in her teens, attended a school, having the dignified name of academy, the first of that order that ever had been taught in Walpole. With other branches I particularly remember that lessons in music were given, and Maria was only too glad to avail herself of this opportunity to gratify her taste in that direction. She had a sweet voice, as I can distinctly remember, as she used frequently to drop in evenings to sing with my mother, who, at that time, took the lead in music both at church and at private musical entertainments, which were quite popular at that period. They did not then, as now, have the assistance of any instrument, unless it were a flute, which was said to accord perfectly with her voice.

At this time, the colonel purchased the first piano that was ever brought into Walpole. It was said that he imported it directly from France. It occasioned no small excitement, as well as curiosity. I cannot resist telling here a little anecdote, although it may slightly compromise dear old Uncle Salmon and Aunt Lydia.

He lived about a mile from the village, and I happened to be there at the time the piano-forte arrived. That word had not been interpreted to many of the inhabitants of that period; and, when the huge box in which it was brought, and labelled in large capitals, was being unloaded, quite a number of people gathered about it, critically examining the letters, and greatly puzzled as to what they might spell. One individual very knowingly informed them that it was the name of an extinct animal, whose bones had been dug up somewhere, and wired together, and were now being carried about for exhibition. Uncle Salmon was not quite satisfied with this explanation; and, when an opportunity presented, he asked his Uncle John what kind of an animal he had got there. The colonel had heard the explanation already given, and replied, it was "a very noisy animal, particularly when there were many spectators about"; and, with a twinkle that did not escape notice, he added, "it had never been known to bite or otherwise harm any one, but, on the contrary, was very much admired by young ladies." Uncle Salmon put this answer in his pocket, and started for home. The mystery of the box remained wholly sealed to him; but he assured himself that Liddy, as he always called his wife, would know something about it, for what did she not know? Greatly, to his astonishment, however, she knew nothing but what he had himself told her.

Her own curiosity now was thoroughly awakened; and she said, before another sun went down, she would see and know what kind of an animal had been imported just for the benefit of the colonel's family. I have no doubt that before the sun set she succeeded in obtaining the desired information. She was a woman, let me say, now her name is mentioned, whose natural abilities were quite remarkable, and I can remember when there was no one who had so many charms for me as my Aunt Liddy. She was particularly fine-looking, and her kindly, winning ways won at once the hearts of children.

I think it would be very amusing, particularly to those who have been accustomed to the grand piano of the present time, if they could see one of those instruments of that early period. This one that was purchased for Cousin Maria was a very large instrument, having a good deal of ornamental work about it; and probably she got all the music out of it that was possible, and in its measure it was sweet music too, but its capacity was very limited as compared with what instruments of to-day furnish to our ear. And now the thought comes over me, how many sweet and loving daughters of our race could be counted up who once kept time with these silver notes in the merry dance in that bright and hospitable mansion, but who now are sleeping where our golden sunsets long ago shed on them their last lingering beams, bidding them good-night.

This instrument that I have referred to was taken to New York, for old acquaintance sake, at the time of Maria's marriage with Mr. Center, and was destroyed in the great fire in that city.

CHAPTER XVIII.

At that period, I think the community might have been called a church-going people, although the meeting-house was located on the top of a steep hill, a mile from the village centre; I have sometimes heard it described as being a mile straight up in the air.

I distinctly remember with what regularity Uncle Colonel's chaise would pass our door at the foot of this long, weary road that lay between him and the place he was seeking. Seated in this vehicle might be seen Aunt Colonel with two of her daughters, the colonel always in advance, on horseback; and, as he had great pride in the feminine portion of his household, it can easily be imagined they were always carefully, and even elegantly, dressed. I think some of the blood of that chivalry, of which we read in the olden time, must in some manner unknown to us have found its way into the colonel's veins; for the knight of the black plume could not have exhibited more gallantry than did the colonel when waiting upon his wife or daughters. He always rode a handsome, high-spirited horse, that would often become restive, when compelled to keep at the side of the carriage, slowly creeping up the hill; and he would allow him to gallop a short distance ahead; then wheel round, and come back to the side of the carriage. He would escort them in this manner until within a short distance of the meeting-house, when he would ride on, and dismount in season to receive the ladies as they drove up to the door. This was no outward show of attention ; the same spirit of courtesy was observed within the retirement of home as well as abroad.

Maria and Harriet, the youngest of nine children, were much petted by their father, who chose to treat them as children when they were old enough to be considered young ladies. When addressing them, he would give them their pet names, Birdie and Dovey. Perhaps Birdie was chosen for Maria, for the reason that she had such a sweet voice for singing; and Harriet's was not less applicable, with her sweet, expressive eyes, and gentle, winning ways. These two daughters remained at home, to cheer and comfort their father's solitude after their mother's death. Although I was quite a child when my uncle died, in 1812, I can recall many incidents that occurred,—one in particular, that occasioned some merriment, as it probably lost nothing by the way Cousin Si related it to the friends. Maria took her mother's place at table, and some friend had joined them at tea. The conversation becoming quite interesting, they lingered around the hospitable board some time after partaking of all the appetizing things that were usually served so bountifully at this last meal of the day ; and, when Maria rose, giving the signal for leaving, she dropped something which she attempted hastily to recover, and caught some portion of her dress on the handle of the teapot, tipping it over directly upon her back. She gave a little shriek, and attempted to escape from the room. Her father, forgetting for the moment that they had lingered at the table sufficiently long to cool all the water in the teapots, supposed she was being scalded, and caught a large pitcher of cold water from the table, and started in quick pursuit, giving a dash of its liquid contents over head and shoulders every time he got sufficiently near, until the water was exhausted. Maria, in her race, had doubled upon her retreat, and returned to the room from which she had started, and sat down, with the water streaming from her clothes, saying, "Why, father, have you really been trying to drown me?" In a moment, the mistake flashed upon the colonel, and the whole ended in a roar of laughter.

I don't think I have related this little episode as well as Cousin Si used to. There are some touches to the picture which I have no power to give, but, as rendered by him, we could see the entire chase.

About this time, a Miss Caldwell came from Boston to Walpole, bringing with her a niece, the daughter of a clergyman, Rev. Mr. Dana, of Barre, Mass. He married, for a second wife, the sister of this Miss Caldwell; and Mrs. Dana had bequeathed to her sister's loving care two little daughters, Sarah and Isabella. When old enough, they were placed in a popular boarding-school, near Boston. Isabella did not live to finish her education; Sarah, when graduated, was brought to Walpole, as I have said, by her aunt, and both were received at Uncle Colonel's as guests.

A beautiful friendship was formed between Maria and this young lady, that strengthened with years, and lasted through life. The most loving and familiar intercourse was kept up during their girlhood, and suffered no interruption after Miss Dana's marriage with Maj. Thomas Bellows, the cousin of her friend.

A few years rolled on, giving time for much to happen in the lives of these two individuals. The first sad event came to Maria in the death of her father, which was a great sorrow to all his surviving children, but especially to Maria and Harriet, who had never left their home. They could not think of their father as an old man, and he was not old as we look upon age. I think he was only a few years more than sixty, a fine, courtly looking gentleman, and just as young to these daughters as he had ever been; and so how could they spare him? But a sad silence now fell upon this home, once the scene of so much activity and gaiety,— a place so often sought by lovers of good society and good cheer; for there was no one of old Col. Benjamin's children who carried out so true to the letter his own ideas of hospitality as his son John had done for long years. There was nothing left of all this now but a memory.

Maria and Harriet took up their abode with their sister, Mrs. David Stone; Hubbard, the youngest son of the colonel, took possession of the homestead, bringing with him a wife to preside where his mother once reigned a queen.

Another change in due time came to Maria. Her sister Harriet slowly drifted into that long and painful illness of which she died; and it was this one who soothed and comforted her through the weary months she lingered.

During this time, her friend had also experienced a deep and life-long sorrow in the death of her husband, who was so suddenly taken away, and also the death of her first child, a daughter six years old. At her husband's death, there was another little one of two or three years of age left, to brighten her lonely pathway. There was now a stronger and more tender friendship, if possible, between these two,— a bond born of that deep sympathy which a few only can ever know.

Some time after all these sad occurrences, Maria was married to Mr. Anson Center, a gentleman who had long been engaged in business with her brother-in-law, Mr. Stone.

On the morning of her marriage, she left Walpole for her distant home, taking the last look upon her native town, and bidding adieu to the lovely home of her childhood and the friends of her girlhood; but probably no thought came to her in this moment of excitement that her adieus were to be forever, as it sadly proved! And thus this most lovely star disappeared from our horizon forever. I could only think of her as such ever after the death of her sister Harriet. They were almost inseparable; wherever one appeared, the other was sure to be seen.

The especial interest I always took in these two daughters of Uncle Colonel was probably connected with the fact, that they were the only ones who remained at home after I was old enough to remember persons and events, and therefore they have been associated with nearly all the memories I have cherished of that grand old place; and this must be accepted as my reason for dwelling so long upon their early and loving life.

I can now distinctly recall, after the lapse of more than seventy years, the expression of each face, the difference in each form, their usual manner of dress; and I can almost hear, at this moment, the different tones of voice in which each would give her friendly greeting. Indeed, any one who had ever known Maria could not easily forget her animated tone, and the bright, playful look of her face; while Harriet, who was much taller, wore a sweet, sad look, and spoke in soft, languid tones, in perfect keeping with her whole bearing: her movements were always slow, but graceful; and, when in repose, she would have been a beautiful model for a painter. Maria was equally interesting, but not in the same way. Her lively, animated manner was always most attractive especially when engaged in conversation, which used to be called brilliant; she was noted for her quickness at repartee. These qualities, joined to her love for music, made her at that period a belle in society. It was some time after Harriet's death that Maria's marriage took place; at what age, I cannot say, but I know she was in no haste to give herself away.

After an absence of some length from my home, in that far-away time when I had something left to return to beside those of my own household, aunts, uncles, and cousins were still in the old places; and the first whom I always sought on these returns was my Aunt Sarah Bellows, that long and true friend of Cousin Maria's, whom I have already mentioned. How vividly I recall my surprise, on that morning, when coming in I found my Aunt Sarah, sitting with a pink and white blossom on her bosom; for lovely indeed as a fresh blown rose was this child of one or two years, resting there; the cordial greeting, too, as she said, "Emily, can you tell me who I have got here?" It only took a moment to recognize those eyes, and I at once exclaimed, "It is Maria Center's child!" She then told me the sad story of Maria's last illness and death, bequeathing to her motherly care and tender love this treasure which she must leave behind! How true she was to the letter and spirit of this trust, we all witnessed; while she herself has long since given her account with joy in heaven to the one from whom she received it.

There is one little episode in her beautiful child-life which comes so clearly to my mind ; and, knowing how pleasant it is sometimes to be set back into the midst of these trifling scenes of our early years, I cannot omit relating it.

This little one always evinced a great partiality for pets. Her feelings in this direction were not in the slightest degree restrained, for this mother thoroughly believed that children's affections could be cultivated through their love for animals as well as for human beings ; and so the child was permitted to have something to pet and take care of, which was usually a kitten, or two kittens, if she so chose. Her first possession of one of these little creatures raised her to the height of human felicity. One of these pets was evidently very fond of music, and whenever the piano was played would leap on the shoulder of the performer and sit there in quiet enjoyment : sometimes she would walk back and forth across the keys, seemingly in order to make music for herself. This cat was a great favorite, and the little Maria thought, one morning, she would take a pleasant walk with her ; so she gathered her up in her arms, and set out towards my home. Little puss was very quiet, suffering no apprehension until she reached the foot of the hill, when a passing team frightened her ; and, without a moment's warning, she made her escape, rushing into a ravine on one side of the road, where it was impossible to follow her. I shall never forget the distress in which the child came in, and no words could at first give her any comfort :

she seemed almost heart-broken. The little cat, however, was afterward recovered, and drawn still closer to the child's loving bosom. Perhaps the one who owned this pet will remember this occurrence better than I do.

Rebecca, the eldest daughter of Col. John, was the wife of Roger Vose. He was a young lawyer, at the time of their marriage, and was one in that literary circle of celebrities that formed a conspicuous part of the society at that early period in Walpole. She was tall, and moved about with much grace and dignity. It was said the colonel was very proud of this daughter, calling her sometimes his queen. She was several years older than my mother. My first recollection of her is when she called upon my mother, one day, bringing Sophia, her oldest child, who was a little younger than myself. I was then not five years old, but I distinctly recollect the comparison made in our size; and, although I was older, she was taller and stouter than myself, which, as I then looked upon it, was quite humiliating to me.

Mrs. Vose had four children, three daughters and a son. The son followed his father's profession, and won for himself the same honors,— the position of judge. Never having married, he made his home with his two unmarried sisters, Sophia and Katherine, who have also passed away. As I now recall these friends and companions of my early years, when the future seemed so full of promise and of happiness to us all, I can hardly realize the sun is now shining upon the graves of all save the one who is telling this story.

Mrs. Vose was a confirmed invalid, for many years before her death. Sophia had hardly attained to young womanhood, when it became necessary for her to direct the domestic affairs of the household, in which her mature judgment and executive ability surprised her older friends. Her face was always like a ray of sunshine, a perfect index of her heart, so full of kindness. She always wore the smile of her grandmother, Aunt Colonel, whom she so much resembled.

There was no place more delightful to visit than the hospitable home of Judge Vose. His three daughters and son all remained with him during his life, but Rebecca was the only one of his four children who ever married.

At that time, there was a pleasant circle of young people, both ladies and gentlemen, and among them were some very fine singers. I can distinctly remember, it was often proposed on warm, bright summer evenings, to go up on the other hill, and sit under those magnificent old trees in the front yard, where were always seats for the family and friends, and there we would exercise our vocal powers, knowing how very fond the judge was of music.

One evening, especially, I recall, when the court was in session, at that time in Keene. The judge usually returned home every night, and frequently brought some of his professional friends with him. I remember, at this particular time, the pleasure he expressed in the unexpected entertainment given to himself and his several guests. Nearly all the old songs they called for were happily quite familiar to us; " Scots Wha Hae" and " Jeptha's Daughter," finding great favor; but we adjourned to the house, to sing our parting song, and a glass of wine was presented, according to custom, with which we took a cup of kindness yet, for auld lang syne.

There are, at this time, but two or three living, to cherish a tender memory of that dear old home, full of old-fashioned furniture and old-fashioned hospitality, and to bear testimony to the patient care and devotion of those daughters, especially of Sophia, upon whose care her father mostly depended, through his long sickness, with paralysis, of years.

I shall never forget her words, when asked if she was not ready to spare him; she replied, that she had never for a moment, in all her own and his long years of weariness, felt that by any possibility she could give him up.

CHAPTER XIX.

ANOTHER son, the eldest of Col. John, was Cousin Si, whom I have only incidentally mentioned. He should have a fuller record in these fragments of our race which I am picking up than I am able to give, as he left Walpole, and went out of my sight, taking his family, many years before he died, locating in northern New Hampshire. The recollections, however, that I still retain of him are, that he was considered one of the most brilliant members of the colonel's family. The elegant and beautiful home he built, in 1812, and in which he lived several years, stands within call of my voice at this moment,— a sacred monument of those who were once with us, but now gone. His house was built directly opposite his father's, commanding the same lovely and extensive prospect.

I have a vivid recollection of the first party given, after taking possession of their new home. Perhaps it was more deeply impressed upon my memory, for the great disappointment I had in being thought too young to be taken with the family, although I was included in the invitation; but I was soon after partially compensated by an invitation to visit, at the new mansion, a young cousin, the daughter of Prof. Hubbard of Dartmouth College, who was here. This visit was made particularly pleasant by having a free passport over the whole house given us. I shall never forget my childish admiration, on entering the drawing-room; something entirely new met our eyes. The walls were covered with paper, representing various scenes,— hunting, fishing, and rural farming; the people and animals all seeming, to my eyes, as large as life. The trees, especially, that represented the forest, quite astonished us. This certainly must be the fairy land,— that enchanted place, which, until now, we only had a vague idea about. As we made ourselves quite satisfied with this conclusion, we passed on to make new discoveries, finding ourselves at last in the kitchen, where old Rachel was evidently the mistress of all she surveyed. She had earned all the privileges accorded her, by long years of faithful service in this family. This colored woman was the first servant they had, when setting up housekeeping. Her physical proportions were quite commanding, and in perfect keeping with her manner of directing all affairs within her jurisdiction. The men who worked on the place used to say, she not only directed affairs in the house, but out of doors also. She was a servant who always stood in high favor with all the household, and had some privileges not often accorded to those of her color. I can remember seeing this woman brought to church with the family, in their handsome equipage; his wife and her sister on the back seat, and the children between that and the front, which Cousin Si occupied, with Rachel sitting at his left hand, arrayed in all the gorgeous colors of the rainbow. That yellow silk bonnet, with its long plume, I can never forget. There was a steep ascent just before reaching the front door of the meeting-house, and a smart crack of the whip would urge the spirited horses to ascend, coming up to the door with quite a dash, and apparently as proud of old Rachel as he was of his horses; and no one drove a handsomer pair.

Many years after old Rachel had left Walpole, when she had finished her work as servant, she longed for one more look at the old home, of which she was so proud, and could never cease talking about; and she was brought here in an easy carriage, one of Cousin Si's daughters, who did not now live in Walpole, coming with her, and taking such nice care of her as was most interesting and touching to see.

All the old families were anxious to make Rachel's visit pleasant and satisfactory, especially those who had bought and were occupying the old home that had once been her pride to take care of. It is gratifying to state, that this faithful servant and friend was as tenderly nursed and cared for during the long period she was unable to perform any labor as any of Cousin Si's own children, and received from their hands her last cup, and the last offices due from the living to the dead.

It is proper to mention, there were three by the name of Josiah Bellows, at one time, in Walpole; and they were distinguished as Si, first; Si, second; and Si, third; and all were heads of large families. The short sketch I have just finished was of Si, the second. His uncle — Si, the first — also had a handsome residence on the opposite hill, but not quite so elevated; therefore the prospect was not so extensive, though wide and very beautiful: but, whatever attractions it may not have had outwardly were sufficiently compensated by those that were always found within. Let me now enter that broad and open door.

As soon as I was old enough to make discriminations, I perfectly understood that this was no common home. Aunt Si, as she was called, to distinguish her from others of the same name, was always dignified in her bearing, and yet without hauteur. Her genial conversation would at once dispel the thought of it; and her remarkable conversational powers were very happily transmitted to her children. I cannot think of one of them who was not gifted with an unusual fluency in use of language, giving fullest force to the clear and sensible ideas on the subjects they were talking upon. All were passionately fond of music, and the taste in that direction was highly cultivated.

I can remember, that Aunt Si for many years led with rare fidelity and success the choir at church, before any of her daughters were old enough to take part. Her brother also, Mr. Oliver Sparhawk, was once a leader there. How vividly I can recall her in her palmy days! Her gracious manner of receiving company; none could ever feel that their visit was inopportune, or that they were unwelcome guests.

Her home was handsome and orderly, seemingly just the same as when they began life. There was no pretence of fashion; you were always surrounded with the same simple elegance; no one could leave the house without feeling both physically and intellectually refreshed.

In the address at the funeral of Aunt Si, in 1869, Dr. Bellows says of her: —

"She knew, face to face, the founder of this town and the large family that bore his honored name, and which she herself wore worthily for three generations; all his sons and daughters, so long pillars of this community; all the successive ministers of the town, who have taught its faith and piety; the venerable physicians, who have watched by its bedsides; the brilliant lawyers and noted men, who have left a traditional glory behind them. She seemed almost a part of the Providence that watches the generations come and go.

"She was a skilful, industrious, unwearied mother and housekeeper; a considerate neighbor; an active servant of all town charities and social duties; a hospitable, friendly heart; a wise and sound adviser; a supporter by example and service of all our higher interests; a woman of a dignified and unreproachable life, extended to an extreme length, but never falling below its own promise, never losing its early direction of probity and self-respect, of virtue and usefulness; and, above all, of humble piety and prayer.

"Through what watchings, cares, and solicitudes must not one, so widely related, have passed during those ninety-six years of life! And what but a noble ambition of duty, a living piety, could have carried her serenely through it all? And has she not been a pattern of all the domestic virtues and graces? With a constitutional pride of character and duty, an inborn industry and thrift, a feeling of competency for all her cares, she has been an example of a true New England woman; strong, patient, industrious; domestic, self-respectful, bearing her own burdens with dignity, and those of others with patience; erect in will and purpose as in person; her mental and moral faculties even clearer than her senses, not one of which really failed her to the last,— for, until within a very few years, she has been a housekeeper, and the centre of her scattered family, so often returning to her own roof.

"What composure, self-respect, and solidity characterized her speech and her deportment; what terseness and good sense and aptness of thought and expression; how living her memory, how wide her circumspection, how manifold her thoughtfulness! Her faith was serene, constant, all-pervading. She loved completeness, and was negligent of no duty.

"What a memory for the immediate and remote descendants of such an ancestress! What a treasure for the recollection of the Church, of which she was so long the most aged member, and of the community of which she was the most venerable representative of her sex!"

The daughters, and there were six of them, were noted for possessing more than a common share of intellectual qualities, which were more fully recognized as each filled so admirably the place of wife and mother.

These six daughters are now all resting in the common bed prepared for their kindred, of whom it is said, nearly one thousand are sleeping within this sacred precinct. These gifted daughters have perpetuated themselves, by leaving their own impress more or less vividly stamped upon their numerous descendants.

I have before me now the record, which was made at the time of the family gathering, under the title of "Our Recent Graves," in which one of these daughters of Uncle Si is thus spoken of: "Catharine, daughter of Josiah Bellows, first, and wife of Judge Bellows, of Concord, N.H., was one of the most exalted and intelligent women our family has produced. She united strength of intellect with gentleness of heart; a large interest in universal themes with a punctilious fidelity to domestic duties. Formed for meditation and study, an admirable talker, and most sympathetic listener, yet she discharged the duties of wife and mother with a true New England loyalty of heart and hand. Duty was her watchword. The beauty of her brow, the heavenly purity and softness of her blue eyes, spoke the fine proportions and transparent purity and celestial aspirations of the soul within. Full of faith and resignation, this gentle and thoughtful woman, large-minded and high-hearted, passed away, leaving the circle of her kindred permanent mourners over so much perished worth and power."

An older daughter, Ellen, was one of those referred to when it was stated that Aunt Si or some one of her daughters sang in the choir, or played the organ, or did both, in the old Walpole church every Sunday during thirty-five consecutive years. Her love of music was akin to her refined tastes in all other directions: to a bright intellect was joined an earnest nature, which led her to interest herself during mature life in various works of benevolence. She was early married to Mr. Gill Wheelock, a Boston merchant. Two of her children are still living: Mary Ellen, whose husband was Nathan Chandler, of New York; and Henry Gassett, who married Harriet Hayward Dorr, whose mother was Eliza Bellows, a granddaughter of the old colonel. The other child of Mrs. Wheelock was George Gill, who became a leading physician in New York City. Mrs. Wheelock after the death of her husband married Jonathan Howe, of Boston, who survives her, she having died in 1859, honored and beloved.

Still another one of those daughters, who, by their voices and the heart with which they sang, made such delightful music for so many years in the old church, was Anne Foster Bellows. She, too, was gifted with all those qualities of mind and soul which give life and happiness to the social circle, and contribute to earnestness of thought and action. She married Rev. Dr. Thomas Hill, at the time minister of the Unitarian church at Waltham, Mass., afterward President of Harvard College. She filled her various responsible positions, private and public, with that grace and dignity which were given by conscious strength and a high and well-defined purpose in life. She died in 1866, leaving five children, who all bear impress of her who moulded their characters and gave them of her own gifts.

Uncle Si's hospitable home witnessed one evening a scene which very few houses can make record of: it was the marriage by one service of three of his children. They were William, the youngest son, whose wife was Miss Sarah H. Giles, of Walpole, their only son now living in Cincinnati; Julia, whose husband was Robert Barnett, of Boston; and Catherine, whom we have before referred to, her husband being Judge Bellows, of Concord, N.H. From but few houses have gone out into the world as many children of the home prepared by intelligence, education, and sound principles to do the work of life.

Uncle Si was the youngest but one of Col. Benjamin's children; and there are yet many living in his native town who distinctly remember him. It is not very long since I heard some one remark that Uncle Si had filled, and filled well, a very large space in the community in which he lived. This was not only true of his ample personal proportions, but he was a man of great energy and great activity, and of the soundest judgment. His presence anywhere always seemed

to mean business, as he paid but few complimentary visits.

I can distinctly remember with what regularity, every Sunday in winter, Uncle Si's great double sleigh might be seen packed to its utmost capacity, winding its way up the long and tedious hill to the old meeting-house. There was not a pew in the church more amply filled; the Sparhawk race, as well as the Bellows race, was emphatically of the church-going sort.

I find myself often contrasting the present with the past, when it was not unusual to see all the pews in the church actually filled with parents and children; whereas we now see only one or two little ones, here and there, looking like stray lambs. But it only requires a look into the homes of our people, to understand this change. Then we could often count from six to a dozen, sitting round the family board; and it apparently required less care and expense to provide for this number than for the one, two, or three, whom we occasionally find in these degenerate days, with habits of modern extravagance. We shall never again see those large square pews, with the seats on hinges, so that all the congregation could stand up in prayer-time, while four or five little ones were anxiously waiting for the amen, to turn the seats down again with a bang; and oh! it was such a relief to us children to get an opportunity to do something!

But to return to Uncle Si. Dr. Bellows, in his address, recalled the fact, that old Gen. Bradlee used to tell of his recollections of once seeing Uncle Si and Col. John's oldest son, while yet boys of sixteen, travel-worn and weary, with their packs on their back, going past his house in Westminster on their way up to the ferry that crossed the river on to the old Walpole homestead. Hailing the boys, he found that they had made their way on foot all the distance from New Haven, whither they had been sent on horseback to college. Impatient of the confinement and dull routine of the place, yearning for the large freedom and exciting life of their half-redeemed forest home, they had run away from college, and were ready to face any amount of domestic reproach rather than endure an unnatural bondage.

In that same address, at the family gathering, Dr. Bellows says of Uncle Si, the people at large respected so much his integrity and his judgment, his plain good sense, and his unpretending honesty, that he wielded a wide and enviable influence. An excellent farmer, his example and advice influenced the agriculture of the place; a good citizen, he always lent a generous support to every public interest,— the church, the school, and the administration of the town. That name, "Uncle Si," was always the synonym of honesty, firmness, judgment, and promptness; of self-respect, independence, and modest worth.

I vividly recall the eldest daughter of Uncle Si, whose name was Louisa. She was the companion of my mother's youngest sister, whose name was also Louisa Bellows, and who usually passed the summer in Walpole, the home of her childhood; her permanent home afterward, for many years, until her marriage, being in Boston, with her oldest brother John. These cousins were very intimate, passing much time together, so long as my aunt remained here.

As I now see them, in that far off time, how different they appear to me from the young ladies whom I meet of the same age, at the present day; they were, at that time, about twenty years old. Perhaps it is because I saw them as a child, being myself only about thirteen. These two Louisas were both fine-looking; not handsome, as that word is generally interpreted, but their faces beamed with intelligence and animation; and when they were in their merriest moods, so full of wit and fun, and dear old grandmother would occasionally indulge in a hearty laugh, I thought there could be no better entertainment.

I wish I could describe one little scene, making it as amusing as it truly was at the time; but that would require the actors themselves.

My uncle had invited a friend, a Mr. Gordon, to pass a few weeks with him. He was a professional man of some distinction, and very much a gentleman. I can remember well his courtly and elegant manners, and also that he was very fine-looking. He, too, was a bachelor, as was my uncle, who endeavored to make his visit as pleasant as possible, by inviting other friends to dinner, or tea, every day. On this particular day, our Cousin Louisa Bellows was invited to dinner, and tea also; and these two discreet young ladies, the two Louisas, so noted for their observance of all the proprieties, had somehow got on their high-heeled shoes. They were both making a pretence of trying to capture this stranger; their badinage on the subject was most amusing, for nobody could say brighter or more witty things than they; and Uncle Abel, who deemed it indecorous to indulge in loud laughter, was compelled to transgress his ideas on that point many times that day, when he would exclaim, "Girls, girls, I am astonished! I shall not dare to take you to the table at dinner. You must be getting the control of your risibles in season, for I cannot permit you to compromise yourselves or myself, and I give you warning." All this was pure fun for me. My young eyes and ears took it all in. I can remember with what interest I watched the progress of the dinner, as all were non-committal, — the girls meeting the remarks, as well as the keen glances, of this handsome stranger, with perfect self-possession. I thought my uncle rather enjoyed the opportunity to show up this brilliant sister and cousin of his, for they could acquit themselves with graceful dignity anywhere.

There was an hour or more of very lively and amusing conversation kept up after dinner, when Uncle Abel proposed taking his friend to visit the Rockingham farm, returning to a late tea. When, however, he noted the lateness of the hour after getting started, he turned toward the Valley farm, which was only half as long a drive.

When the coast was clear, to borrow a phrase, these young ladies picked up the thread of their discourse, which was dropped before dinner, and the contest became warmer than ever. They accused each other of practising all sorts of wiles to capture this unconscious victim, growing more enthusiastic and excited. Cousin Louisa hit upon something so perfectly absurd that there seemed there was no retaliation, excepting a personal attack; and the next moment her high-top shell comb was out of her hair, letting the rich, beautiful mass down over her back and shoulders; the next moment her opponent found herself in the same predicament, and while in this mock contest, with grandmother in a convulsion of laughter, the parlor door suddenly opened, and, to their horror, her brother walked in with his friend : the girls retreated as best they could, leaving poor grandmother, when she could sufficiently compose herself, to explain that the girls were having a game, which they occasionally indulged in, for their own entertainment. The gentleman courteously replied, that nothing would give him more pleasure than to be allowed to join them in their next game. But he never was initiated.

A few years later, this eldest daughter of Uncle Si became the wife of Mr. John Hayward, of Boston, a brother of the celebrated Dr. George Hayward, for many years one of the leading physicians of the city. She brought up, worthy of their ancestry, two sons and one daughter, all of whom are now living, two of them surrounded by children. The daughter, bearing the family name Louisa, married Rev. C. T. Canfield, who for a time was minister of the parish at Walpole; the same parish over which Rev. Pliny Dickinson had been settled more than a half-century before, when he, too, sought as his wife a descendant of the old colonel, the daughter of Col. Caleb Bellows.

Uncle Si died at an earlier age (seventy-nine years) than any of his brothers. He was thrown from his carriage, and received injuries which proved fatal.

Let us now recall one of our great-grandfather's sons, whose memory is still retained fresh even by some of the present inhabitants of Walpole, and will be kept green as long as there is one left in his native town who knew him.

He was like his brothers, always distinguished by his title, the townspeople speaking of him as the Squire, and his relatives addressed him as Uncle Squire, or

Uncle Tom. He lived his whole life where he was born, becoming singularly associated with everything both public and private that belonged to the community in which he dwelt; probably for the reason that he took such a personal interest in all that was going on,— nothing escaping his notice, no opportunity lost when he could give a helping hand, or lend his counsel or advice.

I can now vividly recall that strongly marked face, so full of benevolence and kindness; also, his tall, erect figure, driving in his strongly built old-fashioned vehicle through our street, at a slow pace, and with a loose rein; giving a friendly nod to each person whom he met; stopping often to talk a minute with some acquaintance. There was seemingly no one he had not some business with; but there was no hurry. His horse took the same leisurely pace, which apparently he had followed for years, evidently conscious of the kindness and indulgence of his driver.

I can recollect, also, with what regularity the squire always attended church, where he felt so much at home; he would always make himself comfortable in his own way, during the long sermon: occasionally rising up, and resting his arms over the high top of his great square pew, he would look over the congregation, apparently to see who were there, and who not, yet giving assurance of his devout attention to the sermon, when he had finished his paternal survey, by turning his face up to the speaker in the twostory pulpit with such a look of satisfaction and peace with himself and all mankind as would make a pretty good argument to even such theologians as sometimes preached there against the old doctrine of total depravity.

HOUSE OF THE FOUNDER OF WALPOLE, Co. BENJAMIN BELLOWS (Built 1762.)

I can also remember that his love for young society was proverbial. After he was quite advanced in years, for he lived to be very old, he would gather the young people about him for a game of whist in the long winter evenings, not infrequently ending with a supper, which he knew so well how to provide for young appetites, which never failed to do ample justice on these occasions.

I have many times heard the remark, that our grandfather showed his good judgment and penetration, by selecting this son at such an early age to hold the homestead, made sacred by the memory of so much toil in founding it. He did not like to think that those lovely and fertile meadows, stretching far and wide along the bank of our beautiful river, should be divided and subdivided, passing into the hands of strangers, so long as the affairs of men could wisely keep them as he had left them.

And our Uncle Squire, so true to all his trusts, proved himself worthy of this also, until death released him from all earthly obligations; when the estate was transmitted to his son, bearing his own name, and who still occupies the old ancestral house, which is now standing in all the grandeur which only the hand of time can impress upon these sacred treasures of the past.

This old mansion is set back some distance from the street, on the main road of travel from Walpole to Bellows Falls, and a long line of magnificent elms and maples stand in front, seemingly as gigantic sentinels, to keep watch and ward, as long as there shall be anything left to need their protection.

Uncle Squire held the office of High Sheriff of the

County nearly, or quite, forty years. Perhaps no one else ever did, or ever could, fill that office in the manner he did, and still be retained in it such a succession of years. He could not be accused of any omissions in the performance of official duties, but he would always find a way to be kind and humane to the poor and unfortunate. I can never forget a scene in which I was deeply interested, when I was perhaps fifteen years old. There was a family by the name of Gardner, who occupied many years the house which Mr. William Buffum's family have owned for the last half a century. He was a lawyer of some note, and was sent from this district as a representative to Congress. At this time, my uncle, Abel Bellows, was living in the house now owned by Mrs. Titus; which then stood, before it was moved, on the main street, directly opposite Mr. Gardner's, and so near that conversation could be distinctly carried on between the houses.

Mrs. Gardner was a most genial and pleasant neighbor; she also had a sister residing with her, who was very pretty, and quite a favorite with my bachelor uncle. During the winter preceding this eventful spring, the family seemed encompassed with misfortune. She, or her children, were ill all the time, and her husband away in Washington, seemingly without any care for them. I perfectly remember the devotion of my grandmother at this time, and how often I was called upon to help her. I can also recollect many guarded conversations concerning Mr. Gardner, which was all Greek to me at that time. But the crisis came at last; the spring had arrived, but not Mr. Gardner: instead, a letter was brought, followed by the sheriff.

I can never forget the distress and utter wretchedness of that poor woman, and Uncle Squire's effort to calm and comfort her. He had received orders to attach and remove everything in her house, and all this misery was brought upon her by a gambling debt. The process, however, was staid in some way by Uncle Squire, and I can never forget his denunciations of that man, as he talked with my uncle that morning. Mrs. Gardner was, in some unknown way, protected in the possession of her home by a friend, whose name was never given.

Another memory of him will always live with me; it was when the great sorrow of his life fell upon him. Breakfast was hardly over, one morning, when he came in to my Uncle Abel's so unlike his usual way that my uncle hastily rose, and looked at him searchingly. "Abel," he said, "your aunt has lost her reason; I cannot tell you what a terrible night I have had!" And he seemed entirely exhausted with fatigue, and overcome with grief. My grandmother and uncle could not have been more surprised if he had come to tell them of her death. They endeavored to comfort him, by saying it could not be lasting; that she must be ill, and, when better, this aberration would pass away. But he took a different view, seeming fully impressed that her case was hopeless, which proved only too true. I can well remember how deeply not only the friends, but the whole community, were affected by this calamity; for her place could not well be filled in society, and to her family, never! The thought of placing her in an asylum was not entertained for a moment. The friends were ready to give all possible assistance, especially in caring for her through the long, weary nights; and it was peculiarly touching to hear them tell of

Uncle Squire's great tenderness and indulgence in managing her,— the same as he would a sick child. After a time, she became quite passive, and would see and converse with friends in her old way, which was always most interesting; for she had been highly cultivated, and was a person of great refinement and superior intelligence. She lived many years after this, an object of the most devoted care and indulgence. Her especial fear and dread of darkness occurs to me, and I think it was twelve candles she always wished to have kept burning through the night; and I have no doubt her wish was gratified. It was said, that, when her husband left her remains on the day of her burial, in the darkness of the tomb, he tearfully regretted that he could not have left also some never-failing light with her.

In the annals of our race, perhaps there could not be found a better specimen of one possessing all the virtues imputed to it than our Uncle Squire. His integrity, his benevolence, and kindness were proverbial. There are many charming anecdotes still repeated of him, that will live as long as his native hills remain to cast their shadows over this beautiful valley.

Uncle Squire, as I have said, left the old homestead to the care of his son, Thomas Bellows, and occupied for many years the house nearer the centre of the village, that his brother, Gen. Benjamin Bellows, left at his death. This change brought him very near his two daughters,— Mrs. Buffum's beautiful home, but a short distance above him; and Mrs. Peck, nearly opposite, across the street. There are now but few left who used to know him; but the pleasant memories that cluster round his name are still cherished in this community.

He was born, as I should have mentioned, in 1762, the year the family homestead was erected, which he finally inherited from his father, and to which I have already referred. In the town records, in 1791, he is styled Lieut. Thomas; and it is an evidence of his early weight of character, that, notwithstanding his well-remembered infirmity of speech, he was early appointed moderator in the town meetings, and was sent as State Representative. In 1794, he was appointed Counsellor to the Governor, for five years; and, in 1799, was made High Sheriff of the county. Meanwhile, he had filled every sort of town office, and was a most efficient citizen. As Gen. Bellows seemed to take the old colonel's place, so, at his death, the sheriff took his in the confidence and respect of the town.

Since writing this brief sketch of our good uncle, a friend kindly reminded me of that incident in his life, which illustrated his whole character too fully to allow the story to be lost.

I can vividly recall, as a child, that frosty summer, when the gardens and fields sparkled so often in the morning sun,— not with dewdrops, but with frost and ice; and acres of corn and grain all through the country were cut off, and great apprehension was entertained for the poor, so dependent were they in those days upon the crop of corn. Speculators were active all over the country, and sought this opportunity to purchase, at any price, at which they could get it, all the grain to be found held over from the preceding year's crop. But they could not, at any price they could offer, buy one bushel of the squire's corn, of which he had several hundred bushels on hand. He kept it all, and sold it to the poor people who came from points even fifty miles distant, charging the same price as in years of plenty, or else giving it to them, as he constantly did, without money; and it was proverbial of him, that he never made any one's necessity his opportunity.

When this characteristic incident was told to Mr. George B. Bartlett, he at once saw the beauty of the sentiment expressed, and embodied it in a little poem, which I copy:—

THE SQUIRE'S CORN.

"In the time of the sorrowful famine year,
When crops were scanty, and bread was dear,
The good squire's fertile and sheltered farm
In the valley nestled, secure from harm;
For the Walpole hills, in their rugged might,
Softened the chill winds' deadly blight,
The sweet Connecticut's peaceful stream,
Reflecting the harvest's golden gleam.
And the buyers gathered, with eager greed,
To speculate on the poor man's need;
But the good squire said, ' 'Tis all in vain ;
No man with money can buy my grain:
But he who is hungry may come and take
An ample store for the giver's sake.'
The good old man to his rest has gone,
But his fame still shines in the golden corn ;
For every year, in its ripening grain,
This good old story is told again,
Of him whose treasure was laid away
In the banks that seven-fold interest pay ;
For to feed the hungry, and clothe the poor,
An investment is that's always sure."

When speaking of Col. Benjamin Bellows, the founder, I should have referred to his personal appearance, and manner, and education, and I will introduce it here. This is what we are told of him. He was tall and stout; his weight, in mature life, was three hundred and thirty pounds. It is no small proof of the extraordinary energy of his spirit, that, until within the last few years of his life, this bulk did not encumber his movements or repress in the least his activity. Mounted on a strong sorrel horse, able to carry him and his youngest son, Josiah, who rode behind, and slipped off readily to take down the bars in his visits to his various fields, Col. Bellows rode about his farm, and directed the labor of his men. From him descended, perhaps, our characteristic love of horses; and from him came the Herculean frames which several of the next generation possessed. His great amiability and true benevolence, with a natural suavity and courtliness of manner, procured for him the title of one of nature's noblemen; honest, as he was energetic, rare in judgment, of great self-possession under trying emergencies, strong in mind as well as body, unbounded in hospitality, and sagacious and prophetic in plans, the old colonel united the qualities of his well-known sons, the general and Col. John, and was the large and pure fountain of his numerous and decided race.

Col. Bellows manifested great discretion as a founder, alike in the public spirit and liberality of his own doings, and in the modesty and unobtrusiveness of his conduct. There was nothing to overshadow or wound the pride and independence of the early settlers, in his bearing toward them. He showed, indeed, the same kind of disposition to throw off upon others, as soon as persons could be found to bear them, the honors and dignities of the town, as he did to make his children, at the earliest moment, independent of him in respect of worldly goods. There was no selfishness, no backwardness, in sharing with others his power or place, while there was no ostentation of benevolence, no bustling assertion of paternal authority, no claim to absorb the influence or control of the town.

He was a man of good English education, for those times. His early life evidently threw him into the society of men of education and manners. The country, at that period, contained many persons connected with the army or government who brought the manners and the education of the old country with them. Col. Bellows, through his brothers-in-law, Rev. Mr. Stearns and Col. Blanchard; through the family of his mother, the Willard's, and by his connection with the English officers, as surveyor and purveyor for the army, had formed manners of dignity, and of courtesy and authority. And most of his children were marked by a suavity and courtliness of manner, a carefulness and nicety of dress, indicative of hereditary refinement. Dr. Bellows, in his address, while giving this view of the colonel, adds these words, "It is creditable to the mental constitution of the family, that its hereditary bias is toward intercourse with human beings, rather than books; that it seeks its knowledge at first sight,— by observation, and not at second hand,— by reading; and this strong trait I suppose to be an honest inheritance from the old colonel."

And here, too, let me refer as I think I have omitted to do, to the personal appearance of Gen. Benjamin. The general was a dark-complexioned man, fully six feet high. He carried himself with military erectness and natural grace. Capt. Humphrey, of Portsmouth, told Mr. Abel Bellows, that when in attendance at the seat of Government as senator or counsellor, there was always a rivalry among the different boarding-houses as to who should entertain the general, so much was his attractiveness valued, and so highly did he stand in the good graces of the ladies.

He wore a cocked hat, small clothes, and a cane, and was always nicely and carefully dressed. And here, perhaps, as well as elsewhere, I may introduce what I might have narrated, when speaking of Uncle Thod, who inherited his father's immense size, weighing, as he did, over three hundred pounds. It was generally believed that Uncle Thod, with a strength proportioned to his weight, was the leader and champion in the famous recapture of the town's cannon from the stalwart men of Keene. And here is what is told about the cannon.

It seems that each of the four forts on Connecticut River had been supplied with large iron cannon, by his Majesty the King of England. These cannon, remaining, after our independence, in the several towns where the forts had been, were prized as trophies, and used for purposes of rejoicing on public days. The neighboring towns became jealous of the gun-towns; and, in 1807, some citizens of Keene, led by a young officer, afterwards distinguished in the service of his country, determined to repair to Walpole in the night, and steal the cannon from its unguarded gun-house. This they accomplished. The Walpolians indignantly protested, and attempted to arrest the ringleader in the offence, but in vain. They sought the aid of the law, but the Court decided, that the said cannon was not the property of the town, and the defendants were discharged. Very much irritated, the Walpolians resolved on a recapture of their trophy. They had discovered that it was concealed in a granary, in a back store, on the south side of West Street. On the evening of the 4th of July, 1809, a plot was laid to accomplish their purpose. A stage-driver was sent to Keene in a huge stage-wagon, under the pretence of buying grain, but in reality to discover and arrange for the recapture. He learned the place of its concealment, bargained for his grain, and obtained possession of the key of the place where it was stored, under the plea of taking in his grain very early the next morning, without disturbing the clerks. This done, he went a little way out of town, and met in the dark a cavalcade of thirty Walpole men, led by an officer of high militia rank, and made his report. Tying their horses in the bushes, they stole into town, made their way to the granary, and, after desperate efforts, succeeded in lifting the cannon into their wagon, and started off at a spanking pace for Walpole. The noise of the rescue had, however, aroused some of the people, who rang the town bell, and raised the alarm. A large party of Keene men mounted their horses, and started in hot pursuit; but luckily they took the wrong road, and thus, perhaps, a perilous conflict was avoided. At break of day, the Walpole band were welcomed by the ringing of the village bell, and by the applause of a crowd of their anxious townsmen, who had all night been awaiting their return. This same cannon was afterwards stolen by a party from Westminster, Vt., for use on the 4th of July, and retaken by our citizens while in actual service.

CHAPTER XX.

AND now that I am recalling what I might more fitly have introduced when I first spoke of the old colonel's children, let me say a word more about Aunt Richardson,— Abigail, by name. She lived, as I have mentioned, down to our own day; and, old as she was, she did not outlive her wit, her activity, her independence of feeling. She was a gay and buoyant girl, full of pranks and high spirits; and many are the recollections of her practical jokes and witticisms. When a girl, she possessed a beautiful saddle horse, her father's gift, of which she was not a little proud. She had trained her horse in such a way that, when patted on a certain place in the neck, he grew suddenly restive, and commenced rearing and prancing in a way to exhibit her horsemanship to great advantage and with little danger. When yet a young lady, she rode this horse down to Lunenburg, on a visit to her brother Joseph. While at his house, he buried an infant son, and, on the occasion of the funeral, there proved to be some lack of horses to carry all the party to the burial-ground; and a certain serving maid, one Sarah Anne, at her brother's request, was placed behind Miss Abigail on a pillion. She was not a little chagrined at finding her favorite converted into a family nag, and her horsemanship put at such disadvantage; and, although unable to refuse at the moment the load assigned her, she said, afterwards, "I knew I should never carry Sarah

Anne, if the boy laid above ground all summer." She rode, however, to the horse-block, and the maid mounted behind her. The procession moved on, when suddenly Miss Abigail's horse was seized with an unaccountable restiveness, and reared and plunged until Sarah Anne was thrown off. Miss Abigail returned very soberly to the horse-block, and Sarah Anne, with her rumpled feathers, was placed in her seat again. A second time the procession started; a second time the vicious beast threw up his heels, and a second time Sarah Anne came to the ground. The third experiment had the same result, until Sarah Anne concluded to give up the melancholy ride, and Miss Abigail achieved her somewhat misplaced and mischievous victory.

Her wit continued fresh through life. She had a merry twinkle in her eye, even after it was dimmed with age. Her energy was equal to her spirits. She kept house to the last day of her long life, and only resigned the keys when her breath was but a few hours in her body.

My cousin, Frederick N. Knapp, has just been telling me of the annual dinner, which, during their four college years, Aunt Richardson used to give in vacation time to these four grand-nephews,—himself, and brother, and Herbert Bellows and Rowe Bellows, adding to them Warren Giles, and one or two others who happened to be in college from Walpole at the same time. The table was beautifully spread, and arranged with great care and taste. She, though somewhere between seventy-five and eighty years old, presided at the dinner with all the grace and life of a young woman of thirty; and, by her wit and wisdom, her entertaining stories of incidents in her younger days in the old fort, her account of what the world was doing and thinking about a half-century before that time, she made this dinner most delightful. Never a mortal lived who loved the society of young people more, or did more to contribute to their pleasure.

I have also something now to add to what I have said about Aunt Richardson's sister, Aunt Kinsley; so different as she was in many respects from Abigail; I give the estimate of one who knew her well, and who was a judge of character. Aunt Kinsley, Mary Bellows, the youngest daughter of the old colonel, was a woman of uncommon native power of intellect and force of will.

"She was cast in that mould of the female nature which would have fitted her to be the wife of some resolute old puritan, in the days when wives buckled on their husband's swords, and bade them die, but not dishonor their name and faith. Tall and commanding in person, firm and original in her opinions; of native dignity and elevation, free from frivolous tastes or feminine weaknesses, she carried self-respect with her all her days, and secured the veneration, even more than the love, of others. Those, however, more intimately acquainted with her domestic life, speak gratefully of the depth of tenderness held in her heart, and of the power she possessed to win the warm affections of others; she was efficient in benevolence, from principle and inclination. Possessing unusual business capacity and large experience, she managed her affairs with discretion, and was a helpmate indeed to her husband, whose congressional life carried him much away from home. She was not the ordinary type of the Bellows race, which leans more to mercy than justice, and is rather distinguished for the tender and humane than for the heroic and celestial graces: a certain spontaneous sympathy, ready to burst out at the sight of suffering or wrong, is natural to the race.

"Aunt Kinsley seemed to possess a mind accustomed to weigh its conclusions very deliberately, govern its emotions, and regulate itself by a deliberate principle. In her theology, too, she was an exception to most of the race. She belonged to the sterner school of religion, and did honor to her faith in her practice. Our family would, perhaps, have done better if a larger infusion of the element represented in Aunt Kinsley's character had been poured into it."

Mrs. Kinsley, after the death of her husband, resided chiefly in the family of her only child, Mrs. Gardner; but, after her grandchildren, early bereft of a most interesting mother, ceased to need her care, she followed the family instinct of her race, and repaired to Walpole to end her days.

Here, in the society of her brother, the squire, and with the charge of his household, she passed several years of tranquil usefulness, forming a most important element in her brother's happiness in his old age; and here, in the enjoyment of a firm religious faith, and with a venerated memory, she closed her eyes.

Her grand-daughters, bearing the family names, Mary and Charlotte, live gratefully to recall the inheritance which they received in this strong and noble character, bound in, as it is, to them with the memory of a mother of rare tenderness and beauty of spirit. Their only brother, Dr. Augustus Kinsley Gardner, died but recently, after having made for himself an enviable reputation as a physician and a friend.

CHAPTER XXI.

But to speak of some of another generation. It has been observed in families of children, there is often one wholly unlike the rest, both in looks and characteristics; and our grandmother's family was not an exception to this. In her large flock, numbering fourteen, this one was found. This personage was no other than our Uncle Salmon, the eldest of the family. He was just himself, and no one else. In saying he was entirely different from the rest, it is not to be inferred that he did not possess as many virtues; for it was quite otherwise. Under that butternut colored coat, hanging so loosely on his tall, gaunt figure, and which was spun and woven, and probably cut and made, by his wife's own hands, there beat a kind and honest heart.

He had an intelligent mind, and he always possessed too much self-respect to find any companionship in low company. He held no communication with the world, save what was necessary, in the pursuit of providing for his small family. He was so entirely free, also, from the common habit in those times, of using tobacco, and the daily use of stimulants, that he was considered, by some, almost a social outcast. He lived his own life simply in his own way, perfectly contented if there was a sufficiency for to-day: to-morrow surely would take care of itself, as it always had done; so there was very little trouble in his household. His wife commenced life in this way with him, and had learned the lesson of adaptation. Notwithstanding his many peculiarities, he was thoroughly respected; and not one of our uncles stood higher in favor with the children than our Uncle Salmon.

Perhaps it was his grotesque appearance that first interested us, and then his quaint humor certainly amused us; and there was no one whom we saw approaching that gave us greater delight, for surely somewhere in those capacious pockets there must be a handful of chestnuts or of candy, or a red apple, which we were allowed to fish out for ourselves.

My earliest memory of him and our Aunt Lydia, his wife, is when they lived at the ferry; where, after his own style of employment, he kept boats to take people over the Connecticut River. He followed this humble calling several years, as there was no bridge at that time, though one was eventually built through the enterprise of Col. John, who was the general mover in all public improvements.

I have heard Aunt Lydia relate many hairbreadth escapes, while in the exercise of his river-craft. At one time, there was a violent northeast storm, the wind blowing a gale, when the stage from Boston, full of passengers, came to be ferried over to Vermont.

He took the oars at the head of the boat, while a new hand rowed at the stern. When they got into the current, which was very strong, and some distance from the opposite shore, they began to drift rapidly down stream, while the wind threatened, at each gust, to overturn the carriage. The passengers were in a great fright, but Uncle Salmon, whose self-possession was proverbial, assured them, if they kept quiet, he would land them in safety. He then called upon a man to assist at the oar, for he was himself getting exhausted; it was much harder rowing up-stream than floating down.

Aunt Lydia stood on the river bank all this time, watching the terrible, and, to her, uncertain struggle; she at last had the satisfaction of seeing them landed at the proper place in safety, and then betook herself to the house, and piled on the wood for a hot fire, ready for him when he should come in, as he did after another perilous pull on his return trip, wearing the same composure as though nothing had happened, and making no remark until she said, "You've had a terrific pull, Salmon!" To which he only answered, "Yes, kinder tough; but I cared more for those poor women! They had an awful scare, Liddy."

Another incident she used to relate, but I don't think she voluntarily spoke of it. It was only when we asked her to tell us about the man who was drowned, that we heard it. As nearly as I can recall it, it was this: My uncle never went from home to be gone more than an hour, without leaving some one to take his place at the boats. It was at the close of a hot summer's day he set out on a walk to the village, which was a mile distant, to procure at his brother Joseph's store some articles for the family.

He was picking up his packages, when his brother Thomas, who was then a clerk, went quickly to the door, exclaiming, "What do I hear?" In a moment more, as they listened, there was a repetition, and Uncle Salmon exclaimed, "Why! that's Liddy!" Through the clear, still, evening air, her voice came ringing like a bell; and they all started for the river road, shouting as they ran, to let her know help was coming. She had hastened from the house, but had not gone more than a quarter of a mile before giving the alarm; and, though so distant, her call of distress was heard. It seems that a neighbor across the river, in his attempt to take himself over, had in some way upset his boat when near the shore, and was drowning. His piteous cries for help, she used to say, would ring in her ears forever. When the rescuing party reached the river, they took the man from the water, but all efforts to restore life were unavailing.

Aunt Lydia had many strong attractions for both children and young people. She was the repository of all the girls' love affairs, for she had a pack of cards in which were written all their destinies; and it was only she who had the key to these magic characters. If there was any love affair going on among the young people in the neighborhood, it was she who was in the council. It was very amusing to see how perfectly she could adapt herself to the young folks of both sexes.

I can never forget a little story that was sometimes told of my Aunt Louisa's young life, then fifteen or sixteen years of age, and the youngest of the family. There was, at that time, a young man employed in Mr. Isaiah Thomas' bookstore, which then honored the town of Walpole, where books were not only sold, but published. It was from this press that Parson Fessenden's "Science of Sanctity" was issued. This young clerk became desperately in love with this dark-eyed beauty; and, while she seemed indifferent to his passion, there was no open opposition. Here was just such a field as Aunt Lydia liked for the exercise of her genius; and, not long after, it became known that through her influence these young people met at her house. Uncle Salmon, who always thought just as his wife did, saw no objection to the young man ; but he always took a different view of all temporal things from his brothers ; and the consequences in this case were, that Uncle John banished his young sister to a school, which, as distances were measured in those days, might be said to be located in a foreign country, but, in reality, was no farther off than New Ipswich, where the first academy in the State of New Hampshire was planted. Well, what of the young man ? Why, being unable to remain where disappointed hopes and a broken heart were written upon everything, he suddenly left, seeking a larger place in which to lose himself and his sorrow ! Some years afterward, he was known in Boston as one of the most marked journalists in that city, possessing not only wealth, but fame. I never knew if he were married, but I know that their acquaintance was never renewed, and Aunt Liddy's magic cards were at fault.

When the bridge was built across the river, Uncle Salmon's occupation was gone ; and the next available business was farming. His brother, who owned a farm in Langdon, placed him there to carry it on ; so this faithful old boatman moved to this rural abode, where he took his wife and his integrity, and but a very small portion of anything else.

His oldest daughter was a teacher, and not often at home. There was another, ten years of age; she bore the historic name of Matilda. She was named, as her mother said, for Queen Matilda, the wife of William the Conqueror. Aunt Lydia had a great respect for that personage. I think it was my first real sorrow, when Aunt Lydia and Uncle Salmon went to this far away home, ten miles off, leaving the little house on the bank of the river; which, to my child-mind, was nothing less than a fairy grotto in the Garden of Eden. I was then four or five years old, and I used to find my greatest happiness in running away from school and getting to this lovely place, where my Aunt Lydia and Uncle Salmon lived; the surprise and tenderness with which she took me in her arms, saying to my uncle, "This child has strayed a mile from home to find us, Salmon!" Then supper was soon ready, and I ate my corn cake, with maple syrup, on a bright pewter plate. There were two rows of these plates on the shelves, turned up against the wall, bright as polished silver. A porringer of warm milk completed the repast, and then the bed behind the curtain was turned down, and I was put into the foot; and the bliss of that night's rest, in the foot of Aunt Lydia's bed, I have never forgotten. Meantime, Uncle Salmon would have gone and reported me "all safe in bed," to my mother.

A few more years have rolled away, and we find these excellent people still on the old farm, living their lives in the same old way, looking, if possible, a little more as if they had just left the garden of Eden; they had not reached the time of the ark! Dear old uncle's clothes hang more loosely than ever about him, but there was still the same charm for young people in his kind and genial smile. When I was thirteen or fourteen years old, there was no visit I was permitted to make that I anticipated with so much pleasure as the one to that humble home.

I always chose to make this visit in the winter, usually extending from one day to the next, which gave me one of those long winter evenings that Aunt Lydia knew so well how to make bright and lovely.

Although the same old habits were strictly adhered to, of providing for one day at a time, and, though everybody knew he never had a woodpile to replenish his fire from, there was no fear but that the proverbial tree would be "snaked up" in time, and prepared for the evening fire, which was made about four o'clock in the afternoon. First, would be laid a huge back-log in that fireplace, extending half-across the room; then another log, of a little smaller dimension; next followed a fore-stick from the next cut of the trunk of the tree, not quite so big as the back log; then the small wood was piled on, as much as you please: all this would be set ablaze by the hot coals and brands that remained of the fire built the day before.

While this fire is making, the girl Matilda gets the three-legged stand, with the spectacles and knitting, and Aunt Lydia is ready to commence her duties of hostess. If she has recently read an entertaining book, she relates the whole of it to us in her own easy way; or it is some story from the "Arabian Nights" every word of which she could repeat. If the stories gave out too soon, she could sing such songs as are never heard in these later generations. Dear old Aunt Lyddy! How little she thought, when pouring such a stream of melody and pathos into my young ears, that she was giving me something never to be forgotten, and which would always be associated with her through all these eighty years or more of my life.

I am tempted here, for the amusement of the young readers of these pages, to give the first and last verse of one song, which was my special favorite; and I can assure them the mournful strain of the music was in perfect keeping with the sentiment : —

> "Oh! Polly, Polly, my sweet creeter!
> Come and sit you down by me,
> And relate to me the reason
> Why I'm slighted so by thee!
>
> . . . . .
>
> "Oh, take away that foolish fancy!
> That is what doth break my heart;
> If I should die, oh! pretty Polly,
> Think of me, when I depart."

Foolish, do you say it is for me to repeat this here? Be it so; yet let it stand. It brings back to me days when the fields were green, and bees were gathering honey from the blossoms of clover.

Well, these kind and excellent people are nothing but a memory now! Their graves were made in the far West, but we have heard that they deeply mourned for the home they left, but were never able to return to. Dear old Aunt Lydia and Uncle Salmon, with whom are associated the sweetest and brightest memories of my childhood!

CHAPTER XXII.

Our Uncle John, better known at that time as Uncle Jack, was named for his uncle who was always distinguished as Col. John, his father's brother. He passed many years of his early life in Walpole; and it was said he assumed the dignities of manhood long before it was usually accorded to the youth of that period. It is probable that circumstances helped to an early development of character and practical ability. He assumed, what it had certainly become necessary that some one should take, the lead in this large family of brothers and sisters, after they were deprived of the wise guidance of their father. Our grandmother, when speaking of him in after years, said his forethought and good calculations at this period often surprised her. Perhaps the early exercise of these faculties served to strengthen the foundation upon which was built his success as a merchant prince in Boston, some years afterward. He did not embark in this business until he was thoroughly prepared for it; and then success in all his enterprises soon gave him not only wealth, but marked him as a man of great ability and good judgment, and he was often called upon to fill public offices in the city that were considered quite an honor. When he was well-established in business, and found himself able to provide such a home as he thought worthy the lady he had chosen for a wife, he was married to Miss Betsey Eames, of Sudbury, Mass. Tradition says, when he first saw her, she was in the kitchen; where, according to the wise custom with young ladies of those days, she was assisting her mother in the duties of the household. Her sleeves were rolled up, exposing a pair of beautiful arms; and she was standing before a table, rolling pie-crust in such an expert manner as quite assured him this was not a new business to her, and that, whatever she undertook, she was in earnest about it. He suddenly came to another conclusion also; as he stood for a moment, with his eyes riveted upon her; he thought if she could look so bewitchingly lovely in a long, checked apron, how superb her tall, elegant figure must be when draped in silk and satin! He used to say, that he was indebted to the business transaction, which that day took him to the side door of that house instead of the front, for the loveliest view he ever had of his wife; but he was always sure to say this in her presence. All who ever saw Uncle John can never forget his playful humor, which was ever cropping out.

I have a distinct recollection of the first time I ever saw my Aunt Betsey. I could not have been five years old, when my mother took me, one morning, to see her, having heard of her arrival, in Walpole, the preceding evening. I stood in the hall when she came down the stairs with her train thrown carelessly over her arm,— they were universally worn very long at that time. But what is more distinctly impressed upon my memory is, that beautiful blue silk handkerchief, twisted jauntily as a turban round her head, one end left to hang down over the shoulder; and, through all the years that have intervened, I have brought the memory of that lovely turban,— the long end hanging so gracefully, as did all else she wore. I have heard Aunt Louisa say, that her sister Betsey would look more dressed in a common print than most persons in the richest toilet; and it was very evident her husband was exceedingly proud of her. But she died early, leaving five childen; the two youngest were twin boys, not a year old, when this beautiful mother was called away.

Rev. Dr. Henry W. Bellows was one of these twin boys, of whom we shall speak afterward. His twin brother, Edward, chose the profession of law, and went to Detroit, Mich., to commence practice; but he soon came to a sudden death, overcome by fatigue, as he was making a two days' foot journey through the woods on professional duty to a distant court-house. But of him I shall speak again.

The eldest son, John Nelson Bellows, for many years a successful teacher in different institutions, and a brilliant magazine writer, afterward chose the ministry as his profession, in which he continued until his death. He was a scholar by nature, a ready and graceful writer, a fluent speaker, of great originality of thought and of expression, quick in his perception, tender and responsive in his sympathies, subtle and acute in his discrimination. While he was profoundly interested in philosophical investigations, he took the deepest interest in all matters of social reform and philanthropy. His constant theme was the practical application of Christianity to the work of relieving and educating the poor and ignorant, and elevating the laboring classes. His enjoyment of social life was keen, and his contributions of both wit and wisdom were always acknowledged and sought for. Of a poetic vein and intensely nervous temperament, his mind seemed never to rest;

and, no matter how frequently you met him, you were sure to find in his conversation something fresh and worth listening to. He died many years before his brother Henry, who always insisted that John was superior to himself in intellectual ability and versatility of genius. Early in life he had married, in Copperstown, N.Y., the wife who long blessed his home, and who survives him, holding still in Walpole, in the beautiful cottage on the bank of the ravine, close to the old Caleb Bellows' place, a welcoming home for her sons and daughters. One of these daughters married a son of Dr. Bellows Robeson, of whom I have spoken,— he, the son of Aunt Susan Robeson, whom we all so loved and reverenced; one of these sons married a daughter of Mrs. Allen,— she, the youngest sister of Dr. Henry Bellows,— thus bound by double bonds.

Hamilton, the second son, had also marked ability, and a most genial and delightful nature. Who that ever saw him can forget his marvellous powers of conversation, and his inexhaustible fund of anecdote? His rich and varied tones of voice, as he sang his favorite songs, both of mirth and of pathos, still sound in our ears. But he died in the prime of his manhood. His widow survives him, continuing in her kindly services of charity and mercy in connection with agencies for helping the poor and ignorant in New York City. The eldest daughter of Uncle John, Mary Ann, died early; while the second sister, known and loved throughout the whole family circle as Cousin Eliza, lived till within a few years. As I shall have occasion to speak of her by and by in another connection, I will only say here, wherever she went, she carried life and cheer by her originality and brightness of thought, her keen wit, and genial sympathies. She married Joseph G. Dorr, of Boston, and though living for many years in South America, where her husband was engaged in mercantile business, they both came back to Walpole, to spend in quiet their remaining years; and here they died and were buried, and by their side have been laid one by one all their children, the last who followed them being their only daughter, Harriet Bellows, who married Henry G. Wheelock, of New York, he being a grandson of Uncle Si Bellows. She was one who, with her sweet and winning ways, ever made friends; she scattered sunshine all along her pathway, which, alas! was too short for all of us who knew and loved her.

It was not until some years after the death of Uncle John's wife, and when his youngest sister Louisa, who had made her home with him since his marriage, was preparing for a home of her own, that he gave a thought to providing another mother for his children.

His second choice proved his wise discrimination, and the good fortune which seemed always to attend him; for he brought to his home one of the three celebrated Misses Langdon, who had long been known in their own circle as the three beautiful sisters. And, if they were all as lovely as our Aunt Anne, they certainly merited this appellation. Nothing could exceed her winning gentleness in this family; and, as the children were all young, they must have soon forgotten in her loving tenderness that she was not their own mother. There were three sons and two daughters by this second marriage. The eldest, Francis, a devoted son, brother, and friend, was a merchant in New York, and died some years ago. The youngest

son, George, is a lawyer in Chicago. The youngest
daughter, Harriet, married Mr. William Allen, who for
years was the devoted and efficient parishioner and co-
adjutor of Rev. Dr. Bellows in his New York ministry
of love and philanthropy. Mrs. Allen and her brother
are the only two who now survive in this family of
eleven children.

Uncle John proved himself no exception to the old
saying, that all the Bellows came home to die. When
his business life ended, he naturally turned to the old
home of his race, where so many of them are already
sleeping; and while these hills and valleys remain, and
our beautiful river flows silently on, may our kindred
seek this sacred spot for their last repose! On moving
from Boston to Walpole, our uncle built a handsome
residence, with a view commanding river and valley, and
enjoyed several years of quiet country life, with his last
gentle and loving companion and her four children,
together with those of older birth, who always found
there such a beautiful place of joy and refreshment.

How vividly I can recall that rather short, but stout
figure, in his carefully arranged costume, as he almost
daily came plodding up the steep hill that led to his
sister Louisa's house,— she who had been, in former
times, for many years an inmate of his own household,
and even as a mother to his eldest children! These
morning visits were made most enjoyable by the vivacity
of her conversation, calling out volleys of wit from her
brother. He was full of playful humor, and the quickness and smartness of his repartees were proverbial
wherever he was known; and he imparted in no small
measure his remarkable characteristics to his children.

We, who have known the Rev. Dr. Bellows of New

York, and seen him in his freer moods, will readily admit that he received his full share.

It is now nearly half a century since this uncle, of whom we have so many pleasant memories, was laid away with his kindred, while I am left to relate these few passages in a life so fraught with energy, and that achieved such honorable success.

Since writing what I have of Uncle John, I find in the appendix of the book, which gives the account of the family gathering, a notice of him, which I insert here. "Born in 1768, at Lunenburg, and dying at Walpole, February, 1840, his life was one of extraordinary enterprise and success.

"Fitted for college, but disappointed in going by the sudden misfortune of his father, he started out for himself at seventeen, and, by great activity, accumulated the means of leaving Walpole and trying his fortunes at Boston. Here he soon rose to be the head of an importing house in a few years (Bellows, Cordis, & Co.), and retired from business at fifty years of age, with an ample fortune. The next ten years he devoted himself, as an alderman of the city, to the public interests, with an almost unparalleled zeal, superintending the erection of many of the most important public edifices, and aiding, as his right hand, the labors of that peerless mayor, Josiah Quincy, Sen. The crisis in manufactures largely impaired his fortunes, in 1830; and he made great sacrifices to relieve himself of indebtedness, retiring with a comfortable estate to Walpole, N.H., where he passed ten quiet years, and died, Feb. 10, 1840, aged seventy-two. He was a man of superior intellect, generous sentiments, and spotless integrity. Lavish in the education of his children, stern in his family government, proud and modest, tender at heart, but ashamed of his sensibility, full of public spirit, unsurpassed in sharpness of wit and readiness of repartee, dignified and scrupulous in his costume and manners, elegant in the neatness of his style and his handwriting, admirable as a letter-writer, an excellent talker, fond of speculation and argument, a keen man of business, a philosopher in his sorrows and disappointments, though easily annoyed by trifles, John Bellows deserves this tribute of affectionate respect from his kindred, and the grateful remembrance of his fellow-citizens."

CHAPTER XXIII.

THOSE who were present at the large gathering of the descendants of Col. Benjamin Bellows, in 1854, will perhaps remember a venerable old gentleman, way into the eighties, sitting in their midst with a bright, red cap on his head, looking much like a mandarin. Notwithstanding his great age, he had come all the way from Canada, to see, as he said, "what kind of people represented, at that period, those who once owned and occupied this sacred soil." He was the only one in all that throng, who had seen, and distinctly remembered, this ancestor, to whose memory they were paying that tribute of respect.

This personage, to whom I have referred, was our Uncle Ben. He was always spoken of by this abbreviation of Benjamin, which was his Christian name. His long residence in Canada, where he took his family when the fourth generation were just entering upon the stage of life, made him comparatively a stranger here, as his visits to the home of his childhood were few and far between. But his children did not all remain in Canada; I believe there were ten of them. Yet, wherever they have been, they have maintained the sturdy characteristics of their ancestors, and transmitted them to another generation, now on the stage.

I have some recollections of him, which were gathered in early life; one was his passionate love of music. He would often seek my mother with his singing-book under his arm, wishing her to join him, for more than the hundredth time perhaps, in singing the old anthems, of which he could never tire. In those days, there was but little new music written. The old tunes were so good, they could never wear out; the more they were heard, the better they were liked. I recollect, too, his winning gentleness of manner, doubly impressive as connected with his tall, erect figure. He had not that fluency of expression so natural to many of his race, but whatever he had to say was given slowly and in the most simple language.

His habit of mind was akin to the manly vigor of his body; and, as to that, take this fact as an illustration: An extensive and thorough farmer, to make sure that the work was well done, he made it a rule always to sow his fields of grain himself. And that very season, when we had the family gathering, though he was then, as I have said, way into the eighties, he had sown with his own hand between ninety and a hundred acres of grain. Think of the travel back and forth, back and forth, over that immense tract,— that long, strong arm of his scattering broadcast the seed, while the locks whitened by so many winters were streaming behind him, his face set on thoroughness and duty!

Of his children, one of the eldest sons, who bore the family name of John, went to Canada, where, being successful in business, he planted himself, and thus induced his father with his family to move there. One of the daughters married Charles Towle, a Justice of the Peace, a leading citizen, and a man of high tone and character. His son, Charles Edward Towle, a civil engineer, still lives in Canada, at Lenoxville, where his sister also resides. John Bellows, son of Uncle

Ben, left an only daughter, Harriet, who married Rev. Mr. Scarfe, the Episcopal clergyman at Lenoxville. Another one of our Canada cousins married Mr. Charles Pennoyer, a man substantial in his means and his character. The son of still another of this family of cousins is John Butterfield, of Chicago, whose reputation as an inventor is so well established; and it was a great service that he rendered when he invented, as he did, what is reckoned the best stamp-mill out, for crushing gold quartz. Two of Uncle Ben's sons inherited their father's handsome proportions. One held a commission as an officer in our civil war, and was noted for his splendid personality. His brother was better known by his kindred, because his home was in the vicinity of Walpole. He was a fine specimen of manhood, in his palmy days A short drive would take us to a pretty brown cottage, where we were sure to meet with a most cordial and affectionate welcome. The native kindness and hospitality of these friends were imparted in no small measure to their children.

Two daughters, with whom I have had the privilege and pleasure of a more particular acquaintance within the last few years, have a place with the most remarkable examples of these two leading family characteristics. It is but recently the mother was laid tenderly away, the father having gone many years before. And now, with tearful remembrances of her loving sympathy and tender ministrations,— she whose gentle hands could never weary in doing good,— I have to record the death of the eldest daughter. She has left all too soon that bright and loving circle and beautiful home, but the fragrance of her dear presence must forever remain there.

CHAPTER XXIV.

When our grandmother left the meadow farm, where so many of her boys found occupation until they could do better for themselves, our Uncle Abel was employed by his uncle, Gen. Bellows, in the Register of Deeds Office. He remained there a few years until he had acquired sufficient capital to start himself in the mercantile business. I heard him relate this part of his early history, one evening, to a friend, with whom he had some interest in the Northwestern Fur Company; and it sets before us, in a way we can realize, the difference between those days and the present in the matter of business facilities.

He said his brother John, who was then a successful merchant in Boston, first suggested the idea of his establishing himself in Montreal. Frequent communication between the brothers became necessary, either by letter or personally; and, when the latter, the journey was sometimes made at risk of their lives in crossing Lake Champlain at times when the ice had become very uncertain.

As Uncle John was a wholesale dealer in dry goods, it is probable he furnished the materials for this enterprise. The goods were to be taken on wheels or runners over this long distance, such being the only mode of transportation by land at that period. Uncle Abel took two loads of goods to Canada, driving one of them himself. Here he would explain, that he was neither a born nor bred teamster, quite an unnecessary assertion, as we follow him and his disasters over the long, weary distance that lies between New Hampshire and Montreal.

He said the final arrangements were at length completed, and nothing remained but to receive the last parting words from the family, so full of tender interest and apprehension ; and the last hand-shakes were given by acquaintances and their God bless you ! The next moment we were on our way to that far-off country, so little known to the people who dwelt in the States. We now know as much of the Chinese as was generally known of the Canadians, at that period.

Well, he went on, a deep snow had fallen the preceding day, which did not facilitate our progress ; but, struggling on, we left Bellows Falls a few miles behind, when we approached a place called " Horse Heaven." This place was no other than a deep ravine on one side of the road, with little or no protection to prevent man or beast from rolling to the bottom of the apparently fathomless abyss. We had gone but a short distance on this heavenward way, when we saw a team loaded with wood approaching. As the depth of snow rendered turning out a very difficult operation, my inexperience in such dilemmas made the task somewhat appalling, especially as it was evident the burly teamster was bound to have more than his share of the road ; the consequences were, I found myself and a portion of my merchandise making a hasty descent, and it was only by their great activity, and their knowing how to do it, that the horses saved themselves from following me. The trees and bushes happily rescued me from reaching the bottom ; and it was no easy task for my man to fish me up again with my packages, out of this perilous depth. I had many more adventures before reaching the desired haven, where my partner, Mr. Gates, was awaiting my arrival.

It was about 1804, when Uncle Abel went to Montreal, and he remained there until near the time when peace was declared, after the war of 1812. This war increased their facilities greatly for making money; and a handsome fortune was quickly amassed, but at a fearful sacrifice of health to our uncle. He was compelled to return home before the close of the war, relinquishing all business, which he was never able to resume again.

CHAPTER XXV.

At this time, Uncle Joseph had given up the business he had followed for many years, and Uncle Thomas, his youngest brother, took his place in the store, and Uncle Jo went to the Rockingham farm, which was jointly owned then by himself and his brother Abel. Whoever has seen this lovely meadow, stretching along the western bank of the Connecticut River, nearly or quite two miles, and especially when covered with corn and waving grain, all laid out with precision in squares, each square comprising several acres, can never forget the beauty it presented. This farm was one of the family possessions for nearly a century.

When Uncle Joseph took his family to the farm, he left grandmother and Aunt Susan, as his brother Abel needed all their care; and thus his bachelor home was established, our grandmother dispensing the honors for some years.

At this time, Aunt Susan was engaged to Major Robeson, of Fitzwilliam. He was a merchant, having acquired considerable wealth. He was also a widower with four children. He was a man remarkable for energy; it was apparent in all his movements. That was a superior quality in her estimation, and she would say a man without it could have no attractions for her; and, she would add, "When I see a man, at work, start for his dinner at the first summons, taking his coat, and putting it on as he walks rapidly along, I know that man will get a living, only he must return to his work just as promptly, taking his coat off before he gets there." They were married in a few months after her brother Joseph left. All the incidents of that morning of the wedding are as fresh in my mind as though it happened yesterday.

It was in March, 1814, and a deep snow had fallen, accompanied by a furious blow, drifting the roads so badly that traveling far from home was not attempted. And this explained, to my mind, why a gentleman, who had often come on Saturday and returned home on Monday, didn't go as usual; he was, to my thought, only one of our many frequent guests. There were some other circumstances, however, not so easily interpreted; but, as I was taught that children should never ask questions, I remained silent, keeping my eyes and ears open, as I watched the unusual preparations going on, now and then looking into Becky's quizzical face, as she sat beating the yolks of ten eggs, while my grandmother beat the whites on a large flat dish. I watched Aunt Susan with much curiosity as she separated them; and it required no little restraint not to ask grandmother why she didn't beat them together, as she usually did for custards. Aunt Susan directed all the different operations with her usual air of authority, saying she should not put her fingers to it, as that was always a bad sign. That remark was a greater puzzle than all the rest, and I gave it up.

Tuesday morning dawned brightly, and the circumstance was significantly talked over at the early breakfast; after which, Cyrus, the colored man, opened the north parlor door, where, to my surprise, I saw a bright fire blazing on the hearth. We didn't use this room in winter, excepting on great occasions. As the gentleman passed into the room, I heard my uncle order Cyrus to harness the horses at ten o'clock. After giving a few preliminary orders to Becky, Aunt Susan took me up-stairs, and told me to put on my best frock; she was going to be married, and going home with Maj. Robeson. I could not have been more amazed, if she had told me it was to be her own funeral, and that she was going to the burying-ground. I have often thought how differently such affairs were conducted at that time from the present, always in the strictest privacy. It was too sacred a subject to be made the theme of common conversation, and the sentiment was honored by perfect silence. At any rate, this was the way with our Aunt Susan; and, in later years, I have heard her say, "A wedding was quite as solemn as a funeral."

Precisely at ten o'clock, Cyrus was sent to bring Cousins Maria and Harriet, Col. John's daughters. They were the only friends invited to join the household in witnessing the ceremony. In a short time, Mr. Dickinson was shown in, and, silently bowing, took his seat. I was too young to know then, but I have known since, that he came that morning to give away to another the one he had himself long sought, and would have given much to win for himself. After he had declared the twain made one, when taking her hand to give her her new name, there was such a long hesitation and apparent struggle on his part as to arrest the attention of all present; but a few moments, and he regained his self-control, and spoke calmly and clearly her name, with his congratulations.

Uncle Abel then came quickly to grandmother, and took her into the sitting-room, as he saw she was quite overcome. He then said, in a low tone, "I declare, mother, I think it was cruel for us to ask this service of Dickinson." And grandmother replied, "I think it was; but our regrets are useless now; we should have thought of this before."

As Aunt Susan was married in a cloth habit, she was soon arrayed for her departure. Then, to our surprise, we saw for the first time what had long been concealed for this occasion,— a handsome blue cloak, with a cape cut with deep points, bound with lemon-colored ribbon, and a "repped" silk bonnet of the same color, with two long white plumes. How clearly I can recall that figure bending over her mother as she stood, taking her leave! Then followed her good-by to all, and she was on her way. I ran to the window in time to see those long plumes waving their last adieus, as they were lifted by the breeze, when turning the corner, where they disappeared from view.

When I turned from the last look after my Aunt Susan, Uncle Abel was saying, "I don't know how we can get along, mother; there is no one to fill her place." She returned some comforting words; but they proved quite inadequate to dispel the gloom and loneliness that pervaded the house through all that long and weary day. When evening came, quite a number of the friends called; Cousin Si was one, and Mrs. Gardner another. Those two personages could never be easily forgotten. She had been a brilliant star in Walpole society, but was always spoken of as one of Susan Bellows' satellites,— the last-named being the planet of greater magnitude. This was when they were girls.

The next day Uncle Abel brought a very tall young

gentleman in to dinner, introducing him as Dr. Morse. The after-dinner conversation revealed the fact that he had been invited by my uncle to make his home there for an indefinite time. This proved to be not only a pleasant, but a beneficial arrangement. The young doctor made himself very agreeable company, securing at once confidence in his professional skill. He came to Walpole accredited by old Dr. Twitchell, of Keene, with whom he had studied after graduating from college; and a recommendation from Dr. Twitchell was the surest possible passport to public favor.

It was soon apparent that Uncle Abel was better; he had followed the doctor's humorous advice, to lay his pills and powders on the shelf, where the proverbial old woman put hers, when she wanted to get the best possible effect from them. This was strictly adhered to, while another course of treatment was pursued. The young doctor's lively conversation and wit, which was always ready; and his great love of music, in which he indulged at every leisure moment, kept the house pretty lively. It was found by my dyspeptic uncle to be more pleasant to listen to the sweet strains of the violin, and the grand tones of the bass-viol, than to sit moodily contemplating the process of digestion after a hearty dinner. And so our uncle gradually mended his ways; coming back in process of time to comparatively a new life, under the new doctor's wise instructions.

In the early springtime, another pleasant acquisition was made to the little home circle in the person of my uncle's youngest sister, whose advent always imparted abundant cheerfulness and animation. There was little time, now, for the indulgence of dyspepsia, or any other form of evil that usually awaits people who have nothing to do. Great merriment reigned at the table, particularly at the dinner hour, when a constant fusilade was kept up between the doctor and Aunt Louisa, whose quick and bright repartees the doctor seemed greatly to enjoy; and I perfectly remember there were times when I thought my uncle was very proud of his young sister.

Aunt Susan's first visit home, after her marriage, occurred in July,— when she came in, one day, so unexpectedly, the household was in a state of great commotion. Great joy was expressed on seeing again one who had not only been the controlling spirit, but had given so much brightness to the old home for such a length of time.

The news of her presence seemed to be transmitted on wings through the entire village; and there was such a gathering of friends, after tea, as had not been seen since that forlorn evening after her departure. The house was filled; such was the welcoming in those old times. I recall another incident. Before Aunt Susan returned, it had been arranged that grandmother should make a visit to Fitzwilliam, in August, and, if she made the journey in the stage, I was to accompany her; but a friend took her by a private conveyance. Perhaps this little disappointment, of not riding on the top of a stage over those great hills, thirty miles, served to fix the circumstances in my mind.

It was quite an event for her to take a journey, and all the household were much interested in the preparations. I can see, at this moment, how nice the dear old lady looked, as she tied on her new black silk bonnet, made after the fashion of that time,— called a cottage bonnet, coming close to the face; and I gazed at her, and thought how lovely she looked with her double-cap border, so beautifully crimped, pressed closely to her cheeks; and at the last moment, as she found she had not got her spectacles in her pocket, I was sent to find them for her. When the last goodbys were said, and the carriage was turning away from the door, Becky, who had been watching from the kitchen window, pulled off her moccasin which she had been wearing instead of a shoe, on account of a lame foot, and threw it after them. The young doctor caught a glimpse of it, and said to her, "Didn't you know it was an ill-omen to throw a moccasin? It is only an old shoe that can positively secure good luck." At which she looked down to her feet in utter dismay, and exclaimed, "Oh, jiminy! I took the wrong foot!"

There was one little episode in the domestic department, during grandmother's absence, I can never forget. While Becky was off, one afternoon, I was promoted to the dignity of getting tea; I considered it highly complimentary, and felt myself equal to anything that might be proposed.

The cream biscuit that Becky often made, and which were enjoyed so much, flashed upon my mind; and I determined to make some that would cast all other biscuits quite into the shade. It was only a question of getting leave to do so, to show my skill; and, when I made the proposition, my aunt looked at me so quizzically, I was in great fear she was about to throw cold water upon my enthusiasm; but, when she noticed how eager I was, she consented, promising not to interfere; and, when I had things all my own way, no one could be more sure of success. I first thought over the whole process, as I had seen Becky make them,—the quantity of cream, the soda, and salt.

While stirring these ingredients into the flour, it occurred to me, that unless I put something in that Becky did not, they could not be any different; and I wished to have them very much better than hers. And, as the question arose what I should add, the lovely flavor of my aunt's pound cake came to my mind; and, if rose-water could make that so delicious, why should it not be just as nice in cream biscuit? So I turned a generous portion into the mixture, entirely satisfied with my new discovery. When, at last, I brought them to the table, so nicely baked, there were cordial words of commendation at their attractive appearance; and the young doctor, taking his seat, observed that the agreeable odor of the tea-table reminded him of a bouquet of roses. At this, my aunt took a biscuit, and, opening it, turned to me, saying, "Why! what have you put in here?" I meekly replied, "A little rose-water," and made my escape in the midst of a peal of laughter.

Those who have ever known our good old doctor, who came here as I have already stated when a young physician, and lived the rest of his long life in our midst, becoming, indeed, a part of Walpole itself, can never forget his keen sense of the ridiculous; and it may well be supposed he found many opportunities to remind me of the remarkable efficacy of a little rose-water, and my valuable discovery in the culinary art.

In the early autumn, Aunt Louisa returned to Boston, leaving again a wide vacancy in our little home-circle that nothing could fill.

The misty, frosty mornings came just as they do now,

and the days came earlier and more early to a close, as usual, but the bright and animating spirit, too, of the household, which would have us forget it was not springtime, had departed with the summer, and it was long before we became accustomed to her absence. The long, weary evenings seemed so long without her cheerful presence. The doctor said, "There was no one, now, to beat him every time at backgammon;" and he and Uncle Abel played cribbage until it was an old story, and music was resorted to for a time. The doctor played the violin charmingly; I can recall many of his favorite tunes, every note of which is perfectly familiar to me now.

It was thus the autumn of 1814 was passed in this bachelor home,— the relatives dropping in along through the day,— and there was no end to them at that time. Grandmother, who had returned from Fitzwilliam, was considered common property: each one had a right in her; and she bestowed her kindly words, as she did her pleasant smiles, upon all alike.

At Christmas time, a new star was added to Walpole society: Mrs. Gardner's lovely young sister came to spend the winter; and they both often made a part of the evening circle round our bright hearthstone; and a merry time was had, especially if the doctor was not called off for a professional visit.

At this time, also, Mr. Dickinson had a standing invitation to take tea once a week. This invitation didn't become outlawed for many years. His presence at the tea-table was looked for with as much certainty as his appearance in the pulpit on Sunday; and it was only when Uncle Abel went abroad for two years, which was after his marriage, that these visits of Mr. Dickinson were interrupted.

Mr. Dickinson, at this time, occasionally exchanged pulpits with Rev. Mr. Mason, of Northfield. After one of these exchanges, he made an ominous visit, one day, when he and Uncle Abel were in solemn conclave such a long time as to lead grandmother and myself to form all sorts of conjectures. In a few days, the announcement was made at the breakfast-table that he and Mr. Dickinson were going to take a short journey for recreation and variety; and Jack, a half-mulatto boy, about twenty years old, was ordered to bring the sleigh to the door at ten o'clock. Mr. Dickinson appeared in time to take an additional cup of coffee, as he had taken a hurried breakfast at home.

It was evident that Dr. Morse had not been trusted with the secret of where or what the object of this journey was; and this opportunity for his humorous remarks was not lost. So those two bachelors started off in the most exuberant spirits, that cold, frosty morning, seventy-two years ago. I went into the kitchen, to get a better view from that window to watch their departure, and heard Cyrus, the colored man, saying to Becky, "You better believe Mr. Abel wouldn't been so fussy 'bout his boots, if there wasn't somethin' more'n common in the wind!"

It may be remembered that boots, at that period, were worn over the pantaloons, reaching nearly to the knee; and the tops were made in various patterns, and were highly polished; and sometimes a long silk tassel would be suspended from the top in front. When Becky called Cyrus' attention to the absence of this appendage, he blew a long whistle, saying, "You've lived here long enough to know Mr. Abel don't b'lieve in no such nonsense as that."

It was customary, at this time, when there were so many bearing the name of Bellows, to distinguish them by their Christian names or titles; and when there was a number by the same Christian name, as it happened occasionally, they would be distinguished by their number.

When this mysterious journey was ended, and the parties returned and settled down again to every-day life, our suspicions were forgotten for a time, but only to be revived when the snow had disappeared, and the bright sunshine of spring was giving a new face to everything.

The household was awakened very early, one morning; Mr. Otis Bardwell brought the passengers from Keene to Walpole, and the arrival of the old yellow stage, with its red wheels, drawn by four horses, was regularly announced from the end of a tin horn, before most of the inhabitants had finished their dreams of the night. Grandmother and I occupied a room on the lower floor; and, on this morning, I was awakened by her saying, "You must get up, child; some one has come. Put on my shawl, and go to the door." At this moment, the bang of trunks on the doorstep, and a loud knock on the door from the end of a big whip, accelerated my steps; and the door was quickly opened to one whose coming always brought so much joy and gladness. The cheerful, ringing tones of Aunt Louisa soon brought the whole household out of their beds. Uncle Abel was one of the first to appear, saying, "You have certainly caught me napping, this time; but I have no apology, as it was evidently intended." I think an arrival from Boston occasioned about as much excitement, at that time, as an arrival from any port in Europe does at the present day.

When Becky made her appearance, breakfast was ordered an hour earlier than usual, after which the doctor proposed as a medical prescription to have our young lady guest tucked nicely into bed, and left to her own reflections until she had made up the lost sleep in the two days' and one night's travel on this journey from Boston to Walpole.

Aunt Louisa slipped very easily into her accustomed place in this bachelor home, as matter of course assuming the direction of affairs; and, as her brother was very fastidious in various things, it was a great relief to grandmother, as she was too advanced in years to keep up with the times in many respects, and my own cares were very much lightened; for, although I was in school, I somehow felt myself responsible for whatever was going on at home.

As the summer drew near, there seemed to be some unusual preparations going on, without any explanations. Grandmother looked very wise, but kept her own counsel. When Mr. Bardwell brought a large package to Uncle Abel, one morning, and a bandbox to Aunt Louisa from Boston, things were becoming a good deal complicated; but, when Jack appeared in his new suit, all aglow with bright, brass buttons, our conjectures were at an end.

As they all sat down to tea, that evening, Uncle Abel remarked, that he and Aunt Louisa would set out in the morning on a short journey; they were going to Northampton. The doctor, in his own comical way, inquired if there was any probability they would go by the way of Northfield.

It was very evident, on their return, that the object of their journey, whatever it might be, was satisfactorily attained; and, when Mr. Dickinson and Cousin Si came in the evening, there was a good deal of pretty lively conversation, making great merriment for a time.

It was, now, soon ascertained that the wall-paper in all the lower rooms was soiled, and out of style; it had not been noticed before. There must also be a fresh coat of paint on both the parlors. Mr. Nicanor Townsley,— the man who also reported in the meeting-house all intentions of marriage,— came, one morning, with all his apparatus to hang paper, and to whitewash; Mr. Jacob Brown following with his paint pot and brushes. It can easily be supposed that the house was turned upside down while this work was in progress; but it came to an end, at last; and, when order again reigned in Warsaw, and the household was restored to its usual state of amiability, every member of the family seemed under the happy influence of this peaceful serenity. When we were gathered around the tea-table, for the first time set in its usual place, after this great house-quake, the doctor inquired, in his own quaint way, of Uncle Abel, if matrimonial intentions were usually thus announced by Nicanor Townsend, and were accompanied by such convulsions as had been lately experienced in this abode; that he had a personal interest in the question, as he was intending to be married himself in a few months.

It unexpectedly became necessary for Aunt Louisa to return to Boston in the early autumn,— her brother John claiming to have a larger ownership in her than her younger brother Abel,— and so we were compelled again to submit to the inevitable. It was a great disappointment, as she intended to remain here until her place should be filled by the lovely young stranger who was soon to be installed in that home.

Perhaps I should have explained before this, that it was Rev. Mr. Dickinson who discovered this paragon of all virtues ; it happened the first time he exchanged pulpits with Mr. Mason, of Northfield. On rising, to commence the morning service, the first object his eyes rested upon was, as he expressed it, this vision of beauty ; she occupied a pew directly in front of the desk, and her large lustrous eyes were turned up to his face. At the close of the service, he observed Mrs. Mason conversing with her in the vestibule, and, on joining them, she was introduced as Miss Houghton ; and he learned that she was as lovely in character as she was in person, and he at once decided to interest his friend at Walpole in this young lady on his return ; and the result I have already given.

Should the question arise how I came to the knowledge of all the particulars I have just related, I can readily answer it. It was only a few months after my uncle's marriage that I was myself sent to Northfield, to attend school ; and I soon became acquainted with these families with whom she was always most familiar. I shall never forget the manner in which they always spoke of her, as their lost treasure, and as one whose beauty and refinement were indelibly impressed upon the community in which she was born.

There were three sisters in this family, all of whom were classed with the remarkable women of their time, by all who knew them. The eldest, Lucretia Houghton, became the wife of Judge Prentiss, of Northampton, who was afterward a senator in Congress twelve years. The youngest daughter married Henry Bowen, a merchant of Middlebury, Vt. She was not handsome, but she impressed you at once with her indescribable loveliness of manner, and those large, lustrous, black eyes, so full of sweetness and intelligence. They were her father's eyes. He was a man of dignified bearing, and was justly proud of his daughters, and was not sparing of money in their education.

Well, the autumn months seemed never, as at this time, to pass away so slowly! I had found that this lovely young stranger would be brought to our home some time in December. I remember my uncle was perfectly silent upon this topic; not even Dr. Morse, with all his shrewdness, could obtain any satisfactory information, although several attempts were made to approach the subject. Even after the proclamation for Thanksgiving had been read, as usual, following the Sunday service, Dr. Morse inquired, when sitting down to breakfast, next morning, if it was only the turkey and plum-pudding for which this household were to give thanks on this anniversary. The reply was so equivocal, it was evident my uncle intended to keep his matrimonial affairs to himself.

It was but a few days after this, that an elegant new sleigh was driven into the yard. It was something quite different from anything of the sort ever seen in Walpole before. It was a double sleigh, with a bellows top; and the handsome robes that came with it, and the beautiful bay horses that would take it swiftly over the road, were a theme for no little conversation in the neighborhood. Some other things, out of the usual routine, occurred at this time, which were very suggestive. My uncle maintained a profound silence, and no one presumed to ask any questions; but it was very evident that matters were coming to a crisis. Mr. Dickinson appeared, one evening, earlier than usual for his weekly visit. This was ominous, for he was exceedingly precise in all his habits; and, to come on Tuesday evening instead of Thursday, which he had so long and regularly observed, was surely a suspicious movement; for we had reason to believe he was the repository of all we should so much like to know about,— not, however, to simply gratify curiosity, but we did not wish to be wholly taken by surprise.

Although I had just entered my seventeenth year, I can yet remember how ambitious I was to have every part of the house in order, and appear to the best advantage; and, as my grandmother was nearly eighty, she left it all to myself and Becky to make the necessary preparations for the supposed advent of this young stranger. I think Mr. Dickinson must have been aware that I was giving a little more than my usual attention to the conversation going on, for he looked at me with a questioning smile many times during the evening. When he rose to take his leave, he placed in my uncle's hand something that looked like a letter, without any comment. That I thought was somewhat significant. He then, as usual, bade us good-night; but, as they went to the door, he took my uncle's hand with some ambiguous expressions in his good-by, which brought a hearty laugh from both of them. I was then sure my suspicions were correct, and I told grandmother she must be prepared for startling news in the morning; and when she inquired why I had come to think so, I told her everything I had seen and heard that evening. She was greatly amused at my conclusions.

The next morning was intensely cold; but the bright sun had begun to remove the frost from the window-panes when we sat down to breakfast, and Cyrus had come with some hesitation to the door, saying that Jack had come for his orders. He was bidden to wait until breakfast was over, as there was plenty of time.

I will explain here, that Jack was a colored boy, about twenty, that Cousin Si had kept in his family from early childhood. He was unusually bright, and had been trained to take care of and drive the horses,— an occupation in which he greatly excelled; and, on state occasions, my uncle would borrow him to drive his spirited bays, which he could do as no other one could. Cyrus took care of them, but he was not as good a driver as Jack.

Before rising from the breakfast-table, my uncle quietly said, "I am going to Northfield, to-day, and shall return to-morrow afternoon." He then called Jack, and told him to be ready to start at eleven o'clock. Well, to my great satisfaction, the way was made clear to me now; and we only waited their departure to commence operations.

The doctor, all this time, was evidently aware of what was going on, but wisely kept his own counsel. At the precise moment, Jack, with a mighty flourish and crack of his whip, dashed up to the door. It was quite difficult to determine of which he was most proud, the beautiful bays in their gilded harness, or the elegant sleigh with its splendid appendages; but Cyrus, a little jealous of Jack's privilege, said he was more proud of himself, for had he not got a new fur cap with long tails hanging down behind, and a new bright yellow silk bandanna for a muffler round his neck? And it was not probable he would forget the number of gilt buttons he wore under his overcoat, and which he would take the first opportunity to display!

My uncle didn't keep this equipage long in waiting; those pawing, dancing creatures were too impatient of delay; and he soon made his appearance, arrayed in the warm and handsome outside garments he usually wore; which was a brown surtout, made in the fashion of that time,— something like a frock coat of the present day, with the skirt reaching a little more than halfway below the knee. Over this was thrown an elegant black broadcloth cloak, lined with fur.

As they left the door, Mrs. Gardner and her sister, across the street, were waving their adieus, and the doctor gave a warning word to Becky, that if she threw anything after them, to let it be her shoe and not the moccasin, which she still wore, and which once, in her haste, she had sent after departing friends to secure good luck for them; and which, because it was a moccasin, involved the terrible possibility of bringing bad luck upon them for life.

I soon followed my grandmother into the sitting-room, to ask her advice about a few things, and also tell her of my own plans; for she always liked to know what was going on, and she seldom objected to whatever I proposed to do. As we had so recently prepared for Thanksgiving, in the manner of that time, when there were pies and puddings made sufficient for any number of weeks, it was not thought necessary to do anything more than make a batch of pound cake. As this was my first experiment, my ambition was now raised to its highest point: the thought of failure was too terrible to entertain for a moment; but I had not much fear, for I had thoroughly learned the quantity of each article of which it was composed, not forgetting the rose-water, which once brought me to grief. I will here inform my readers, who perhaps may indulge in a little curiosity, that my cake on this occasion was a perfect success, and was complimented by the one for whom it was particularly made.

The next in order was to see that my uncle's chamber was suitably prepared. Although there was an open fireplace, I could not remember ever having seen a fire lighted in it; and, when Becky had polished a pair of brass andirons, and Cyrus had made a bright fire, I took grandmother up to see how comfortable it all looked. When I proposed opening the great north parlor, there were at first some objections made; it was such a cold day grandmother thought we couldn't get the room sufficiently warm; but, after some argument in favor, and Becky had respectfully reminded her that the "fore-room" was always used for weddings and funerals, she changed her opinion. And when I had decorated the sideboard with all the cut glass, and trimmed the silver candlesticks with curled papers, giving a few more extra touches here and there, Becky became quite enthusiastic, and declared the room looked like a paradise. When I thought the air sufficiently warmed, I took grandmother in, telling her we would give them a warm reception, if it were possible; to which she replied, a bright, glowing fire would be the most fitting expression of our warm and cordial welcome on such a bitter cold day; and she complimented Cyrus on his remarkable skill in that department.

The next day, as we were to look for the arrival as early as four o'clock, my attention was given to what I considered of much importance,—I wanted my grandmother to look as smart as possible, and proposed that she should put on her black silk; but the early impression she received of a silk dress, probably when her blue damask was purchased, was not yet obliterated, and I could not persuade her that any circumstances could make it proper for her to wear a silk dress at home; so the matter was compromised by her putting on a nice bombazine. Her cap was the next in importance. The double border, about half a finger in width, was never more perfectly crimped; and, when she folded the book-muslin handkerchief across her bosom, I thought she was fit to be presented to a queen; and, when at last she was seated with her knitting in her own especial corner in the sitting-room, I took the opportunity to prepare myself—but not without some trepidation—to meet the one who had lived in my imagination the last three months, and oh! could she be all my fancy had painted her?

As I now turn to that day, so long ago, how vividly I can recall each hour, as we completed our preparations with feverish haste; the intense cold seeming to make the day even shorter than it really was! But at length the hand on the old clock, which had stood in that corner since long before I was born, pointed the hour of four. I had completed my own toilet, not forgetting to remind Becky to make herself look as neat and tidy as possible, giving her at the same time a new, bright calico apron, that grandmother had made for this special occasion.

When I recall the way in which young misses in their teens dressed at that period, I think it was in better taste than the present manner. There certainly was a childlike simplicity, which we do not often see at the present day. As an illustration, I will describe my own costume, on that especial afternoon. My dress was a dark woolen fabric, called bombazette; the skirt was gored, and reached a little below the ankle, and the waist was made precisely in the form we now make a baby's slip. A linen cambric ruffle, plaited very fine, and turned down over the edge, was the only bit of trimming upon it, and the sleeves were long and made with small puffs reaching half-way to the elbow. There was no decoration for the skirt, save a broad ribbon, the same color with which the gathers were tied back in a large bow with long ends at the bottom of the waist behind.

As combs were an appendage seldom used to confine the hair, it was either cut short, or rolled on papers at night, which were removed at the proper time next day, letting the hair fall loosely about the neck in curls, which was all the covering considered necessary for the neck of young girls at that time. And so I was thus arrayed, that long remembered afternoon, when I took my place at the window, to catch the first glimpse of those we were so anxiously awaiting; and we were not kept long in suspense. First came the music of those clear bells; and then the bays, half-covered with frost, dashed round the corner of the street below us, and the next moment they were at the door, which I had already opened. My uncle alighted, and stood waiting for a figure to emerge from the depths beneath that bellows top. She soon appeared, and stepped lightly to the ground, and he led her up the steps, saying to me, "Here is an aunt for you;" and then, taking her into the sitting-room, said: "Mother, I have brought you a new daughter." She then stooped down, and pressed her cheek against mother's without a word.

This greeting, so unlike the usual manner, impressed me in a way I have never forgotten.

The salutations over, I then assisted in taking off a blue flannel pelisse that was trimmed with white down. This garment was worn over a cloth habit, the jacket embroidered with black silk braid. Her bonnet, which was made of green silk, completed this travelling costume. As soon as she had disrobed, grandmother placed her in her own chair, in the warmest corner, as she saw she was very much chilled. Uncle Abel bustled about, calling Becky for hot water, with which he prepared a cordial for her, and something for himself also; and now, sitting down before the fire, which Cyrus said had been kept roaring all day, he pulled out his watch, saying, "Harrit, we have not been three hours coming from Northfield!" I will say, here, that he always pronounced her Christian name with two syllables; and once, when she remonstrated with him, a friend who was present said, "A rose by any name was just as sweet."

As I have already said, this was one of the coldest days of the season, and it took some time to make those who had been out so long in the frosty air comparatively comfortable; but, when quiet was restored, and I ventured to give my first scrutinizing glance, she rose at the same moment, asking grandmother, as she then kissed her for the first time, to take her own chair again: and, as I placed another for herself, she kissed me also, saying that she was too much chilled when she first came in to greet us as she wished to. I thought, then, as I did ever afterward, how sweet and lovely she was! As the usual tea hour was very near, I said to my uncle, the parlor was nice and warm, perhaps he would like to sit there while the tea was prepared. He expressed some surprise that I had thought of warming that room, in words which implied a little doubt of the possibility, as he took our guest — as we chose for the moment to consider her — across the hall, and opened the door, saying, "Well, well, Harrit, I declare, this is more comfortable than I could have expected!"

When tea was ready, a question arose, in my mind, of great importance. My grandmother had always presided at dinner, but I had served the tea and coffee, and should I, at this first repast, offer the new wife this seat, or treat her as company? It did not occur to me that I could ask my uncle, and so the question remained quite a puzzle, and was left to decide itself. When my uncle brought her in, I stood where he could give her my seat, if he should choose to do so, but he placed a chair for her at his right hand, saying, "We shall treat you, my dear, as our guest to-night." And so, to my infinite relief, this momentous question was put to rest.

The intense cold did not prevent several of the nearest friends from dropping in after tea. Uncle Thomas brought his wife with her aunt, Mrs. Dana, and Mrs. Gardner and her sister. Mr. Dickinson also came in at a later hour. He gave the young bride a cordial greeting, and took his seat in the merry circle around the fire, apparently in a high state of satisfaction, as he joined in the lively conversation that was going on. Perhaps there were, at that moment, some pleasant anticipations for himself awakened. It had certainly become known, there was another in Northfield who had been sought; but it yet remained to be seen if she had been won. I will here inform those who may wish to know, that another minister, more fortunate than Mr. Dickinson — his name was Shepherd — persuaded this lamb to come within his own fold, at Ashfield; and thus Walpole and Mr. Dickinson were deprived of a most lovely and efficient pastor's wife.

As our visitors took an early leave, my uncle called me to go up-stairs with him, supposing there might be some arrangements necessary for the comfort of this new aunt, as he called her; but, when he opened his chamber-door, and saw a bright blazing fire in the chimney, which Cyrus had carefully tended all day, he expressed his surprise in the usual way, saying, "I declare! this is very nice and thoughtful of you. Go and ask your aunt to come here, and stay with her; she may need your assistance."

As I have been inscribing on this white sheet, in visible characters, all these little incidents — some of them so trivial, as I am aware they are — that have been written on the pages of memory alone, I have lived over again the day I can never forget. Each person who participated in the simple occurrences I have described has stood visibly before me, making this realized dream of that long ago seem more like an event of yesterday.

When we gathered around the breakfast-table, next morning, my uncle led her to the seat I was very willing to relinquish; and, as I watched the manner she dispensed the honors of the table, her beautiful hands attracted my notice, and I afterward saw that a delicate foot corresponded with her hand. She, however, always seemed unconscious of her own personal charms. No one more studiously avoided anything which would induce flattery; it was most distasteful to her; she was a lady by nature, as well as by education.

How well I remember the first Sunday she went to church! My uncle's health prevented his accompanying her, and she avoided all pretence of coming out as a bride; and when she entered the parlor prepared to go, with her green silk bonnet on, my uncle remonstrated with her. She had a white velvet hat, decorated with two long, elegant white plumes, in which she looked exceedingly lovely, and he wanted her to wear it; but his argument proved unavailing. She sweetly told him that, when he could go with her, she would wear it. He was evidently a little disappointed, and, as he went out to put her in the sleigh, he caught an old green plaid cloak from a nail in the entry, and laughingly threw it over her, saying, "Everybody now will know who you belong to; for I have worn that about town the last ten years."

She thanked him, and kept it on, which he did not expect her to do; but she wrapped it about her, saying she would find it very comfortable. And, as we rode a mile up-hill to the meeting-house, she made not a word of comment, but quietly left it in the sleigh, and wrapped it about her again when we returned home.

I will say, here, that I think my uncle discovered, through this little episode, one phase of her character with which he was wholly unacquainted: she did not come to her conclusions hastily, but, when her decisions were made, one might as well attempt to move the rock of Gibraltar as to change her decision; and how calmly she would defend herself against any amount of opposition! I never heard her raise her voice, or exhibit any excitement upon any occasion, but showed always perfect self-control, and calmness of voice and manner. I can now see my grandmother, as she sat calmly and silently with a suppressed smile, listening to a lively discussion upon some point of difference, each maintaining their own view of the question; and it was often amusing to notice with what pertinacity she would hold her argument, making it apparent there was no possibility of changing her opinion. He would then say, "Well, well, Harrit, I think the better part of valor will be for me to surrender; but it must be upon such conditions as an old general I once heard of. He was willing to surrender, but he would never own beat."

In the second year of his marriage, Uncle Abel began to relapse, and the old trouble, dyspepsia, seemed to take a firmer hold than ever. This was a new disease, at that period, and it was not treated as at the present day. He declined so rapidly, that a change of climate was recommended as the only hope of recovery.

In all that lovely woman's life, I think this was the most trying ordeal, save one. She had a lovely babe, a little girl about eight months old. This precious little one she must leave behind. It was necessary she should devote herself wholly to her husband, and she was not one who ever allowed any personal feeling to prevent her performing whatever she considered a duty. It was in 1819 that preparations were made for this journey: they were to sail from Boston for England, early in September.

I can never forget the last few days that intervened before the parting. How often, in those weary hours, she would press the lovely little creature to her bosom, the tears falling upon its face like rain; but the last sad moments came, and oh! what a tempest of agony was wholly suppressed when, with a face white as marble, and with no word nor tears, she pressed the little one again to her bosom, and then put her in my arms, saying, "Oh! take her away!" Every one who witnessed this struggle was in tears, and there were many friends present who had come to take, as they supposed, their last leave of my uncle. He travelled in his own carriage, and was so weak and prostrated he could only reach Boston by going a few miles each day. It will be remembered, at that period, steamboats were not known; and the voyage across the Atlantic was made in a sailing vessel, taking a number of weeks to go from Boston to Liverpool.

The first letter that was received gave us the pleasant intelligence that they reached port without accident, and there was hope that the change would be beneficial. It was two years and a half, when again they set foot upon their own native soil: their absence had been prolonged by the birth of a son, born in London, and he was six months old when they returned. How clearly the occurrences of that day are present to my mind! There seemed but one thought to have taken possession of us all. That sweet, loving mother was not coming home to the same little one she had left with so much pain: two-and-a-half years had wrought an entire change, and she now pressed to her throbbing heart a little girl of more than three years old, — a perfect image of herself, in feature and complexion; she was a vision of loveliness, and again the thought now impresses itself upon me, I am the only one living upon whose memory is mirrored the image of that beautiful child that had been my especial care during their absence! It had been arranged, before they left home, that Uncle Thomas and wife should fill the vacancy made in the household by their departure, and have the general supervision of the family. I cannot leave that dear little one yet, who has been enshrined in my heart through all these long years, but I have only a little way farther to follow her; for her stay with us was not long. She lived only three years more, to give sunshine to that home. She bore the sweet name of Charlotte,— a name made doubly sweet to me by association, for years afterward I gave it to my own and only little one, to perpetuate that child's name and memory; but she also stayed here but a little while, and died at the same age as her little cousin.

Another great sorrow awaited this household a few years later. A little daughter had again been placed in the arms of this loving mother; and how joyfully it was received,— a little sunbeam whose brightness seemed never dimmed! She was unlike her elder sister; she had great beauty, but it was of a different type, resembling more her father's family. During her brief life, she was the light and joy of that home, afterward made so desolate by her death, when little more than sixteen years old.

Our cousin, Rev. Dr. H. W. Bellows, better describes this sad blow, when speaking of others who belonged to us that were cut off in all the loveliness of youth and beauty. He continued: "We add to this necklace of our family jewels, with which Death has arrayed himself, one fitting in lustre and worth to be its clasp: Harriet Louisa Bellows, in maiden maturity, and in the bloom of her loveliness, was cut off by sudden and violent illness, when at school at Lenox, Mass., in 1850. Charming in form and feature, mild and docile in temper and manners, formed to cheer and adorn the home of which she made the life and hope, this lovely girl had won the admiration and respect of the village, of which she promised to be its brightest ornament. She was privileged beyond others, but never envied; an only daughter, and yet not spoiled; beautiful, but unaffected; gay, yet innocent. Unspeakably necessary to the happiness of her parents, death could not spare her who could least be spared by us. God took her whom everybody wanted, and desolated the hopes of a life, the light of a father's old age, a mother's pride and joy, an only brother's companion. Faith has consoled, and time has familiarized, and a hope beyond the grave more and more lightens the dreadfulness of that loss; but it is fitting, when God smites so hard, we should recognize the full severity of his blow, meekly bowing before his majesty and goodness, in our direst afflictions."

Thirty-seven years have elapsed since that dark cloud enwrapped this household. What agony of grief when that daughter was brought home to her father in her coffin! The mother who had gone to her returned with her dead child, nearly paralyzed by this blow.

On hearing the sad news, Dr. Bellows hastened from New York to Lenox, and was there to help sustain the mother through those sad hours. He then hastened to Walpole in advance of the others, to prepare and help support our uncle, who was entirely broken down by this sudden calamity, and never again during all his after years seemed like his former self, but more like a child that needed to be soothed and cared for. It was not many weary years that he was kept in waiting, when he was laid to rest beside the two lovely children who made so much of his happiness while they were here on earth ; and what one of us shall attempt to tell how much these two may now contribute to his joy in the heavenly home? The dear mother remained a few years longer with the loving friends below, when she, too, bade adieu to all earthly scenes, and joined the family above.

The only son, Abel Herbert Bellows, is still living. He graduated at Harvard in 1842, and then studied law, and practised for several years at Concord, N.H. His interest in his native town and in the family were manifest by his efficient and devoted services at the time of the gathering of the clan, at the dedication of the founders' monument. On that occasion Dr. Bellows, when extending his thanks to those who had specially aided him in his preparation of his address, said : " Far beyond any thanks due to other kindly helpers is my gratitude to Cousin Herbert, who for weeks has kept the mail freighted with his contributions of new facts and incidents bearing on the family history. Beside general historical information, he has contributed some of the best characterization, and some of the happiest narratives in the address. I should be most ungrateful not to make our kinsmen aware that, though deprived of Cousin Herbert's presence to-day, no one has contributed more substantially to the interest of the occasion, or had at heart a livelier sympathy with the ceremonies of the day."

A VILLAGE STREET, WALPOLE, N.H.

CHAPTER XXVI.

THERE was much in our Aunt Susan's life worthy of note, beside her wedding, which I have already described, taking place when her brother Abel assumed the proprietorship of the old home in which she had passed the greater part of her life since her childhood. She had always been the presiding genius in her brother Joseph's household. It has been truly said, some people were created for leaders; and she was a fair specimen of that class. Not only in the household, but in society, Susan Bellows was one of the reigning queens, not for the reason that she was a beauty, for she was not that, but her face was beaming with intelligence, and she possessed a dignity and superiority of manner that none could mistake. But what was most charming in her young life was her vivacity and brilliant wit and humor, cropping out always in her own inimitable manner.

I have already stated that her marriage made her the stepmother of four children. There were two daughters and two sons: Eliza was the oldest, and about seventeen; Jonas, named for his father, was the eldest son; Maria was the second daughter, and not quite fifteen; another, who was the youngest, and called John, was a lad of twelve years.

It can readily be seen, it would take no small amount of good judgment, good sense, and nice discrimination, and we will add a little tact, to manage all those half-matured children; but these qualities she possessed in no small measure.

The daughters were amiable and pretty, and the sons were fine-looking boys. I think their stepmother was very proud of her family, particularly when following her up the broad aisle to the family pew, their father always leading the way. Of our Aunt Susan it was often said, she was the best type of the old Puritan in the Bellows family. She was a strict observer of the Sabbath. Not one in her household was permitted to remain at home, if by any possibility able to go to church on Sunday. Anything that pertained to dress was of secondary consideration; and her lessons to us girls upon the display of fine clothes at church were worthy of being handed down to posterity.

There were some clearly-defined rules established, which the young people were required by her very strictly to observe. Perhaps I cannot better illustrate the original and happy manner in which she governed this family without their knowing it, than by giving one or two examples. If she wished to correct a bad habit, or establish a good one, she would take the opportunity when all were present to express her own views, upon that and kindred ones, and then request them to give theirs, always treating their opinions with as much respect as if they were equals in age and judgment. When she had gained her point, of enlisting their interest, and committing them to the side of right action, she would propose some penalty or forfeit, to which they should all assent, for the non-observance of the more important rules. Thus, there must be no delay at the breakfast-hour. For this, there was an especial penalty; and Jonas, the big boy, was most sure to be the culprit, when no small amount of fun was anticipated and fully realized during the whole day following.

As no apology could be accepted save that of real sickness, when found guilty in the first degree, the culprit was sentenced to wear through the livelong day a pair of boots which had been handed down from a remote generation. They had been carefully put away, evidently for preservation. Their history ever remained an impenetrable mystery, for no questioning threw any light upon it. It was difficult to determine which excited our mirth most, those boots, or the mock penitence with which the wearer would walk round in them. Even his father, with all his gravity and dignity, could not withstand the grotesque attitudes and the comical expressions. Jonas was unusually tall, and these boots came to the top of his knee; a broad band of red morocco, six inches wide, turned down over the top; the heels were very high, and the toes were run to a sharp point, three inches in length, and turned over on to the instep. The thought of these boots would ever create a smile; associated as they always were with that fun-loving, fine-looking, good-natured boy, who always treated his stepmother with respect and kindness so long as he remained at home, to receive her kindness and discipline.

As Uncle Robeson was much the wealthiest man in Fitzwilliam, he was also the leading man in business and all public enterprises; and Aunt Susan thought his influence and effort should extend beyond the mere getting of money; they should also be looked upon as examples and leaders in all the moral excellencies. Perhaps no one was better qualified by nature to lead in that direction than she; for her good, strong common sense pervaded everything she attempted; and to her deep, religious nature was added a dignity and persuasive power of appeal that usually proved irresistible.

There is nothing I can recall more vividly than the way she would dissuade her young people from indulging in whatever she considered demoralizing; their choice of amusements, and plans for visiting; those also whom they selected for companionship: nothing seemed to escape her vigilance.

I think it was in the year preceding her marriage, that Maj. Robeson built the Turnpike between Fitzwilliam and Keene, thereby greatly lessening the number of hills that were the terror of travellers and teamsters on the old road from Keene to Boston. This enterprise also greatly benefited his own town, by turning the travel through it. It was also principally by his efforts that a new meeting-house was built in the same year of their marriage, taking upon himself the work of soliciting subscriptions for that purpose, and contributing very largely himself. There may be a few now living, who, if they should read this, will remember its destruction, a few months after it was completed. Strangely enough, in the month of January, there was a violent thunder storm, when this house was struck by lightning, and burned to the ground. The comments that were made upon this calamity, by a certain class of the inhabitants, were more amusing than reasonable; and it may well be supposed it was most discouraging to those who had given all they could afford for its erection. But it took more than this to discourage or dampen the ardor of Maj. Robeson, who told them, whatever had been once done could be done again; and in due time he commenced with more zeal than ever to get funds for the rebuilding of this house. And the next autumn, old Mr. Sabin, the minister, found himself with his small but zealous congregation in a new house, superior to the one which had been destroyed.

I have only given this account as one specimen of his energy; and these, by her own confession, were the qualities that first engaged her attention. How well I remember, one boisterous, stormy evening, when Aunt Susan and the two girls and I were sitting alone, the bright, blazing fire seeming more grateful by the contrast of what was outside! We congratulated ourselves on having an uninterrupted time for work and conversation; for Aunt Susan always improved such opportunities to make herself entertaining, besides giving some of her never-to-be-forgotten moral lessons. Any one, now living, who knew her at that period in her life, will be able to recall the sudden manner with which she would sometimes startle you with an unexpected question, or give some vigorous word of advice. A brief silence was broken at this time, when she quickly looked up, saying, "O girls! are we not all going to meet in heaven?" This was followed by some remarks that were suggested by the question. After this followed an examination of our work, upon which some pretty sharp criticism was made on Eliza's careless way of doing some things, for sewing she always declared was her abomination. Her stepmother, however, insisted that whatever she did should be done well. After this colloquy, we worked steadily a short time; when she again spoke suddenly, and with much emphasis, "Girls, remember what I say to you now; never make yourselves too cheap!" This reminded us at once of her conversation the evening before,— endeavoring to impress upon our minds all the maidenly proprieties and improprieties, which no one perhaps understood better, or could point out more clearly than she could.

As I recall the manner in which she obtained such a remarkable influence over others, I can more clearly, at this distance of time, understand the wonderfully winning and compelling qualities that gave her this power. One was that sweet musical laugh you would often hear; another was that tone of authority in which she would direct all those who assisted in the duties of the household. There was nothing imperious in it, only the voice of one who used her native right to dictate with the assurance her orders could not but be obeyed, because they were always based on what was right. It was six years after her marriage, when she had two children of her own,— a little girl named Mary Ann, and a son who was only three years old, when Maj. Robeson was taken with typhoid fever, and died.

This unlooked-for calamity occurred a few months before the eldest daughter's marriage was to have taken place with Dr. Wells, at that time a resident in South Carolina. He had commenced the practice of his profession in Fitzwilliam, but sought a wider field at the South. The wedding was consequently delayed more than a year.

I cannot forget the many long conversations of Aunt Susan with Eliza upon the new life she was about entering on. Her religious counsel, particularly, was most earnest and impressive; and she did not forget the poor slaves with whom they would be in contact in that southern home. This was long before the slavery agitation. Wendell Phillips and his colleagues were not born ; but there were a great many northern people who were as strongly opposed to that deplorable institution as he, but who had not his ability or enthusiasm, or the courage of William Lloyd Garrison, to fight it.

With many other things which she said to this stepdaughter, as I recollect perfectly, she made the following remark, "Eliza, it somehow is impressed upon my mind that the Lord is about sending you into the midst of these selfish and cruel slaveholders as an example of pitying kindness ; teach them to temper their discipline with mercy, in the correction of their slaves. Above all other things, and under all circumstances, my daughter, dare to do right."

When Dr. Wells came on, in the early part of December, it was soon apparent that he was pretty thoroughly imbued with southern ideas. For a short time, Aunt Susan was silently tolerant; I knew, however, that the crisis would soon arrive; she had too much respect for herself to allow her opinions to be treated with contempt, or tolerate any undue liberties in her household. And when Dr. Wells ordered her colored man, in a dictatorial manner, to harness for him her horse for a drive, without so much as even saying, With your leave, madam, she verified her belief in the old saying, "There is a point beyond which forbearance ceases to be a virtue." She overheard the order and the tone of it, and went directly into the sitting-room. I can now recall the flash in those large, expressive black eyes, also the calm dignity and perfect fearlessness of her manner, when she said to him, "Dr. Wells, I have taught my young people, when they want a favor, to ask for it. If it is the custom down South to take whatever you wish, and whenever you like, such lawlessness cannot be tolerated here; and I may as well remind you now, that our colored people at the North are not slaves. Whenever you want boots or shoes blacked, please take them to John. It is no part of Lot's duty to perform such work as you seem to impose upon her." This colored girl, Lot, was one Aunt Susan brought into the family when she came. She was a relative of Cousin Si's faithful old Rachel, and proved to be most efficient and devoted help; and no one's personal rights were more scrupulously guarded than hers, in this family. And this young doctor found he had brought his southern ideas and southern airs to the wrong market. Although this rebuke was what he might have expected,— for he had been an inmate of this household two years before going to the South,— he seemed, however, much surprised, and made an awkward apology. When Eliza heard what had happened,— for the doctor told her as soon as she came in,— she laughingly replied, "Better have left your bad manners at home; I am glad there is an opportunity for your improvement." She was amiable, gentle, and pretty in all her ways; her stepmother was very fond of her, and often indulged in many painful forebodings, as she prepared this child of her dead father, as she expressed it, to go so far away from her. "Eliza," she would say, "I never felt the need of your father so much as now; do you think he would approve of all we are doing?"

The wedding-day came at last. A few friends were invited to witness the ceremony performed by old Parson Sabin, the evening previous to her departure.

How well I remember that cold leaden morning in December, so portentous of a storm! It was a perfect index of the feeling within that household, so busy in this last hour, making everything comfortable as possible for the long, cold ride in their own conveyance, before taking the stage. When the last words were spoken, and the last silent pressure of the hand given, she went to her mother, and laid her head upon her bosom for a few moments, receiving there her benediction. She then cast a long, lingering glance around the room, as if, as it truly proved to be, it was her last look upon her childhood's home. She then gave her hand to Dr. Wells, who led her out, putting her into the covered sleigh, thus shutting her from our sight forevermore. Aunt Susan turned from the door, and went directly to Maria's room, who had taken her leave the night before of her sister, and did not come down to breakfast, or see her again. The poor child had wept herself quite ill, and it was evidently necessary something should be done for her. It had occurred to me that I had not seen Lot since breakfast, and went into the kitchen to look for her. She had gathered little Bellows up in her arms,— he was then a child of three years, and of whom she was very fond,— and sat weeping violently, declaring she would never see Miss Eliza's dear face again, and she would rue the day she ever went off with that man.

CHAPTER XXVII.

THERE was nothing, now, to prevent Aunt Susan from returning to the old home of her race, where so many of her kindred were still living. John Robeson, a boy of thirteen years, was placed in a military school; and Maria, the youngest daughter, was at Miss Fiske's boarding-school, in Keene. She had nothing to leave but her two graves,— those of her husband and daughter,— she who died when six years old; and now she bade adieu forever to the place where she had lived so much in such a brief space of time.

It was not long after coming home that she built a new house, fashioned after her own taste. I have heard it remarked, that people often express something of their individuality in the structures they build. I think this must be true; for I can never pass this house, although so many years have elapsed since she went away, without becoming suddenly conscious of the one who for so many years filled it with the life of a noble Christian woman.

Her one earthly treasure, as she would often express it, was her little boy, to whom was given her own name, Bellows. I can never forget the impressive way she would teach him his moral lessons, and how strictly, also, she taught him the observance of good manners. There is no one of our race, whom I have known, who had a higher appreciation of good breeding. She could never find any apology for the want of it. I have known her to seek opportunities to say, in the presence of those who were careless, that, whatever their occupation, be it ever so humble, it would lend an additional grace to possess polite and agreeable manners. "Why," she laughingly said, on one occasion, "I would rather have, as a husband, a blacksmith who is a gentleman than a professional man who is a clown!"

When her son had reached a suitable age, she placed him at a school, in Amherst, going with him herself to choose his boarding-place, and secure the especial care of some one of the teachers, to whom she presented him as the "only son of his mother, and she a widow." He graduated at Yale College. While at New Haven, he became acquainted with Miss Susan Taylor, daughter of Prof. Taylor, the distinguished theologian. She became his wife, after he had studied his profession, and established himself in the city of New York as a physician. His marriage was particularly gratifying to his mother; for to this young lady's personal graces were added the charms of a bright intellect and lovely character. Who that ever saw her can forget the peculiar sweetness and loveliness of her manner? Alas! the memories of that household always fill my heart with tearful sadness!

How distinctly I can recall the words with which Aunt Susan described to me the fulfilment of a long-promised visit to the old home! The professional duties of her son, on whom were centred all of a mother's love and pride, had detained him year after year, each one rendering it still more difficult for him to leave. "He came at last," she said, with her hands pressed tightly together, and her eyes raised toward heaven, "he came home in his coffin ; and, when they had brought him in, and placed him in the parlor, I seated myself close beside him, and the only words my lips could form were, 'Be still, and know that I am God!' and it was thus I received my lesson of submission."

It can easily be conceived how crushing must have been this terrible blow. All her bright hopes and high expectations for future years were thus suddenly ended in the death of this only son. The dark shadow of disappointment seemed ever after brooding over her spirit; it was apparent that, to be cheerful, required an effort; that sweet, musical laugh was forever silenced. It was not very long afterward that this son's widow, the sweet, young mother, was called away, leaving her four orphaned children to the tender and loving care of relatives and friends. How warmly and lovingly these little ones were taken into the hearts of those who assumed the care of them was manifested in everything that pertained to their future as well as present welfare.

It had been an unspeakable happiness to Aunt Susan to have the three little boys with her much of the time, when old enough to leave their mother; but she was too far advanced in years, when the dear mother went away, to have the entire charge of them; but the lessons she impressed upon their young hearts and minds, by precept and example, I have reason to think have never been forgotten by these grandchildren, who still cherish her memory with reverence. And if she is permitted to watch, from her heavenly home, the footsteps of those she loved so much on earth, she must feel assured her daily morning and evening prayers for them were not in vain.

At the time of this writing, there are only a few nephews and nieces left, to hold in veneration the memory of this aunt, and who can distinctly recall the closing scenes of her life, and her last illness and death.

It was the night before she died, that there was to be a brilliant torch-light procession, to encourage the election of Lincoln as President of the United States. She had been all her life one of the most ardent of patriots, and thoroughly informed upon all political subjects. During this day, she had heard whispers in her sick room about an illumination, and the necessity of keeping the house dark and perfectly quiet. Just at night, when they thought her near her end, she roused from a lethargy, and asked why the windows were not lighted? It was explained to her that it was because she was so sick, and they thought it might disturb her: she said, in her feeble whisper, but still with an authority that no one for a moment dared to question, "Let every pane of glass, in every window of this house, be lighted at once, if there are candles enough in town to do it. It is my order!" It was the last order she gave, and it was obeyed to the letter. That very night, to her another order came, which she was waiting cheerfully to hear, and was glad to obey: it summoned her where they need no candle, neither light of the sun.

Her obituary, which I append to the sketch I have given of her, was written by Uncle Knapp, and furnishes a more adequate conception of her character than I am capable of doing.

OBITUARY.

"Died, in Walpole, N.H., Oct. 3, 1860, Mrs. Susan Robeson, widow of Col. Jonas Robeson, of Fitzwilliam, and daughter of Col. Joseph Bellows, and granddaughter of Col. Benjamin Bellows, the founder of Walpole. Rectitude, intellectual strength, and decision early marked her character; followed in maturer years by deep piety, and a comprehensive view of the duties of religion, she united in her character the peculiar traits of Mary to Martha's devotion to duty; was active and influential in advancing the temporal and spiritual prosperity of the religious society of which she was a conspicuous member, never sparing of money or of labor.

That the children of the parish might have the benefit of her knowledge and experience, she continued to instruct a Sunday-school class until nearly the end of her life. The respectful manners, the kind-heartedness and manly characters of her early orphaned grandchildren, bear striking testimony to the wisdom of her loving care. Private and local objects did not absorb her interests, or limit her exertion.

Temperance found in her a strenuous and eloquent advocate, and human suffering of every description a deeply sympathizing friend. The sick and the destitute were relieved by the interest she took in their suffering and wants. Her relatives and neighbors all join in admiration of her noble spirit and consistent life. Her strong, constant, and unwavering faith had long since removed terror from death and darkness from the grave, and imparted sustaining strength to spiritual vision."

To this I will append a letter written by our cousin, Rev. Dr. Bellows, to my Aunt and Uncle Knapp, immediately after Aunt Robeson's death. It sets forth, in strong light, the marked features of her character.

NEW YORK, Oct. 6, 1860.

Dear Uncle and Aunt,—Frederick's letter, announcing Aunt Susan's decease, came yesterday; and, as I suppose he is at Boston, I thought it best to direct my reply to you. I was, of course, prepared to hear this, as Sister Eliza has kept me informed of her gradual decline; but the death of the most aged and infirm is always, at the last, a surprise and a shock! The candle cannot go out so quietly that the darkness does not make itself sensibly felt. I have not waited for the sanctifying influence of death before appreciating the rare force and steadfast worth of Aunt Susan! Her puritan sternness and self-relying though God-fearing graces have commanded the reverence of her neighbors, and the admiration of her kindred; the strength of her mind, the vigor of her conscience, the determination of her will, the depth and persistency of her convictions, the proud self-respect, the wide and sleepless sense of responsibility for the good of others, the willingness to do her duty, however costly to her purse or her inclinations, her uncomplaining heroism in all her sorrows, her wide family sympathies, her native wit and humor,— all these things make me feel that Aunt Susan was one of the most memorable women in our family record, and one whose death, though timely and blessed, will be deeply felt in Walpole, and by her friends. It is impossible not to follow her to the abode which she had so long anticipated with Christian confidence as the scene of her final reward! I believe her eyes are already opened to many misconceptions, and to some practical mistakes; but I think very few will carry a cleaner record, or can show a sincerer and more consistent life. If my dear aunt had, earlier in life, been under a different influence, I think her views would have been softer, milder, truer, but nothing could have made her a braver, more conscientious, or more truly venerable character. I am proud to be her nephew. I shall hold her memory in lifelong affection and respect.

May we not hope, dear uncle and aunt, that family ties, so strong as ours have proved, will survive the power of death? I could not contemplate the probable changes in the next ten years with any serenity, did I not confidently hope that our friendships and affections are superior to the short interruption of the grave! God bless you both, and preserve you to us all!

Your affectionate nephew,
H. W. BELLOWS.

CHAPTER XXVIII.

WHEN conversing with friends, grandmother would occasionally speak of her large family; when she usually improved the opportunity to say, she had ten boys, before the advent of a little daughter, who was received with great demonstrations of joy by her big brothers, some of whom had quite reached manhood. And they were permitted to find a name for her, which all should unite in choosing. They were not long in deciding upon the name of Susan. It was one held in veneration, as it was the name of their mother's only sister, who had long before passed away, and it was particularly gratifying that they should have chosen this for the little stranger; and it was seldom spoken, without recalling the one whose memory was very dear to them, and to whom it was said she bore a striking resemblance.

Two years have elapsed, and now another daughter is placed in the arms of our grandmother. To this one was given the name of her Grandmother Whitney, whose maiden name was Sarah Farr. She was called Sarah during a few of her early years, after which it was changed to Sally; and this name she bore through the remainder of her long life, of over ninety years; and there is no name in this great family that can awaken more tender memories than that of Aunt Sally. She was very unlike her sister Susan, who was so full of vivacity, and so conscious, always, of her ability to do and to dare; while this one was painfully shy, and never quite sure of herself in whatever she might attempt. But this did not prove her inferiority; for, in reality, her natural gifts, in many ways, were quite equal to those of her elder sister.

As I have already recalled a few incidents in her life, we will pick up the thread again where we dropped it, at the age of thirteen or fourteen, where we still find her an inmate in her Cousin Caleb's family. And I think she must have been serviceable, as well as agreeable; for when teaching me the use of my needle, at an early age, she would entertain me by describing the marvellously beautiful work her cousin would do, and how proud she herself would feel when complimented by her for having done her own work unusually nice.

I will say here, for the benefit of the young people who may read these pages, that those who invented sewing machines were not born at that time. All the beautiful stitching and hemming was done with the fingers, and Mrs. Caleb Bellows was no less distinguished in the art of sewing than she was in many kinds of cookery, which she also endeavored to teach my mother when old enough to assist her. And it became the dream of my childhood, that, when I became a woman, I should make just such lovely pound cake as that which was baked in scolloped tins and in the shape of a heart; and my pies, also, should be seasoned and decorated in all imaginary forms like hers. I think it was when describing a Thanksgiving dinner, that I received this lasting impression of our cousin's cookery.

At this time, there was no one in our family who could give more elegant entertainments than were given by our Cousin Caleb and his wife, who was one of the especial leaders in society. She was tall and dignified, with a face not handsome, but beaming with intelligence. Her brilliant conversational powers always drew about her a circle of admiring gentlemen, who liked to talk with a sensible woman. It was said she was quite as much of a theologian as Parson Fessenden, who was at that time their spiritual teacher. She was also very fond of music, and would often invite friends who could sing to come and practise sacred music with her, when Uncle Josiah would usually join them with his bass-viol. At this time, their Cousin Sally was nearly fifteen, and her remarkably clear, sweet voice was fully appreciated; and it was at this time she was persuaded to attend a singing-school. I have already spoken of her shy and retiring ways; and it was only when her Cousin Caleb promised to go with her that she consented to join.

In telling me the story of some portion of her young life, this singing-school had a prominent place. She would always shrink from meeting unfamiliar faces, and had an especial dislike to going where, as she would say, she had not been once before. After her cousin had formally introduced her into the school, she became greatly interested in learning to read music, and would have enjoyed it much more, if she had not been made so conspicuous.

Thomas Fessenden, the parson's eldest son, but better known as Tom Fessenden, played the flute, having a seat by himself; and she was placed beside him, for the reason that her voice accorded so well with that instrument; and he greatly added to her confusion by complimenting her singing, keeping her face, as she said, in a blaze much of the time; and, to her unsophisticated mind, he seemed to enjoy it: and, what added still more to her annoyance, he always came prepared to take her home, by putting the pillion on behind his saddle. It will be borne in mind, perhaps, that the only mode of transportation, at that period, was on horseback; and it was quite customary for two to ride on one horse, making a pillion a necessary appendage to the saddle. She used to say, he followed her so closely, she found it impossible to escape from what she considered a persecution, but what proved to be, in truth, his sincere admiration for this very young lassie; and, when he became aware of her aversion to him, there was no little disappointment expressed.

During this winter, Mrs. Caleb Bellows received a visit from her father and mother, Squire Hartwell and his wife, of New Ipswich. It was not the first time they had visited her since her marriage, and these dear old people could not too often visit this child, on whom they had lavished such a wealth of love as well as worldly goods; and the burden of their conversation was, how lonely, now, was the old home, since her departure. Her young life had filled the household with so much light and joy, that nothing then seemed wanting to make up their sum of happiness; and now, on their return, could they persuade the young Cousin Sally to go home with them? She could attend the school which had become quite popular, and the only one in the State dignified at that time with the title of academy.

This opportunity filled the child with delight, but her cousins thought best she should wait a few weeks; it was necessary to prepare her wardrobe for the coming summer. The roads would then be better settled, making the travel not only easy, but pleasant; for those accustomed to travel on horseback found little fatigue in the exercise, and a fine opportunity was given for enjoying the scenery.

When Esquire Hartwell and his wife returned to New Ipswich, it was arranged that she would come some time in April, and attend school one term, which was as long as she could be spared, or rather as long as it would benefit her to study at one time. Mrs. Bellow's theory of education was, to mix a good deal of practical training with intellectual acquirement; and, as I look back upon that far-off time, I think that must have been the general theory; and, in my own early life, the mixture savored much more of the practical than the intellectual.

This anticipated journey — the first since her babyhood — was a dream of delight, by day and by night, as she used to describe it to us. Her cousins at the colonel's were in full sympathy with her, particularly Sophia, who entered deeply into this plan for her to attend this celebrated school. Her aunt expressed her pleasure, by measuring off a dress for her from a piece of striped blue and white linen. It was a home manufacture, for which Aunt Colonel's establishment, as I have told you, had become quite celebrated. The fabric was noted for the fineness and delicacy of its texture. She was very grateful for this substantial evidence of their kindness; and, when returning home with her precious bundle, if she did not step as lightly as Walter Scott's "Lady of the Lake," she certainly stepped as quickly; for her hurry to reach home, and exhibit her present, increased every minute. And, when she came bounding in, nearly breathless, her dignified cousin was greatly surprised to find so much enthusiasm in one who was usually so quiet and undemonstrative.

The days and weeks seemed never before so long as now, when waiting for this last winter month to pass away. But, like all things else, it came to an end at last; and now this first spring month brought its usual work of the season, with an important addition: Sally's wardrobe was to be made in readiness for an early departure in April.

Perhaps some of my young readers may like to know more than I have already told, of the way girls of fourteen or fifteen were dressed at that period, near the beginning of the century; and I will tell them, though possibly I may repeat something I have already said.

There were only a few materials from which dresses were made. Silks, and all the fabrics that were made from cotton, were imported; but linen was generally used for all purposes, and was manufactured at home, by persons of all classes,— the poor and the rich alike. Very few were so poor they could not make a web of cloth, which they knew so well how to spin from tow; but that made from the beautiful soft flax was very handsome, and worn at home by ladies as well as by children. It was admirably fitting for school garments. The blue and white stripe was fadeless, and always new when clean; and, what was of more importance, would bear the wear and tear of the wildest games that boys and girls were apt to indulge in, especially those who lived so far away as to make it necessary to take their dinner, and pass the noon hour at the schoolhouse.

We will now attend to the preparations for Sally's

departure to that far-off school, necessitating a two days' journey to reach the institution. There were many discussions as to what and how much would be needful to take; for nothing could be carried that a pair of saddle-bags could not accommodate. And so it was decided, that her white dimity, which she had already worn two seasons to church, could be made sufficiently long, by putting on a wide flounce at the bottom. This bit of trimming was allowed, as a matter of necessity. Her cousin's ideas of simplicity in the manner of dressing children were strictly adhered to; but Sally thought she should not be included any longer in that category, for was she not nearly fifteen years old? So this flounce, in her mind, was a great acquisition, and greatly served in reconciling her to wear a dress she had nearly outgrown. There was also an appendage to this dress, called at that time a vandyke, and which we now would call a cape. This also must have a ruffle at the edge, to enlarge it sufficiently to cover the neck; for all dresses for children and misses were cut with a slip waist,— that is, such as are made on baby's long dresses; and, as the sleeves were nearly always made short, and gathered into a band above the elbow, an extra pair of sleeves were usually made to draw over the arms, and fastened up with a button, for common dresses, but a pair of long, soft kid gloves, tied up with a bit of ribbon, was deemed indispensable to complete a nice dress. As we have now got Sally's white dimity sufficiently enlarged to be wearable, we will finish this, her Sunday costume, by putting on a straw hat with a broad brim, and a ribbon carried over the crown, tying it down closely to her face; while her wealth of long brown hair is fastened up low down at the back of her head. And now, in imagination, I have my own mother standing before me, as she was at the age of fifteen. After mature deliberation, it was at length concluded, that two more dresses beside her nankeen habit, which was only worn for a riding dress, was all that were necessary for her to take, or that could possibly be carried in such a limited space as one side of a pair of saddle-bags; for the other side must be reserved for various things quite as necessary as dresses. One of these last two dresses was the lovely blue and white striped linen her Aunt Colonel had given her, which was yet to be made; the other, a calico print, which was in a fair state of preservation, having been made in the autumn, and worn as prints only were worn at that period,— for visiting and receiving company. This print was much admired, having a large bright flower stamped upon it, the name of which I cannot now recall, as it is many long years since I heard it from my mother's lips in childhood, as she described its beauty to us children when old enough to understand her, and take an interest in the simple stories which she would relate connected with herself. It was seldom she dealt in fiction for our entertainment. She could always find enough in her own life sufficiently interesting for that purpose. It is to this strict adherence to what was true, and our interest in these home-details, that I am indebted for the little episodes in her early life that I am now relating.

Well, the weeks had all passed, and the days were now counted that intervened before this long anticipated journey was to be commenced. The importance of fair weather, while on this horseback trip, can readily be understoood, and the weather-wise, as well as the skies, were often consulted; for it is well known that April skies, with their fair promises, often prove treacherous. As the roads were now settled, it was deemed safe to decide upon the day for their departure. How eagerly, now, were the heavens scanned, and with what a thrill of joy, as Sally watched the sun on that last day, sink gloriously without a cloud behind the Westminster hills,— the sure harbinger of a pleasant day on the morrow! And now the last things were done, on that last evening, preparatory to an early start on the following morning.

Old Pacer, as Sally's horse was called, was carefully groomed, as was also the colonel's saddle-horse, which he took great pride in, for he was a high-spirited, beautiful creature; and, before the sun was fully risen above the hill-top, they were dashing along the highway at a speed few ladies could indulge in at the present time,— for old Pacer was bound to keep up with Dick, who, if not checked, would always go as if on a steeple-chase.

We cannot follow them all the way on that two days' journey, but we know of the warm reception that awaited them, when at length they alighted at Squire Hartwell's door, which they reached just after nightfall of the second day: while, meantime, many anxious glances had been turned toward the windows by the kind hearts within, as they listened for the approach of the travellers. Nothing could exceed the motherly tenderness with which Mrs. Hartwell cared for both, especially Sally,— her poor tired child, as she would say, when winding the soft linen bandage around her ancle, but more especially where the saddle-horn had worn pretty deep into the flesh. And now supper, which had waited for these necessary attentions, was ready. How grateful was this repast can easily be imagined, for they had partaken of an early but not very sumptuous dinner, according to the Bellows' estimation of that mid-day meal!

It would be useless to attempt a description of all the substantials and dainties that were prepared for this repast; but we must not omit the beefsteak, broiled on a gridiron, set over the live rock-maple coals, on the great kitchen hearth, and turned every half-minute until done to a turn; when it was put upon a long deep, dish, heated hot for this purpose, then cut in strips about an inch wide, and then seasoned with a shake of pepper and salt, while a generous slice of butter was added. This was a favorite dish for breakfast as well as supper, which was always made a substantial meal; and nothing could be more appetizing, as this was brought in steaming, and abounding in rare gravy after the company were seated at table.

As soon as this refreshing meal was disposed of, Mrs. Hartwell said Sally must come with her; so, leading the way up-stairs, she took her to a room, saying, "This is Mary's room;" then going to the bed, and patting it tenderly, "and this was her bed; it will be very pleasant to have it occupied once more." She then called to a young colored girl to bring the warming-pan, with a handful of sugar, which she sprinkled over the coals, and, shutting it quickly, put it in the bed, telling the girl to move it slowly about, and saying to Sally, that the smoke from the burnt sugar would take all the pain and soreness out of her limbs, and she would be bright as a new pin in the morning. And so, with many more soothing words, she drew a chair, and sat down by her; but it was only for a few moments; for, nearly as soon as the child's head touched the pillow, she was wandering in dreamland.

When she opened her eyes, in the morning, and commenced emerging from the depths of this downy bed, she was suddenly conscious of some one in the room, and, the next moment, saw Mrs. Hartwell adjusting the curtains at the window. She had come, she said, to see how it was with her little girl, and was much gratified to find how well her warming-pan had done its work. Dressing herself quickly, she was ready to go down with Mrs. Hartwell, where she found the family had gathered, to listen to the morning prayer,— a service that was always attended before breakfast.

The colonel was apparently as much refreshed by his night's rest as his cousin was; and this, her first day in that family, whose memory was kept bright through her long life, by often relating some incident that occurred while she was an inmate of their household, was made very enjoyable to her; for she was taken all about the premises, the colored girl delighted to have some one help her hunt the hens' eggs in the barn; and she was greatly amused to hear Dick and old Pacer's loud whinnies, as soon as they saw their young friend, and their loud calls to come back, when she left them.

Mrs. Hartwell placed no restraints upon her young guest, as she chose to consider her on that first day. She evidently thought that children could best entertain themselves in their own way; but, on the second day, after completing her rounds — for she superintended every department of her household personally —

calling Sally, she said, she had been thinking it would be better for her to have some light duties assigned to her, and she was going to propose that she take those which Mary used to attend to: one of more especial importance was cutting the roses every morning while the dew was on; as she distilled them, making a quantity of rose water every year. Another was, to draw a fresh mug of beer at noon, which the squire always took with his dinner, and also to dust the sitting-room and have it nicely done before the time for morning devotions, which were never omitted, and at which all the family, with all the servants, were expected to be present. There was the same observance before retiring at night; the addition of a hymn would often be proposed, in which all who could sing would join. When, for the first time, Sally's clear, sweet voice rang out, they were all surprised and delighted; it seemed like an inspiration. She did not sing with a trained and cultured voice, but she sang as the birds do, for the gift of song was native as her breath; and she took great delight in the exercise of this power.

Col. Caleb's visit at Col. Hartwell's was necessarily a short one; but before he returned, the preceptor, who I think was Mr. Hubbard, was invited to tea, as the colonel wished to introduce his little cousin to her new teacher before leaving; he at once took a deep interest in her, which was manifested as long as she remained his pupil.

There were many little episodes that my mother used to relate, when telling her children the story of her school-life in New Ipswich. Every day was full of happiness, made so by the unsparing kindness bestowed upon her.

At that period, stoves were nearly unknown, and elderly people often used one of the sitting-rooms for a sleeping apartment, during the coldest winter months; and a bedstead that could be turned up against the wall was generally used for that purpose; and it was made quite ornamental, by hanging a handsome curtain before it. At the morning and evening services, it was expected, as I have mentioned, that all the household would be present. On this particular evening, their colored girl came in somewhat weary, and, slipping behind the curtain unnoticed, seated herself upon a roll of cloth that was placed there during the day; and, probably thinking it was more restful to sit than to stand during the reading of the scriptures and the singing of a hymn, and then a long prayer, which constituted the usual evening devotions, she fell asleep, unfortunately, and did not wake at the close of the service. When it was time to attend to the last duties of the household, before retiring, she was nowhere to be found. Search was made in all directions, loudly calling her name, but there was no response. When they returned to the sitting-room, expressing their surprise and anxiety, the bed-curtains parted, and she stood there with a look of bewildered astonishment, asking what had happened. As Mr. and Mrs. Hartwell were very sensible people, this girl was not sent to bed with a reprimand, but with a hearty laugh; also a mild admonition not to hide again in prayer-time behind the bed-curtains.

It was now June, the time Sally had waited for with a pleasant anticipation; for she was then to assume a task her Cousin Mary had always performed in her girlhood, and only relinquished when she left the dare old home for the new home at Walpole. This duty, before referred to, was, as I have said, to gather the roses, each morning, while the dew was on them, as fast as they opened their lovely petals to the morning sun.

During her long life, she could vividly recall the delight she took in the preparation for her first morning's experience in her new employment. Equipped with a pair of scissors and a new and pretty deep basket, and well-protected from the dew, she entered upon her work with all the enthusiasm of a child, that she was. Her basket was soon filled, when she returned to the house from the great garden, to spread the roses upon a long table prepared for the purpose; when she became so intoxicated with their abundance and their beauty and fragrance, her exuberance was so great, that Mrs. Hartwell laughingly threatened to give the work to some other one who had not such a wild passion for roses as she had. And when, at breakfast, she related the morning's exercise to the squire, he looked at her a moment, and replied, that he could see no harm in a little girl so near of kin to themselves having a love of flowers!

CHAPTER XXIX.

It was during this month of June, information was received that Gov. Strong would pass through the town on his way to some place, where he was invited to be present, on some particular occasion. As the governor desired no public demonstrations on his way, he was simply invited to breakfast at Esquire Hartwell's, with a few of the leading citizens of the place. It will perhaps be remembered, that the governor's sister was the wife of Gen. Bellows, and their son married Miss Mary Hartwell, their only child. It is probable he was indebted to this relationship for the breakfast which was served on this occasion. Mrs. Hartwell was the queen of housekeepers; and, as was customary with New England ladies, in those days, she directed this department personally. In childhood, our mother related many times the story of this breakfast, which she always described with great minuteness. Probably it was more vividly impressed upon her memory for the part which she, as a young girl, took in it. She said, I cannot recall the number and variety of dishes that were prepared for this occasion; but I distinctly remember there was an antique vessel, of some kind, filled with roses of every hue and variety, placed in the centre of the table. Breakfast was served at nine o'clock. Mrs. Hartwell had arrayed herself in her highest crowned cap and black silk dress. She had also interested herself in Sally's toilet, telling her to put on her white dimity, which was made with low neck and short sleeves. A bunch of rosebuds was in her hair, and a bouquet of buds fastened on her bosom. They then awaited, in the proper place, the arrival of their guests. The governor, with a few of his staff, was escorted from the hotel by the invited citizens; and, on entering the breakfast-room, he and his aids were presented to Mrs. Hartwell and to the little girl at her side, with great formality. They were then seated at table, when the squire, in his most impressive manner, invoked a blessing. The ceremonies over, all seemed prepared in the highest degree to enjoy the banquet so bountifully provided for them. When the party rose from the table, it was announced that, before they separated, the National Ode would be sung by Miss Bellows and a gentleman, whose name I have forgotten. At this point of her narrative, my mother would say she never sang better, for she was filled with enthusiasm with which the words always inspired her: "Hail, Columbia! happy land"; and she was accompanied by one with whom she often sang, who always filled her with confidence and courage. After speaking a few moments with Esquire Hartwell, the governor came directly to her, and, taking her hand, thanked her cordially for the song she had so charmingly rendered; saying also, that he had just learned she was a niece of Gen. Bellows, his brother-in-law, whom he held in high esteem, and of whom he had ever been justly proud.

The six months that she remained at school in New Ipswich were filled with incidents, from which she could always select something to relate, which she could make as marvellously interesting to our childhood comprehension as anything she could have read from the "Arabian Night's" entertainment. She visited in some of the most delightful families of that place, where there was a specially refined social circle, and also made some acquaintances that were not so easily dropped. A young gentleman, a graduate of that academy, by the name of Emerson, was one. Her friends considered her too much of a child to receive the attention of any one in that way, and she availed herself of their advice, — that she make no return to the ardor she had so unfortunately kindled in this most excellent, but sensitive youth's heart. He afterward became a distinguished clergyman in Massachusetts; and many years later, when my mother's hair was silvered with age, she often saw his name attached to some article she had been reading with interest in her religious paper, when, with a look of abstraction, she would say, "It was all for the best."

Having finished her school education, she returned to the old home, ever ready to give her a warm welcome, bringing with her many tender and lifelong memories of those she had left, especially her dear old friends, Mr. and Mrs. Hartwell. Through her long life, she cherished a grateful memory of their loving and unfailing kindness to her. In a few weeks after her return, Dr. Sparhawk, at that time the most popular physician of Walpole, although he lived three miles out of the village, was called to visit one of the family professionally; and, when he saw her come into the room, greeting her with surprise, he exclaimed, "Well, I think that I have found the schoolmarm I have been looking for. How would you like, Sally, to come and teach the school in our district?" I think he must have had a wonderful gift of penetration, to discover in her any of those qualities that were deemed at that period necessary to make a born "schoolmarm." Knowledge was of secondary importance to discipline. The number of switches successfully used became qualifications for that position. Happily, for the little urchins who have their letters to learn now, public sentiment upon that subject has been greatly modified. The little girl so suddenly called upon to answer an important question could only express her surprise that any one should think her capable of teaching a school. She was persuaded, however, to accept the invitation, the doctor promising that she should board at his house; and, under his protection and encouragement, she got through with her school with more credit than she thought really belonged to her.

I think she must have been sixteen at that time, as I can recall many incidents which she said occurred in the summer that followed her first and last attempt at teaching school. I will relate but one of these. It was proposed that the young people make up a party for a berrying excursion. It was in August, and report said that blueberries were in great abundance, that season, on the plains, which were about three miles distant from the village. According to the necessity and custom of the time, they all went on horseback, carrying baskets and pails,—the latter being filled with the lunch that each took; and when spread upon the grass, as they prepared for their dinner, such a variety of good things were not often seen at one feast. But most conspicuous was Aunt Colonel's election cake, for which she had become so famous, and to which all were ready to pay their respects; but Sophia declared they should only have a bite, in exchange for something they had brought. Great merriment prevailed at this feast for a time, but they were suddenly warned by a clap of thunder that a tempest was gathering, looking at that moment very portentous. All was changed; there was nothing, now, but to gather their effects, and make a hasty retreat. For a few moments, all was excitement, as the storm seemed rapidly approaching. To add to this dismay, the young school-teacher could not find her hat. She had taken it off, and put it under a bush, where she was quite sure she could go directly to it; but she was so intent upon filling her basket with this favorite fruit, she had wandered farther away than she was aware. All joined in the search for a few minutes, when she told them to leave her, and she would soon overtake them. Her brother Thomas remained, and another young gentleman, who was too deeply interested in the situation to give up the hunt, but all effort proved fruitless; and the favorite little hat was abandoned, when the big drops began to fall ruthlessly upon her uncovered head. Her brother threw her hastily upon the saddle, and all three started as if upon a steeple-chase, for she was a fearless rider. They had not gone far, however, when she became aware that her saddle-girth was loose, and she was slipping on one side of her horse; but her brother, with a dexterous movement, righted her without checking their speed. At this moment, all the artillery of heaven seemed opened upon them, and the rain was pouring in torrents, drenching them through. In this plight, they reached home, terrifying all the household who saw them coming; for why was Sally bareheaded, soaked through and through, with the water streaming from her long hair hanging down upon her back? When this adventure got abroad, it was long before Sally Bellows heard the last of her great loss ; reports came from various sources. The little hat was sometimes seen on the head of a pretty young fox, capering about in the fields in great glee at his newly-found treasure; then, again, it was said to have occasioned great jealousy and strife among the denizens of the woods, which was happily ended by the interference of an owl, who captured it, and, putting it on his own head, flew up into a tree so high that no rival ventured to follow him.

The following winter, in February, my mother was married. It was three months before she was eighteen years old. This early marriage was not fully approved by some of her friends; while a few others took a different view.

Her two brothers, John and Joseph, were in favor of it. They had become acquainted with the young man who had not been in town very long; but he was enterprising, and soon established himself in business, and was desirous to have a home of his own. And so it was decided that she should be married without further delay. He then purchased a pretty cottage, owned and occupied by her cousin, Josiah Bellows, Jr., and not long afterward she was installed mistress of the household, thus assuming, at the age of seventeen, the cares of housekeeping. At this period, girls of that age are usually attending school, not having received their first lesson in any of the domestic arts, which formed part of the education of girls in those days.

I have nothing to relate in the way of a list of expensive wedding gifts. It was not customary, at that time, for the guests to bring a fortune in the shape of presents for the bride; but I have heard my mother say, she was "quite respectably set up in housekeeping." I have reason to think that her housekeeping would compare favorably with many others much older than herself, for she was ambitious, and not wanting in capacity to accomplish whatever she attempted.

CHAPTER XXX.

We will now pick up the thread of our mother's life, when, after varied experiences, at the age of thirty, she was left with seven children. Her tender and anxious care of our childhood, and ever-increasing watchfulness for our welfare in maturer years, have sometimes been themes for tears as well as laughter, at her unnecessary apprehensions. It is pleasant to recall the last forty or fifty years of her life. We can only look upon them as her long earthly repose. Free from worldly cares and the unpleasant vicissitudes of life, her serene temperament enabled her to attain the great age of ninety-six years, retaining to the last her clear intellect, and to a remarkable degree her physical powers. Her children, save one, were all living at the time of her death, and saw in her lengthened years their most precious blessing. Five of these had the old family names, originally taken, of course, from the Bible,— the youngest rightfully bearing the name of Joseph. He, perhaps, more than any other, inherited her exquisite taste for music, and her voice also; which, joined to his ready wit, and genial humor, and versatile gifts, made him a most delightful companion, as he was a most faithful friend. The eldest son of the family, Lewis by name, filled a large place in our circle, and has left several children to inherit and transmit his sterling qualities of mind and heart. He had a rare amount of inventive genius, which he turned to valuable, practical ends.

He took the greatest interest in studying and discussing questions of philosophy and social science. My Uncle Knapp used to say of him, that for clear and close argument, and forcible expression of his views, he seldom conversed with any one who surpassed him. But he also has gone.

To give an idea of the estimation in which my mother was held by her kindred, I will append to these fragments her obituary by Rev. Frederick N. Knapp, who from earliest childhood had known and loved his "Aunt Sally." I will then add the letter received at the time of her death, written by her nephew, Rev. Henry W. Bellows.

" Obituary.
IN MEMORIAM.
Died in Walpole, N.H.,
March 11, 1878,

Mrs. Sarah Bellows Ripley, aged ninety-five years, nine months, and twenty-three days. She was the granddaughter of the first settler of Walpole, and daughter of Col. Joseph Bellows, whose large family lived, most of them, to a very advanced age, but left her, for several years, the only representative of that generation.

And she represented it well, by those genuine traits of character, which marked so many of the men and women born in those early New England homes a century ago. She had a mind of clear and keen comprehension; a conscience sensitive and vigilant; a religious nature, deep in its instincts, and toned by thought and discipline; a heart full to the brim of love and sympathy. During her long life, she had many trials; she reared and buried children; she saw days of prosperity and adversity; yet her heart to the end was as loving and fresh as the heart of a little child, so that it was a joy always and a benediction to hear her voice, so peculiarly sweet and gentle. All her words were of good cheer and kindly charity. She was ever patient with the faults of others, and hopeful.

A beautiful quietness and serenity habitually rested upon her countenance. It seemed, somehow, as if to her were entrusted, unconscious to herself, messages of loving tenderness and affection from the fathers and mothers of a past generation to their children's children. She retained, until after ninety years of age, her clearness and activity of mind, and to the very end all her freshness of heart. She died, as for years she had lived,— surrounded by her children, whose devoted care gave brightness to her home; and she was sustained by a faith and hope full of immortality.

F. N. K."

The following is the letter of Dr. Bellows : —

NEW YORK, March 12, 1878.

MRS. E. R. BARNES, Walpole, N.H. :

Dear Cousin Emily,— I wish, at once, to send you and Cousin Sarah an expression of my respectful sympathy in the loss of your venerable mother.

To you who have watched over her long protracted decline with so much tenderness, there must be a grateful satisfaction, mingled with the sorrow at the rupture of so strong and sacred a bond. You both have done the best that daughters could to show your gratitude, respect, and affection for so excellent, meek, wise, and venerable a mother.

Her life had been greatly extended by this watchful care, and you have both had the pride and comfort of her revered presence long after the period when children are commonly allowed the privilege of using the sacred word, mother.

I really dread the effect of this loss upon Cousin Sarah, who had eked out her mother's life by a surrender of her own! A great care is also a strong crutch! We lean upon it, and, when it is suddenly taken away, we are unbalanced and upset. I hope Sarah will escape this reaction! I know how submissive she is in her nature, and what support she will find in her faith and piety. Give her my admiring regards for the beautiful spirit of constancy and devotion she has ever shown to her mother, and let her find consolation, now, in remembering the never-failing patience and love with which she has beguiled the weariness of that now released "prisoner in the flesh."

Your mother was the last link that bound the present to the past in our family history; the last of her own family of brothers and sisters! As such, her death seems to be a sort of separation between this generation and the first generation of the Bellows race, hitherto kept up by living witnesses. The last eyes are closed that looked upon the original settlers of Walpole. I think that whole heap of our dust that reposes in Walpole graveyard must be stirred with the coming of the ashes of the last of the original stock,— of one who has known almost all the whole thousand said to be sleeping in that sacred mound of our race! I cannot help recalling my own father's memory with special tenderness, and Aunt Robeson's and Aunt Knapp's, as I think that the only and last of that family is now, at nearly a century of years, gone to rejoin her original kindred.

Your mother bears a spotless memory! "Blessed are the meek," who so humble, so placid, so gentle, so sweet-voiced, so unexacting; and few more intelligent, more lady-like, courteous, and venerable women have I known.

I recall my last interview with her with great gratitude. It was her benediction. She has gone to her reward. Heaven rest her weary bones, and receive her pure and childlike spirit!

     Affectionately yours,

       HENRY W. BELLOWS.

CHAPTER XXXI.

I WISH to recall to the minds of those who may read these pages, that, in my grandfather's family, there were ten sons and four daughters, belonging to his household. The youngest daughter, whose name was Mary, and who died in early infancy, completed this number of fourteen children. I used to think my grandmother, when giving this number, would always name it with some degree of pride.

As I have related the incidents most vividly impressed upon my mind, in the lives of the two eldest sisters, also whatever might be connected with them which I deemed most worthy of note, and interesting to our kindred, and illustrating the life of those olden days, I will now speak of the third daughter, who was given the name of her mother, Louisa,— a name made sacred to me by so many associations, and around which clusters the brightest and happiest memories of my girlhood. I have already introduced her in various connections; she was so inwoven with my memory of those days. I can now recall how impatiently I awaited her coming from her Boston home, after the winter was over. She usually came the last of May, or first of June, to spend the summer with her mother and bachelor brother. The march of time seemed never so slow as in these intervening weeks; and, when at last we reached the day of her expected arrival, how delightful was the preparation of many little delicacies, that were not indulged in every day! But over this happiness there hung a little cloud. The stage-coach, that thing of the past, was not due until five o'clock the next morning. Grandmother could not array herself in her daintiest cap and black silk apron, and sit down with her knitting, serenely awaiting her guest; nor could I don my pretty new print and white apron, that was so neatly pointed across the bottom. No stage-coach was heard rattling through the street when the sun was setting, bringing to us the loved one, so long waited for. How could we pass a long, sleepless night, and then, just at daybreak, when our eyes should have been wide open, and the front door also, we be caught napping so soundly that the driver's terrific knocks on the door were necessary to awaken us! Now for the hurry, and skurry,—sticking our naked toes into our slippers, and only too happy that we did not lose both of them off, in our haste to admit one whom we knew was listening for our footsteps. I seem, at this moment, to hear again the clear rich tones óf that voice in her kindly greeting, and also saying, she had been creeping three hours, at a snail's pace, over these interminable hills. This last sentence was spoken, as she was hastily approaching grandmother's room. The dear old lady was sitting up in bed, her face beaming with delight, to see again her youngest daughter, who always brought so much life into the household. This was the last summer she ever spent with this bachelor brother; for another bachelor had laid claim to this sister of my uncle, as I presently found out; and her brother had retrieved his loss, by filling her place with another, whom I have already described too minutely to need further comment.

As I now look back, I can recall one incident that took place at that time, which to my inexperienced mind was very mystifying. I was puzzled by the sudden arrival of a stranger, between eight and nine o'clock in the evening. It was a lovely moonlight night in June, and we were sitting with windows and doors open, when a chaise suddenly stopped at the side-door, and a gentleman alighted. My uncle rose, and at the same time I saw my Aunt Louisa suddenly retreating through a door that led into the hall. This was certainly a very strange movement for her, who was always ready with her graceful courtesy, whenever her brother received a guest.

My uncle called to Cyrus, the colored man, to take care of the horse, as he went out to bring the stranger in. I quickly learned, by the conversation, that, to my uncle, he was not an unexpected visitor; for he was inquiring, with some surprise, why his brother John was not with him; to which he replied, that the little boys had become so very tired with their two days' drive, he had decided to remain with them in Keene, and drive over the hills the next morning. As for myself, he added, I did not choose to remain so near to Walpole over night, and this moonlight drive over the hills has been delightful. At this moment, my Aunt Louisa entered the room, but not just in her usual manner; I was quite sure there was a little constraint in the way she welcomed our guest. My curiosity was now at its height, and the mystery deepened, as I heard him say, calling her by her first name, "Louisa, I owe you an apology for the part I have taken in your brother John's plan, to give you a little surprise; I did not fully approve it, and notified your brother here to do as he pleased about informing you." There was a general laugh, when Uncle Abel said, he saw no reason for spoiling his brother John's little joke. I had watched this scene, from its beginning to the end, with an indescribable feeling of injury, as every word and every look caused it to dawn more clearly upon my mind that this man was something more to my aunt than a common acquaintance, and she had not so much as whispered to me a word about it, when she surely was free to tell me all. But I had not then learned it was much easier to talk about the common occurrences of life than these deeper and more sacred sentiments of the heart.

When the old clock, that had stood like a tall sentinel in the corner of that sitting-room since long before I was born, struck the hour of nine, it was an invariable custom, as perhaps I have told you before, for each member of this household to be in readiness for the night's rest. Grandmother, adhering to her usual custom, rose, bidding them good-night; and, following her example, we went to our rooms. As soon as the door was closed, she dropped into her chair, saying, " I do believe there is something on foot!" The next morning, Uncle John arrived with his two boys, John and Hamilton; they were home from school, having a few weeks' vacation; and their father said, they gave him no peace until he had promised to bring them to Walpole. And so he had planned this surprise for his sister, who had been an inmate of his household many years, and had nearly the same love and care for his children as their mother. I can never forget this visit, for two circumstances served to stamp it indelibly upon my memory. It was the first time I saw him who was to become my Uncle Knapp,— one whom I have always since held in the highest respect and veneration. And it was high carnival in that house, from the time my Uncle John came until that memorable visit was ended. His merciless raillery, and lively jokes at his sister's expense, were dealt out more freely, for the reason she had a champion quite equal to himself and ready to meet him on his own ground.

I have many times regretted I did not learn more about Aunt Louisa's earlier years. I think it must have been an interesting period with those who had the opportunity to watch her, as she merged from childhood into young womanhood. Her quick perceptions and keen sensibility made her peculiarly alive to all that was about her; and then always to be noticed were the remarkable conversational powers with which she was gifted, to which the rich, sweet tones of her voice added a peculiar charm. I remember that my grandmother, in speaking of her once, said, she was much inclined to have her own way in her childhood; and her brothers — there being seven of them — had always petted her as the baby of the household, and could never see why her wishes should not be gratified.

As some incidents in these later years of her life vividly impress me, at this moment, I am inclined to think her brother's views, at that time, have since been entertained by others, for all that she could ever wish or ask seemed ready to be brought to her hand. Four or five of the first years of her married life were passed in Roxbury, Mass., but ever after his very first visit to Walpole, Uncle Knapp fully intended to make this place his home. He was enabled, much sooner than he anticipated, to realize his cherished plan. The spot he would have chosen above all others, and which fully realized his dream of earthly beauty, was for sale; and no time was lost in making it his own. It was the beautiful house which had been built, at large cost, by Cousin Josiah Bellows, Si, 2d, son of Col. John. How clearly I can recall that bright and lovely day, when preparations were being made for their reception, in which we all took a lively and active part! They were received at her brother Thomas's, where they were to remain until their own house was made ready for them. I have a good and sufficient reason for thinking it must have been the last of May, or the first of June, when Uncle Knapp brought my Aunt Louisa, with their two little boys, one, about four, the other, two-and-a-half, years old.

Perhaps some curiosity may be awakened as to what my reasons may be for giving this particular date of their coming, and the temptation to tell my little story that I have told verbally so often before is at the present time irresistible; and it will furnish a sufficient proof that I am correct in my figures. On this memorable day, I was assisting my Aunt Sarah Bellows, Uncle Thomas' wife, in all possible ways, in her various arrangements, for these dear friends; and I took, as a part of my duty, the preparation of a generous dish of rhubarb sauce. It was the first we had obtained from the garden that season, and therefore a rarity. When this was prepared, and ready to be placed upon the table, in a long cut-glass dish, I, to make sure of its safety, set it upon a high shelf in the pantry, which, to give point to my story, it becomes necessary I should describe.

It was an old-fashioned, spacious pantry, full of cupboards, drawers, and all kinds of convenient places. On one side of the room was a cupboard with two doors ; above this was a row of deep drawers, and then a broad shelf, which was called a dresser; and above this were four very narrow shelves, with narrow spaces between them. It was upon the second shelf, above the dresser, that I placed this choice dish, fully assured that its height would insure its safety. We had not long to wait after the dinner hour for the expected guests. They came in their own carriage ; and what a joyful welcome was given these weary and dusty travellers, after their long drive of a hundred miles and more from Jamaica Plain! How delighted were the little ones, to have their freedom again, after being cramped in a close carriage two-and-a-half days! They scampered everywhere; the youngest particularly was a marvel of life and activity, which was very amusing to his Uncle Thomas, who said he was nearly as large, and full as spry, as a big grasshopper. In the first flow of conversation, in which all were so deeply interested, the children for some time were left to amuse themselves, but it was soon observed that the oldest one was by himself ; and where could the little two-and-a-half-year old one have strayed ? In a few minutes, we all were searching in every direction. I could never tell what led me to look in the pantry; but, when I opened the door, the first object that met my view was that little fellow, stretched at full length high up on the second narrow shelf, his face directly over the dish of rhubarb, with which he was regaling himself with evident satisfaction. That was a sight too good to be lost, and I left him to continue his repast, while I called the household to come and see him. The first exclamations were, "How did that child ever get there?"

As there was apparently nothing that could aid him in climbing, how, indeed, did that child of two-and-a half years get up on that high shelf? I will here inform my readers, that to this day it has remained an inexplicable mystery. There was a little light thrown upon this transaction, two or three years later, when his Cousin Susan saw him, one morning, climb to the top of a stone wall, several feet in height, with no visible places for a foothold; and her remark on that occasion was, she had never entertained a doubt but he would, some day, get into heaven.

As the subject of this little story is still living, I shall hope to be pardoned for thus presenting him as a culprit,— the only one of our race whom I have known to receive that appellation. I have no doubt, however, that the consideration of his extreme youth will serve to modify the judgment of his kindred!

In the early part of the next day might have been seen a small and joyous party, toiling up a rather steep acclivity, but, happily, not a very lengthy one,— only just long enough to complete the delightful purpose for which nature seemed to have intended it. On this eminence, situated at the southern extremity of the village, stands a handsome brick edifice, which was built for the oldest son of Col. John Bellows, in 1812. Much satisfaction had been expressed, that this lovely place was still to be occupied by one of the family, who was so near of kin. The little party scrambling up the hill were going to pay their first visit to this newly purchased home. I can, at this moment, hear again my aunt's voice, ringing through those empty rooms, as she called the attention of her husband to every new discovery, as they went from one lofty room to another. And then the spacious hall, extending through the whole length of the house, from north to south, and in which the little boys were in full chase, greatly delighted with the clatter of their feet upon the hard floor. And now the spacious drawing-room is reached. The large open fireplace, made of polished marble, and the beautiful landscape paper on the walls were the first objects that met the eye; and these, at that time, — going on seventy or eighty years ago — were certainly marvels of grandeur, surpassing anything that had before been seen in Walpole.

From this lower hall, a long flight of stairs took the explorers to the upper hall, nearly as spacious as the one below, with a large window looking to the north, and made with special reference to the view that could be obtained from it. My aunt was the first to reach this spot; and, with an exclamation of rapture and surprise, she turned, as I remember so well, looking my uncle in the face without speaking a single word: they were both silent for a moment, when he said, with a perceptible quivering of his voice, "Louisa, this surpasses anything that can be found in Switzerland!" From this window can be obtained such a view as seldom blesses the eyes of mortals! The village is spread out before you in all its picturesque beauty; the surrounding hills and lovely valleys, the green meadows, mountain, and river,— Bellows Falls Mountain, and the beautiful Connecticut River. Here they stood for the first time together, in silent admiration, neither uttering a word to break the charm. When, at last, they turned away, he said, "My vision of a home is more than realized; I must write, Louisa, to my friend this afternoon, and I must sit by this very window, if a table can be improvised for me."

As despatch was a marked quality in her character, it did not need a second visit to this establishment to ascertain all that was necessary to be done before the furniture was arranged. It was decided to give the lower hall and sitting-room a fresh coat of paint. This, with a slight alteration in the china closet, could soon be accomplished. Jacob Brown, the man of all such work, was sought; who, as usual, engaged that it should be done without delay. Our experience, however, proved the contrary. When we saw this quaint individual, the next morning, with his brush in one hand and paint-pot in the other, hurrying in his grotesque manner,— walking a few paces, and then starting upon a full run as many more,— we hastened to follow him. He was soon hard at work, and we ourselves were busy measuring and fitting carpets, when we were suddenly conscious there was no one at work in the house but ourselves. I had a slight acquaintance with this man's mode of operations,— doing things by jerks, and never finishing. I assured my aunt that I believed I could paint that hall as well as Jacob Brown. I took the brush, and went to work with a bold hand, and with a success that surprised myself. When he returned, in the afternoon, and found what progress had been made, and that a girl had done it, he was somewhat crestfallen; and, when told if he left it again in that manner he need not return, he thought best to complete his work as he had engaged to do.

We will now take a look into this lovely home, all its appointments in perfect keeping with those who were to dwell in it. It was the home of culture and refinement. How tasteful were all its arrangements within, and how beautiful its surroundings without! And now what a throng of memories are awakened of that dear old time, when there were so many to enjoy the hospitality that for long years was so generously dispensed there! To friends and acquaintances, and especially nephews and nieces, of whom there were so many, this home had a marvellous attraction. The warm and genial welcome of the host, and no less kindly greeting of the hostess, were something never to be forgotten! That dear old home seemed always alive with the happy ringing voices of the young people of the village, all of whom seemed to share the feelings of one who, in her own phraseology, said, " The toes of my shoes will always turn in that direction."

HOUSE OF JOSIAH BELLOWS, 2d.
Afs. wird, owned by Jacob N. Knapp.

(Buii: 8'2)

CHAPTER XXXII.

This was also a special resort for the children of her eldest brother John. During their childhood, as we have seen, Aunt Louisa was a member of his household. Their mother died when the twin boys were babies, Henry and Edward. As I take the last name upon my lips, the thought of his tragic death in earliest manhood fills my heart with sadness. And Henry, to whom this brother was a second self, for nearly forty years kept his memory fresh and green, as if it had all happened but yesterday. How much these children's lives were influenced by the noble, dignified, and Christian example of their uncle, and the deep and tender interest of their aunt, in all that pertained to their welfare, was beautifully acknowledged by the surviving brother, Rev. Dr. Henry W. Bellows, in his letters to his uncle on each successive birthday, which was ever kept sacred, in memory of that twin brother, thus early lost.

It was not the two youngest only, but also the two eldest sons, John and Hamilton, who were the objects of tender interest and care. His Uncle Knapp saw great promise in the talent so early developed in John. Hamilton was full of life and spirit, but shown in his own peculiar way. He was wholly unlike his brother. Although it is now a half-century since I saw him, I have not forgotten his marvellous conversational powers. Eliza, the eldest sister, who retained only a vague remembrance of any other mother than this aunt, always received the welcome a daughter might have had. She had gone but a little way in her teens, which must be the apology for such an amount of wild exuberance as she brought with her. I have alluded to her before, but I should like, if I could, to give our kindred a perfect description of this remarkable woman's personality and bright intellectual qualities. She had no beauty, and needed none. Her other powers of attraction more than compensated for the lack of that. As soon as she spoke, the plainness of her face vanished, and lighted up with animation, expressing more than words could have done; and she would soon surround herself with a group of admiring listeners of her brilliant conversation and sparkling wit.

I cannot forbear relating one of the many incidents that I vividly remember of her young girlhood; she was not sixteen, and I think it was the first visit she made to her Aunt Louisa, after coming to Walpole, and the first reception given at this new home. There were enough of our kindred, at that time, to make up as large a party as could conveniently be entertained in any one house, however spacious, — brothers and sisters, uncles and aunts, not forgetting the great uncles and aunts, and cousins innumerable.

As indicating the numbers of these kindred, whose permanent home was in Walpole, say forty or fifty years ago, I may mention that my Aunt Knapp, at one time, said that from her parlor window, where she was sitting, overlooking the village, the floor of the house just on a level with the top of the church-spires, she could see the houses in which could be counted sixty-five immediate relatives. This count included five of her own brothers and sisters, heads of families, she the youngest of six children then living, and her age was nearly sixty years.

At the reception, which I began to tell about, a general invitation was given. How splendidly the four large rooms, opening into one another and into the entry, were decorated, especially the drawing-room! How elegant was that long table, reaching the length of the dining-room! I especially recall the glass pyramid in the centre, towering up still higher with a vase of beautiful flowers set upon the top. Upon this was arranged all imaginable delicacies. Here, indeed, was prepared a most sumptuous repast, which I will not spoil by attempting to describe, but will pass to another feature of this entertainment. A little surprise had been prepared for the guests, by stationing in the upper hall two or three persons, with musical instruments; and, at a given signal, they were to strike a lively tune, and at the same time, by some magic, the lower hall carpet was rolled up, and now everything was in readiness for the dance. All now were on their feet, and the gentlemen seeking partners. One unfortunate swain, whom I have now forgotten, sought Eliza; and she excused herself, by saying she was engaged; she then came hastily into the sitting-room, where quite a number of the elderly gentlemen had congregated, and, going directly to Uncle Squire Bellows, she said, "I am in a terrible dilemma, Uncle Tom, which I can't explain to you now,— you must take it on faith, — but you must help me out of it, you must dance with me. I can't take a refusal!" As he was then between sixty and seventy years old, and it was well known that he never danced a step in his life, this occasioned a general laugh. He quickly rose, however, most graciously saying, he "never refused a lady's appeal when in distress," and led her with a great show of gallantry on to the floor. If any were now living who witnessed the wild exuberance of this young girl, as she helped her uncle through the mazes of that dance, they would smile at least at the recollection! But, alas! of all that merry throng, I am the only one left to tell this story.

Well, I must not tarry too long at this shrine of domestic happiness, where my heart loves so well to linger, and around which cluster many of the happiest memories I have brought through my lengthened life, now verging toward the nineties; I can yet vividly recall so many scenes, which at the time appeared of little consequence, but now so full of interest. Perhaps there never was a father who found more happiness in rearing his children than our Uncle Knapp. There were no bounds to his indulgence, save in what he thought would prove an injury to them. And with what interest he watched the unfolding of their physical and mental faculties! An example of his indulgence comes to my mind, at this moment, which will show the pleasure he took in gratifying their wishes. The two little boys, one three and the other four-and-a-half years old, saw, one morning, something which deeply interested them. Their cousin was using a mortar. This was something new, and must be thoroughly investigated, as well also as the manner of using it; and they insisted upon having it, which was decidedly refused. They went, with many tears, to their father, who, coming to understand their trouble, assured them he could make a mortar, and they should assist him. We saw him depart, with the little fellows, toward the woodshed for that purpose. An hour or two passed, as we sat by the window sewing, when my aunt suddenly arose to look for the children. In a few minutes, I heard my uncle calling, "Louisa, I have solved many problems in Euclid, and some knotty questions in metaphysics, but I think this is the knottiest job I have ever undertaken." No one who saw him could doubt it; his face was very red, and covered with perspiration, in his effort to make a hole deep enough in the end of a hard piece of wood for the boys to pound in. "Well, my dear," she replied, playing upon the word knottiest, "the naughtiest thing I see about it is, the effort you are making for such an unnecessary end; but, if it gives you an appetite, and the boys pleasure, we will not call it so very bad after all." I can never forget the unceasing watchfulness of this mother over the children, or the tender and loving administrations of the father. Their manner of discipline was a beautiful illustration of the power of love and gentleness, and, as the youthful intellect unfolded, it was delightful to listen to his long conversations with them upon the various questions the little fellows always had to propose; and it was in this way those two precious lives were led up to that point where boyhood ends and manhood begins. And here we find them prepared to enter the University in Cambridge, where their father graduated in his early life, with high honors. He had assumed the whole charge of his sons' education, teaching them himself, not only in all the branches they were to pursue for entrance to college, but in all those virtues that dignify a noble and useful life on entering the world.

The time was now fast approaching, when they would

commence their college life. How well I remember those intervening days, so full of the last preparations; and, when all was completed, as we sat in the twilight of that last evening, each seeming full of his own thoughts, my uncle, in a voice full of emotion, said, " Louisa, this is an epoch in the life of our sons, as also in our own. Our children are leaving, for the first time, the home they have loved so well, and to which they have given so much life and happiness; and we must now make this sacrifice, in view of the importance of this great change, to prepare them for the pursuits they may choose, which we will hope may lead to noble and useful lives." And thus it was he sought to comfort her, and himself also.

Everything seemed propitious for an early start in the morning. My uncle remarked, when at tea, that a mackerel sky was the sure precursor of a pleasant day on the morrow; and, as they were going to take their sons to Cambridge in their own carriage, the weather was worthy of consideration. The prediction certainly proved true, this time, for a brighter morning never greeted waking eyes than that which followed the preceding evening, saddened with the thought of their leaving, yet made cheerful with the hopes of the future. When the early breakfast was over, my aunt sought the opportunity to say to Cousin Susan Knapp and myself, " Bid the boys good-by as if you were to see them again to-morrow; I can bear nothing more." The thought was pressing upon her, at the moment, this is the first break in our long happy home-life; and, at the last moment, we bade as cheerful good-by as we could simulate; and, as the carriage wheels rolled through the gate, Susan sat down upon the doorstep, and relieved her heart by the long pent-up tears. It may be well to say here, this cousin was an inmate of the household before these children were born, and a daughter of our Uncle Knapp's brother Benjamin; she had enshrined them in her kindly heart with a love that lasted until her death.

Well, this lovely home, although deprived of its younger attractions for a time, still held a potent charm for all acquaintances and friends; and there was no place more frequently sought by distinguished strangers, or where they found a more graceful and generous hospitality, or a richer intellectual treat. There was still another charm, which to fully understand should have been witnessed; for any description of it must prove entirely inadequate. It was the tender and delicate courtesy my uncle and aunt always showed each other; it was nothing put on, for the reason it had never been laid aside. Always addressing each other by some endearing term, the playful gallantry he would sometimes indulge in nearly surpassed Chesterfield himself.

A little scene occurs to me at this moment. I had been commissioned to purchase for my aunt a bonnet, and had come to bring it. Taking it from the box with some trepidation, lest it should not meet in all respects her exquisite taste, I waited the verdict. She held it up, and, turning it round upon her hand, expressed her approbation in strong terms; then she placed it on her head, when I saw my uncle rise, and, walking across the room with the grand air, presented his arm with a request that she would grant him the supreme happiness of escorting her, naming some place. She at once caught the spirit; and they paced across the room once or twice, in a manner very few could imitate. I think, at this time, he was eighty-five or six years old, a period when such buoyancy of spirit is seldom retained.

Another incident, which occurred still later in life,— I think he must have been ninety-one or two: I happened in at the time he had just completed a letter to his little grand-daughter, Louisa, in which he had endeavored to impress upon her young mind, in a manner she could never forget, the remarkable qualities and virtues of her grandmother, which in earlier years had kindled that flame in his own heart which had never ceased to burn as brightly as on the first day he saw her. He had been reading this letter to her; and, when I came in, he said, "I am now going to read this to Emily." She playfully caught it from his hand, saying, "There is too much flattery in it"; when she looked up, she saw an injured expression upon his face, and quickly restored the letter, saying, "Do as you please, dear; I only feared the sentiment which I appreciate so much might suffer some loss."

I hope it will be borne in mind, that I am giving these recollections just as I proposed in the beginning, in no other order than as they occur to me; were I to attempt anything more, I fear many of these fragments would not have found a place here.

I recall, too, another visit I made one morning to this dear old house, but a very few years ago, when it stood tenantless,— no living thing to be seen or heard within or without.

I first wandered about the grounds. Although shorn of so many of their former attractions, there were traces still left of the taste and beauty that once reigned there.

As I approach the door, I cast an involuntary glance at the window, where I so often saw my aunt sitting at her work, clad in her white dimity wrapper; and in imagination I heard again the clear tones of her voice calling me to come up-stairs to her. As I enter the hall, my heart takes me at once to the sitting-room door, which I find open, and one glance within assures me that nothing is changed, but every article kept in its place, with religious care, just as they left it. There stands the vacant chair beside her pretty worktable, with its crimson satin bag, sufficiently deep to hold the work upon which she had busied herself. Directly over this table hangs the clock, that for more than half a century measured the hours of her precious life. At a window near by stands my uncle's easy chair, where, in dreamy meditation, or in contemplation of the lovely scenery, of which he could never tire, he sat many hours in the day, fully conscious of the presence he always liked to have at his side.

There, too, in its own place, stands the mahogany bookcase, filled with a choice collection of volumes; and there, with the leaf of the desk turned down, he always sat to write his letters. There, also, are the dear old pictures I loved so well,— the exquisite engravings, from Claude de Lorraine paintings, — still hanging on the walls. But most eloquent of the past is the large open fireplace, with its polished marble jams, and brass firedogs, the charred brands lying just as they had burned themselves out long ago. And now with my heart throbbing with the old memories, newly-awakened, I climb slowly up the stairs. Here, too, it is obvious that, as far as possible, everything has been preserved in the same manner that they were arranged by those busy hands now folded forever from our sight.

As I look into this lofty, airy chamber, how vividly I recall my first experience, sixty odd years ago, in assisting my aunt to hang on this high-post bedstead, still here, the dimity curtains trimmed with broad, netted fringe, while we found it still more difficult to arrange the blue silk canopy overhead. Here are the old-fashioned mahogany chairs, the seats covered with the traces of her taste and industry. Turning from these objects of tender interest, I retrace my steps through the long hall, up-stairs and down, listening for some sound to break the oppressive silence; but nothing comes to my ear save the echo of my own footsteps, and the sound of my own voice, as I repeated the fragment of an old familiar song, that seemed so applicable at that moment: —

> "When I remember well,
> The friends so linked together,
> I've seen around me fall,
> Like leaves in winter weather,
> I seem like one who treads alone
> Some banquet hall deserted,
> Whose lights are fled, whose garland's dead,
> And all but me departed."

CHAPTER XXXIII.

I WISH to append to the brief sketch I have given of our venerated Uncle and Aunt Knapp some extracts from a sermon, written on the occasion of her death, by Dr. Bellows, and preached in All Souls Church, New York, on his return from attending her funeral, at Walpole. She died March 16, 1872, aged eighty-six. Says Dr. Bellows, "This venerable aunt was my father's youngest sister. She passed her girlhood in his house, and, on the death of our mother in my infancy, she became virtually the mother of my brothers and sister. I had been at school to her husband,— a most gifted and excellent man,— and for my whole life enjoyed a frequent and most familiar intercourse with this venerable and beautiful couple; he closing his spotless life in nearly full possession of his mental powers, three years ago, at ninety-five, and she surviving until last week at eighty-six, in possession of an equally remarkable understanding.

In the summer vacation, my house was within a few rods of theirs; and it was love and reverence for them that drew me to the spot, and made it such a refreshment and delight to go there season after season.

Her devotion to her husband was complete. She appeared to think him perfect, which indeed he almost seemed to others, and the nearest thing on earth to her Saviour; and he repaid her homage by a love and gallantry, a trust and reverence, which is usually seen only among those not in daily and long contact with each other. What is written in books of poetry might be daily witnessed in their lives. They delighted above everything in each other's society, which was not the mere intercourse of habit, it was the daily and hourly interchange of thought, the obvious and intentional ministration to each other's mental and moral improvement and pleasure. They read the same books together, they studied the Scriptures, and discussed the principles and ideas of the day, and knew all that was going on in the great world of affairs, although seldom leaving their country home. Until over ninety, he worked in his garden a couple of hours daily; and then, clothed in spotless garments, he sat down to his books,— the classics, and the elegant and solid literature of the past. He was a poet, sage, and saint, by original endowment, and by culture as a student in theology, and as a teacher who had had the first men in Boston and Salem under his charge,— the Prescotts, the Peabodys, Grays, and Amorys.

His spiritual mind, profoundly interested in the present and in the actual, was equally at home in speculation, and in aspiration. The future of society on earth, for which he had the boldest and noblest hopes, and the future of the soul in heaven, were his favorite themes; and on both he talked with such beauty and wisdom, that his conversation up to ninety was the attraction of men of taste and culture from far about. She almost or quite equalled him in the gift of graceful expression, and was fascinating and charming in the acuteness, fluency, and fervor of her spirit. Together, they made a couple such as I have never seen in life, in respect of the high level of their intercourse, the equality of their powers, and their complete and increasing happiness in each other.

"But I will not place her by the partiality of my affections in a light that may discourage imitation; I wish her example to shine in upon you, not only to dignify and sweeten your ideas of the possibilities of domestic union and blessedness, but also to bear witness to the possibilities of making old age green and growing.

"She fulfilled the promise of the Psalmist, 'They shall bear fruit in old age.' How large and full and sweet the harvest was, I cannot make you know; but if you could read the gratitude and affection that swell my heart, and other hearts, to whom her name is a bond and spell, you would appreciate the force of all the arguments I have used in this discourse, on the duty and possibility of preparing in youth and middle life for a happy, serene, and triumphant old age."

When copying the last words of this loving and beautiful tribute to our revered Uncle and Aunt Knapp by our cousin, Rev. Dr. Bellows, the thought came to me, how few years elapsed, after those words were written, when other lips as eloquent in praise pronounced his own eulogy. From every pulpit, far and near, at home and abroad, tearful voices were raised in expressions of no common sorrow; for one had suddenly gone who it seemed, of all men, could least be spared by friends and by the world. Wherever he had been — and where had he not been?— he so impressed himself upon the minds and hearts of those who saw and heard him they could fully realize those beautiful words of scripture, "When he went up to the holy altar, he made the garment of holiness honorable."

And now this bright, particular star had set forever! It could no longer illumine our earthly pathway with the words of hope and encouragement that so often fell from his prophetic lips; no longer can we have in our midst one whose presence ever brought a thrill of pleasure and pride, that in our race was one in whom were combined so many noble virtues with such brilliant talents, used indiscriminately for the benefit of all that came within his reach. Whoever had looked upon that stately figure, clothed with a grace and charm that nothing but heaven could have given him, could feel surprise at the unusual demonstrations of grief, when death took him whom all loved! For indeed he was the common friend of all humanity, as was witnessed when he was borne away from the city where for more than forty years he had ministered so faithfully to his own people and to the community at large; for no creed or nationality ever set up a barrier to his kindly ministrations, or checked the bounties of his hand. It was no wonder that the heart of the great city gave such tokens of grief at his departure. He was borne far away from them, to be laid where his dust would mingle with the ashes of his kindred. He sleeps beneath the trees he loved so well, and where the last rays of our glorious sunset cover his bed with their golden radiance.

Lest my own expressions in regard to Dr. Bellows should seem colored by the partiality of family affection, I desire to make an extract from a discourse which was delivered by one whose kinship with him was simply that of heart and of mind.

Speaking of Dr. Bellows, he says, "Around the lifeless dust of him we loved was gathered a body of mourners such as rarely meet to do honor to the dead.

Clergymen from every household of faith, Jewish Rabbis, men of letters, philanthropists, artists, actors, statesmen, and merchants mingled their tears with ours. Amid the throng of gifted, brilliant men that sprung up on every side, he had still maintained the place that he early won for himself in the foremost ranks of her citizens,— not one stain upon his shield ; not one whispered reproach upon his memory. The intense glare of public life found him spotless ; and he is borne to his last rest, not only by the loving arms of his religious disciples, but by an unnumbered multitude of loyal hearts, by all who cherish the highest interests of the city that is proud to claim him for her son.

" His overpowering eloquence is the first great quality that rises to our minds as we think of him! What pictures he could paint upon the passive soul of his listeners ! How they would palpitate and start into life at his word ! The images that he invoked were not mere dead figures of rhetoric ; they seemed to breathe and to move through the circumambient air,— mighty magician, calling forth invisible spirits from far off realms, obedient to his will, and endowing their ethereal substance with form and meaning. It was not the grace and beauty of what he said that so affected us ; I have heard as polished orators and equal masters in the art of mere speech, but never one that went so directly to the mind and heart. And why? Because his words were realities to him while he uttered them. Not sentences, but things, emanated from his presence. He looked within his own consciousness, and what he saw there active he delivered to us. Unstudied, with an almost reckless indiscrimination, the contents of his great personality were poured into ours, and deep answered to deep. . . .

"But again, Dr. Bellows' power rested on thought. He was not a profound scholar, nor a subtile logician, but he had the faculty of seizing upon a subject, disentangling its intricacies, cutting away unessential elements, and then conducting his hearers by broad, plain channels to a practical result. His sermons were written with an amazing rapidity, frequently in the few hours of a single day, but they seemed nevertheless to spring forth in full armor from his brain. Doubtless they bore some of the defects as well as all the merits of their hasty composition, but they were never wanting in arrangement, harmony, or proportion. As a combination of spontaneity and sound reasoning, I believe that they are unexcelled. The topics of which he treated had been so long maturing in his rich mind, that, when he did come to speak of them, all he needed was the garb of language for ideas and arguments which had already marshalled themselves in due order.

"His native thought-germs were also fructified by contact with a wide range of men and books. His wit and geniality made him the most charming of companions; and from every person whom he thus encountered he seemed unconsciously to absorb the best essence into his own hospitable organization. The extent of his reading was simply prodigious for one so preoccupied and distracted with cares. It was recreation for him, when exhausted by other labors, to plunge into abstruse questions of theology or philosophy. He read swiftly and eagerly, assimilating what he needed, rejecting what had no relation to himself; but, when he laid a volume down, it had been forced to yield its fullest supply of mental nourishment. The infinite variety and compass of his utterances and the intellectual freshness of his old age are largely traceable to this regimen of the study. He believed its discipline to be hardly secondary in importance to the actual ministrations of the pulpit. . . .

"Once more, Dr. Bellows' power rested upon a sensitive, generous heart. It was that which set him all aflame. Touch his sympathies, and you held *him*. How closely in him the forces of the intellect were wedded to human tenderness and love!"

Rev. Dr. Bartol, of Boston, a life-long friend of Dr. Bellows, near to him almost as a brother, thus speaks of him: —

. . . "What was the mission of the man here named? I answer, He was born to be a leader of other men. His genius was not philosophic or poetic, but social. His gift was fellowship; his power, sympathy. He was constituted to observe and study, but to read and think no longer than was needful to prepare him to act. His destiny was not so much to originate conceptions in politics or religion as to organize and apply them to the case in hand. If not a man pre-eminently of ideas, he was their officer on a scale so true, in a manner so lively, and through a range so various and vast, and with so versatile a skill, that he may be called in his aspiring an ideal man. The founder, the institutor, as well as the metaphysical explorer, or the artist with language, canvas, or stone for his vehicle, deserves praise; and Dr. Bellows was an incarnate, perpetual, irrepealable act of incorporation in his very nature for all good, Christian, public things. Consider the rank and importance to the community of this faculty. . . . His talent, his temper, was to mediate, harmonize, reconcile. He admitted he was on board to trim the ship, to unfurl or reef the sail, to roll the heavy, iron-laden car on trucks from side to side of the main deck, to keep from careening and maintain an even keel. To what was peculiar and sometimes seemed inconsistent in his position, this was the key. He had no notion of letting any enterprise he was embarked in, by following extreme counsels or by any exclusive tendency, go to excess. His mind was a compensating pendulum of the theological clock. According to the wind and weather, his hand moved the tiller, and made it continually veer.

"How extraordinary was his tact! What a composer of strife he was! How worldly-wise, yet utterly unselfish in what he did and said! Not for his own sake was he prudent and adroit, but for everybody's sake. But in his diplomacy was no hypocrisy. He never hid: he was always ready to show his hand, and there was no false bottom to his mind. What a candid cunning was his, how artless and astute! An essential nobility in his frame, an unfailing self-respect, an intrinsic honor, a pride that could not be distinguished from lowliness, and a love impossible for any wrong or provocation to turn into hate, were the sustenance of his purity and the secret of his strength.

"Never was a man whom abstractions were less adequate to content. He wanted principles to be put into gear. If a tool would not work, or a constitution march, or a plan succeed, it might be very fine on paper, but was a contrivance of no value to him; and the sort of person he in this wise was is beyond all price for a Church or a State. One likes to see not only water-springs far away in upland solitudes or woodland glens, but cisterns and reservoirs too. The fountains suffice not without service-pipes. Parnassus, Helicon, and

Siloa would be forsaken and despised, if they did not flow down afar and abroad to fertilize and refresh. Dr. Bellows had uncommon intellect, a fine fancy, great reasoning power, and a persuasive eloquence scarce exceeded in our day. But all was for practice and use. His metal was not for ornament: it must be coined, come from the mint and circulate. Yet it was virgin gold without slag or dross. He was tried in many ways, but I never could see that he did not go into the furnace as pure as he came out. A more perfect temper, less capable of being embroiled, embittered, or soured, of better proof against irritation or exhaustion, I never have known. Was he disposed to appear and lead? Never was like ambition conjoined with more marked ability or a fitter gift. Indeed, as 'Talbot' in the play showed his proportions only when heading his soldiers' troop, Dr. Bellows was himself completely only when in company, on the platform, in the desk; and was lost or bereft if left utterly alone. From a sympathetic audience, or perhaps single companion sometimes, his own genius came. His magnetic presence, open countenance, beaming eye, animated gesture, and melodious voice,— every one of his properties,— would have been a talent wrapped in a napkin but for the assembly or committee, convention, conference, or institute he consulted with and addressed. Else, he would have been as helpless and unmusical as an Æolian harp without a breeze. He must not be laid on the table, but put into the window when the wind blew! He was resonant; not 'a voice in the wilderness': he responded like Memnon to the sun.

"Because he was constituted so much by and in this correspondence with others, and had, as he told me, a great deal of the woman in him, as his understanding was suited to or undertook no virile tasks of systematic speculative toil, but met with matchless equipment of wit and eloquence every occasion as it came, therefore he has left no one literary monument which can disclose to us the full measure of his strength. He was as one all the time prepared for actual emergency, no matter how public or private it might be. He answered the door-bell of every summons of human need. With equal competency and the same satisfaction, he helped obscurely or was a hero on the stage. . . .

"The feeling at his demise is not only of grief, but dismay, as if the pilot were overboard on whose orders the safety of crew and passengers depends; or, to use the prophet's ancient figure, the standard-bearer of an army had fainted and fallen on the field. . . . Dr. Bellows was a servant of morals, religion, country, and philanthropy rather than a special or original contributor to theological truth. In opinion, he held less the straight course of a steamship than one of tacking like a sailing-vessel, which, though zigzag, yet makes headway across the sea. But his was no skiff turning to and fro on a creek. How majestically, with all its lurches, his frigate came up to the wind! . . .

"The deep religiousness of the man explains his deeds. Every kind or measure of work has, in a right intent, the same worth. But he has extraordinarily, by his gifts and their manifestation, affected the age in which he lived. Yet who more than he prized his own kith and kin? Some persons care not for their genealogy. Of these, he was not one. *Bellows,—belles eaux*, beautiful waters,—that is the name; and a hand uplifted in the air, and pouring from a cup, is the escutcheon and the shield. The *Bellows Falls* his ancestry gave the title to furnish a curious and apt suggestion of the pure, rapid, and wholesome stream in their descendant's career, beneficent as the flood, clear as the light, and open as the day. . . . His remains were taken to Walpole in New Hampshire, the home of his ancestors, and his own summer home,* and lay there over night in his familiar study, with watchers of his friends and kin in the next room. How silently ticked the clock! At the funeral, before the burial in that town, all the stores were closed. . . .

"My conclusion is that Dr. Bellows will stand in history, and have long repute in our American country, not as the discoverer or signal illuminator of any truth, but inventor of methods, founder of associations, deviser of ways and means, mover of his fellows to his proposed ends, adventurer of church reform, strategist in time of war, not to destroy but save life, in the boldness of his operations showing the old heritage of Norman blood, which for something better than battle he was born with and of again, philanthropist in every diverse, ingenious, and manifold way of doing good, believer in God, sanctified by his spirit, and consecrated to his will."

I shall conclude my reference to our cousin Dr. Bellows with the following extracts from a discourse delivered by Rev. James Freeman Clarke, whose estimate of men and things is always based on calmest thought and keenest discrimination : —

"I can hardly think of any man whose departure from the midst of life would leave such a vacancy in

---

*A large delegation of his New York parish came on to Walpole to take part in these final, farewell services, under the guidance of Dr. Bellows' life-long friend and devoted parishioner, William M. Pritchard. There had previously been a funeral service in his own church in New York.

our society. . . . All the amenities and all the humanities of life caught inspiration from his vicinity. Every one interested in art, literature, education, moral and social reform, felt strong from knowing that his eloquence was near to help them. He could be checked by no sectarian prejudices: he could not be deterred by any partisan resistance, nor daunted by great names opposed to him. His courage was indomitable; his zeal for justice and humanity always to be relied on. Years of untiring devotion to the best interests had accumulated in his mind a great power. . . . He illustrated the heroism of which man is capable to-day. This is the chief work of the hero of our times — to set his face like a flint against popular falsehood. Dr. Bellows did not follow, though he often led, the multitude: he was ready to oppose any man at any moment when he thought him in the wrong. I remember his withstanding Webster to his face, and denying his conclusions, when the great statesman said in his presence something which seemed to him too much like a concession to slavery. . . .

"He was a born preacher. He showed how a preacher may mold and direct opinion in such a city as New York, just as Chrysostom did in Constantinople and as Latimer did in London. . . .

"The essential element in heroism is the readiness to attack difficult problems. This Dr. Bellows had, and it came from deep convictions. It was by faith in God that he did so much. He was a grand type of religious convictions. Although of an inquiring mind, and reading everything of interest that was published on controverted points, he never let go his hold on the foundations of Christian faith. His anchor was a profound Christian experience."

Rev Dr HENRY W BELLOWS

CHAPTER XXXIV.

How vividly, in connection with this mention of Dr. Bellows, do I recall at this moment a scene that reaches far back to a certain bright morning in May, more than half a century ago, when the air was filled with the fragrance of early blossoms! My Uncle Thomas had risen at daybreak, and I had also to await the Keene stage, due at five o'clock. It was to bring two little passengers from Boston, ticketed for Walpole, and intrusted to the care of the driver. Their father, wishing to give these little boys, Henry and Edward, twin brothers, the benefit of country air during the summer, had sent them to his brother Thomas. We soon heard the shrill blast of the tin horn, the usual warning of approach of the stage, and our uncle stood at the gate when they arrived. I can see him now, tenderly taking the sleepy, weary, and dusty little fellows from the stage, leading them to me, as I stood on the door-step. I took them to their room, brushed the dust from their jackets and trousers, and bathed their faces; which Edward had the courage to tell me had not been done before since they left home. Henry was more shy; both, however, looked about as if they were realizing a little too keenly that they were in a strange place, and with those whom they had never seen before. They were ten years old, and this was the first time they had left their city home. Our Aunt Sarah, who was so bright and cheerful, and, we may add, so lovely, was soon down stairs, and spoke such kind and tender words as quite reassured the little boys. After being refreshed with a nice breakfast, it was proposed they should go to bed for two or three hours, and make up for the lost sleep; but they evidently had much rather keep their eyes open, and be looking around; so they had permission to go about the premises wherever they liked, and amuse themselves in their own way. Our uncle, sitting by the window, watched them with interest for some time, and then took up his morning paper. A few minutes had elapsed, when I saw him suddenly lay down his paper and hasten to the door. There was Henry standing alone in the yard, and evidently in trouble. When asked where his brother was, bursting into tears, he replied, "Ned don't like Walpole, and has *started for home*, and I am afraid he will get lost." The little fellow had evidently been thinking how he could impart this information, and yet save his brother from rebuke. His uncle took him merrily by the hand, saying, "We will go and bring Edward back, and I am sure you will both very soon like Walpole." When reaching the foot of the hill, that turns from the main street, the runaway was found and captured, behind a wood-pile that was close to the highway. He was soon induced to return willingly, when his uncle told him how much he had in store for their pleasure; and he devoted himself wholly to them during that day. He procured for each a small hoe, and, taking them into the garden, he marked off a square piece of ground, which they might plant and take care of wholly themselves, and he would buy all they would raise on it, and pay them in silver. This was surely something new, and required no small amount of instruction, for the handling of any implement of labor was a novel experience to these children; but they entered with none the less enthusiasm into their work, which proved a source of lasting enjoyment. Their waiting for the product of their toil was something to be remembered, taking them out of their bed many times at an early hour in the morning to see, as Henry would say, "what might have happened in the night"; and, when the first seed peeping from the ground bade them good-morning, their joy was not to be restrained.

It took but a few days for these little fellows to become deeply interested in country affairs. The marvellous discoveries they often made required much explanation! They were not satisfied with merely seeing; they wished to know all about it, showing at this period an unusual desire for knowledge. Their first Sunday in the country was a memorable day to me. I recall the pride I had in taking them to church, in their blue cloth suits trimmed with gilt buttons, but made in a very different style from the present time,— their trousers coming down to the instep, and buttoned on to the jacket round the waist; a broad collar, that formed a part of the shirt, and which was trimmed with a linen cambric ruffle, three inches in width, laid in fine plaits, and turned down upon the back, tied in front, with a blue ribbon to match. Knowing that, as strangers from the city in a country meeting-house, they would be sharply criticised, I looked them carefully over, to make sure all was right; but I recollect I had a feeling of regret that, being twins, their faces were so unlike: otherwise, there was little difference. At that time, there was both a morning and afternoon service; and, as the church was a mile distant from the village, attendance upon both services occupied pretty much all the day, when we chose to walk, as it happened on this day. The little boys were delighted with the idea of climbing the long hill, upon the top of which stood the meeting-house, near the edge of a forest stretching far and wide. In the spring and early summer, when the woods were fresh, and all the world seemed new and charming, the young people often put some crackers in their pockets, and passed the two hours' intermission roaming about in the edge of this grand old wood, or sitting under the giant oaks and chestnut trees that stood near the meeting-house, their long branches affording ample shelter and shade.

Our uncle and aunt readily assented to my proposal to be allowed to remain with the children until the services of the day were over, and, as the others were to ride, a generous basket of lunch was put up, which they could carry in the chaise-box, for our benefit. So, at an early hour on that bright sweet morning in May, we set out with all the freshness of childhood,— for I was but a child myself,— and the blessedness of youthful vigor and strength, to walk up this long ascent without a thought of fatigue; but so exhilarated were the boys by the clear, bracing air, so full of oxygen, I found some difficulty in restraining the exuberance of my young companions. Edward was bound to give chase to every butterfly, and, when passing a house that stood near the highway, where an old hen with a very young family was providing breakfast for them, Edward attempted to make a more close investigation of her domestic affairs, which was furiously resented, the old hen flying at once into his face. Henry went quickly to the rescue, no thought of his own safety seeming to have crossed his mind. Our observation soon disclosed the fact, that Henry was always a shield and protector, forgetting himself in the presence of others' danger or trouble of any kind. He would save Edward from harm or blame when possible; not because he was himself superior, but it was always Edward who got in danger, and always did the mischief. After assuring myself that the children's eyes were not pecked out, and securing Edward's cap, that disappeared in the fray, we proceeded on our way to church, and stepped into the vestibule just as Mr. Apollos Gilmore was winding the rope round his arm for a pull upon the bell, which for nearly half a century he had rung on Sunday and every week-day, both at noon and at nine o'clock at night.

We were quite early; very few had entered the church when we took our seats in one of the square pews near the pulpit. I looked at the boys, to see how they were impressed with the great, high-up pulpit and the deacon's pew under it, built in so as only to have the tops of their heads exposed to view. Edward had discovered the hinges on each individual seat, and stood up experimenting upon his own, lifting it up and down; while Henry, with a show of authority, bade him sit down, which he only did after I explained it all to him. His next discovery was the open work round the tops of the pews, seeming to have been especially designed to give children an opportunity to take a peep at their neighbors, and to have something to play with during the long sermon time,— a privilege of which Edward soon availed himself. People were now fast assembling, for the tones of the last bell were dying away, when a family from far over the hills, with a number of youngsters, arrayed as only the genius of country people can fix up the little ones to go to meeting, took their seats in the pew adjoining ours. This proved an irresistible attraction, and I saw, with dismay, that Edward seemed intent upon mischief; but our uncle and aunt came into the pew at that moment, to my great relief: he took the little boys into his own keeping, with a significant smile as he looked at our aunt. Uncle Thomas was always more amused than annoyed with Ned's mischief, which was never wanton, but perpetrated in a spirit of roguery and fun that was hard to resist.

When the morning service was ended, the children were told to come out to the carriage, and take their basket that was brought for us. I soon joined them, as they stood in waiting, and led them to my favorite tree, — an old oak, that looked as if it might have stood there for centuries. It was certainly tall enough, and its branches wide enough, to give shelter and shade to a much larger number than those who were now about to refresh themselves under its inviting canopy. How bright and happy were those two young faces, as they helped me take from the basket the generous quantity of dinner, and particularly when we found something at the bottom that was intended for a pleasant surprise! It was a small bottle of metheglin,—a very choice and delicious beverage made with honey and other things I have forgotten, as I have never tasted it since my girlhood. I have not forgotten, however, with what keen appetites the little fellows partook of this repast, looking so attractive as we spread it out upon the ground.

After refreshing ourselves, there were many fragments remaining to be disposed of, and Henry proposed that we should prepare a banquet for the squirrels. Perhaps he didn't call it by that name,— more probably supper,— but by any name it would be just as sweet to those pretty creatures, running about in the woods everywhere around us and close to us. The proposition was readily assented to, and the boys commenced gathering the acorns that lay plentifully about. Although they had fallen from the branches the preceding year, many were in perfect preservation; and, with much enthusiasm, they commenced filling the tiny saucers — the acorn cups — with choice bits, placing them on the ground and in all the little nooks they could spy, gleefully anticipating the surprise of the squirrels, when they should return from their wanderings through the day to the old tree, in the depths of which they were probably born, and find their dainty supper ready and awaiting them.

Henry grew quite animated at the thought of this unexpectedness, as he chose to express it, and would like to have remained to witness the curiosity the squirrels would manifest when investigating this new article of food; but we had already lingered so long, at our repast and the preparations for the squirrels' supper, that very little time was left for our walk in the woods, and it was finally decided to leave that for another time.

Once, in later years, after he had become a Doctor of Divinity, when talking with me, Henry recalled the incidents of this day, his first Sunday at church in the country with his brother Edward,— all of which he recollected perfectly as one of his joyous days. But now it awakened memories evidently too painful to dwell upon ; the wound that never could be healed on earth, made by the untimely death of this twin brother — his other self — was opened afresh. The scenes in their young life were too vividly brought to mind for him to regain composure without a struggle.

A few more years, and these children of so much promise are graduates of Harvard, prepared to enter upon the study of their professions ; each was permitted to choose for himself.

It was no surprise that Henry should have chosen the ministry, for which he always seemed so eminently fitted ; while Edward was equally fitted for the bar. He only lived long enough to prove he had not mistaken his vocation.

The beautiful tribute paid to his memory by our venerated Uncle Knapp, in 1854, when the monument to our noble ancestor, Col. Benjamin Bellows, was consecrated, will afford more knowledge of this sad event, and also give to our readers a more perfect idea of the character and brilliant qualities of this young cousin. I copy it here.

After a few preliminary remarks, Uncle Knapp said, "There is one grave I cannot pass in silence ; my heart demands an utterance. In that grave rest the remains of a gifted son of the family and of the name. Many of you remember his commanding person and manly bearing. His mind was of a high order; he seized subjects with a strong intellectual grasp. Truth had in him a champion ; falsehood was quickly stripped of its counterfeit robes, and its deformity exposed. Nature had formed him for an orator and statesman. In addition to the properties just named, he had an ardent temperament, a strongly marked countenance, good memory, brilliant imagination, deep, well-toned voice, and graceful gesture. He was a well-read lawyer, and acquainted with the civil and political history of our country. He had at his command playful humor, stinging sarcasm, and keen-edged satire. Had he lived, the halls of Congress would have listened to his eloquence, and the confidence of the public have been secured by his integrity and firmness.

"Just as he entered upon the stage for a life of usefulness, in the western wilds, far from any habitation, and in the discharge of an arduous professional duty, the curtain of life dropped, and concealed him from our view. His grave is solitary. No friends nor kindred lie near him; the winds, yea, the pitying winds of heaven, as they breathe among the trees of the dark western forests, mourn the sudden fall, and continually, night and day, sing a requiem over the early grave of Edward Stearns Bellows, a twin brother by birth and in spirit to the gifted orator of the day."

It seems most especially fitting, to speak here of another grave. It was made far from the dark western forest, to which our thought involuntarily turns. In that grave was laid the lovely form of one, to whom this twin brother's heart had long been pledged; and, had he lived, she would have borne his name, and shared his fortunes. When the sad tidings of his sudden death were broken to her, the shock proved too great for her gentle, loving spirit, and from that time she faded away.

I can never forget how tender and deep was the sympathy his family gave her, sending for her to attend church with them on the Sabbath following the arrival of the sad news, the father supporting her on his arm to a seat with his wife and children, thus acknowledging her a daughter of his household. Many hearts were deeply touched, when they saw this stricken family take their accustomed seats; but, for this drooping, smitten flower, there was a rain of tears!

She was the daughter of Josiah Bellows, 3d, who was distinguished for his manly beauty and for his energy as a leader in the business community. He was the son of "Uncle Si," of whom I have spoken; hence, grandson of the founder.

There is nothing in our history that awakens more saddened thoughts than the memory of this lovely family, so untimely swept away by that fatal disease, consumption, which they inherited from their mother. Her maiden name was Stella Bradley, daughter of Gen. Bradley. She died first; then followed the three daughters, in all the fresh young beauty of their girlhood. Stephen Rowe — and who that saw can ever forget that handsome boy? taking with him the exuberance and beauty of his childhood into his earliest manhood — was the next to follow, thus completing the desolation of a father's heart and home!

After a lapse of time, Col. Josiah, as he was called, sought another companion to brighten his desolate home. He married the widow of Dr. Alfred Hosmer, whose brother, Dr. Hiram Hosmer, had married Phœbe Bellows Grant, the grand-daughter of Gen. Benjamin Bellows. But it was not long after this before Col. Josiah died, leaving with its widowed mother an infant son; who now, in manhood, is living with his charming family in the old mansion, the only surviving representatives of that refined and delightful household. As a lawyer, judge, and citizen, he renders faithful service to his native town, and receives that respect and confidence which were wont of old to be given to those of his name.

CHAPTER XXXV.

When preparing to make a call, this morning, I was suddenly and strongly impressed with a desire to say, "I am going up to Cousin Caleb's"; just as we used to say; for nearly all who lived in the village at that time were cousins. Waking from this dream, I found I had been travelling backward more than sixty years, and the house I was intending to visit was owned and occupied by those, who, if they have no claim to kinship, have certainly a claim to gratitude for the perfection in which this old landmark is kept, both without and within. Should a dry leaf, or straw, borne on the breeze, drop upon grass-plot or gravel walk, we should pick it up at once, hiding it away in our pocket; there could be no other place to put it. As this old family residence is but a few rods from my own dwelling, I often find myself recalling the scenes of earlier years, when our Cousin Caleb, for whom this house was built, occupied it with his wife and a family of twelve boys and girls. Those near my own age were my schoolmates and familiar friends. Strong, the eldest child, of whom I have a dim recollection, was killed by being thrown from a horse, when very young. Mary Lyman and Phebe were my companions. In those years, how full of buoyant life and activity was that household! Mr. Dickinson, who was Parson Fessenden's colleague, and at his death installed over this parish, made his home in this family until Mary, whom he saw grow from babyhood to childhood, and from that to womanhood, became his wife. He took her to the parsonage, which was near the old meeting-house on the hill, in which he continued to preach until his death; and there they reared a large family of children, who by their lives have honored their parents. Most of them are scattered through the West, where their spirit of enterprise took them; one, Dr. William Dickinson, is to-day a valued and influential physician in St. Louis.

Another daughter marrying Dr. Barr, of New Ipswich, found her home for life, by happy coincidence, near the delightful home from which her mother had gone, years before, as a bride, upon her beautiful "Sappho," by the side of Col. Caleb Bellows, to adorn and bless his own home in Walpole. She carried with her to New Ipswich not only the affection and interest of all the long list of Walpole kindred, but likewise a character and gifts of mind and heart inherited from both her father and her mother, which made her, what she proved to be, the helpful physician's wife, the active and sympathizing neighbor and friend, the wise and devoted mother of her children. And these children, and even their children following them, are to-day filling places of trust and duty with an ability and faithfulness which, though probably never once thought of by them, came down from the old original New Ipswich home of Col. Hartwell, but "by the way of" Walpole. And it is pleasant to be able to add, that New Ipswich still retains its hold upon the affections of the family; some residing there permanently, others seeking there a summer home. Mrs. Ames, one of the daughters of Mrs. Barr, and mother of Prof. Ames, of Cambridge, has just been building there a delightful summer residence, surrounded by charming scenery and more charming associations.

The youngest of the many children of Aunt Caleb were twins, Caroline and Charles. She, in her girlhood life was full of attractive beauty; her married life was spent mostly at the West, distant from her native place, where we who remained in the old town almost lost sight of her, though from time to time she, with her sisters, who were also distant, made pilgrimages to their birthplace, to renew their love and allegiance.

We must not fail to mention the devoted and efficient service which the brother, Charles Bellows, rendered during the Civil War, as one of the agents in the field of the U. S. Sanitary Commission: I am told by Mr. Knapp, who was the Associate Secretary of the Commission, and in whose department of "Special Relief" Charles labored, that he was unwearied day and night, in his work for the sick and wounded soldiers. Here he spent his time and strength, and, like so many who were engaged in that same arduous work, died soon after he finished this valuable service.

Aunt Caleb Bellows stood high in the religious community. She was well-read in the civil and religious history of the day, while at the same time she was a most efficient housekeeper.

I had many opportunities to verify the stories told me in childhood of the way this house was furnished, at the time of their marriage, as I was familiar with every part of the house.

I think the long array of brass kettles could not have been exaggerated, looking, it was said, "like a full company of soldiers in bright uniforms;" for any size that was desired was always at hand.

The closet, in which the sets of choicest china were arranged, would be a feast for any one in this later generation who has a love for antiquities. One of the sets, I recollect, was so transparent that objects could be discerned through it, and the cups were most diminutive in size.

The number of feather beds that were said to be provided was probably correct; provision was made, not only for the present, but future emergencies. In that age, people were not supposed to be comfortable on straw and hair, as in these degenerate times! and springs were unknown; so that twenty-six feather beds were none too many for family use, reserving the usual number for spare beds.

The saddle which was placed upon her beautiful Sappho, and upon which she rode from her native town, New Ipswich, to Walpole, at the time of her marriage, bore many evidences, when I used to see it, of its original beauty at the time. Phebe, who was tall and finely proportioned, filled her mother's place in the saddle, and was usually one of the party who in the pleasant summer time made frequent and long excursions on horseback. I used to watch for her appearance at the appointed hour; and, punctual to the moment, she would be seen turning from the foot of the hill on to the main street, seated upon Mr. Dickenson's sorrel colt walking upon his hind legs, and pawing the air with his forefeet; but she was not in the least intimidated, for she would manage him perfectly, and as no other one could. Then, riding across the common to Mr. Stone's residence, Fanny and Sophia Stone, with one or two young gentlemen, would join the party, which usually numbered six or eight. As I now recall this family, on whose memory, as you see, I love to dwell, then so prominent in our large family circle, I think there were none who stood higher in the estimation of the Christian community than this one.

At one time, when paying a visit of two or three days, I can distinctly remember how deeply I was impressed with Aunt Caleb's manner of leading the morning devotions, in the absence of Mr. Dickinson, who always assumed that duty when at home. Her reading of the Scriptures seemed to give it a new significance, and her extemporaneous and heartfelt prayer was eloquent and impressive! My young mind was filled with great reverence and respect for this gifted woman. Her tall, erect figure now rises before me. Her face was not handsome, but strongly marked with intelligence, varying in expression, when conversing upon her favorite themes, and always emphasizing her conversation with one of her forefingers.

I remember that my Uncle Abel Bellows held her in high esteem, not only for her own personal qualities, but as the wife of his Cousin Caleb, with whom in his early life he so long had companionship; for he had his home in the general's family while employed in his uncle's office. Soon after his marriage, I heard him say, one morning, that while waiting for his sister Louisa, who was coming before they had their wedding reception, there was one family whom he wished to invite for an informal visit as an especial mark of his friendship; and so the Col. and Mrs. Bellows were the first invited guests after his marriage, and I thought my uncle manifested a good deal of pride when presenting his handsome wife to these cousins.

A few more years, and the colonel died, leaving the greater number of this large family still at home; and, as time elapsed, these children one by one drifted away, and widely apart from each other, and from the place where in infancy they were cradled. One sad event I recall, in this connection, the death of their son Lyman, in the far West. He seems to have gone, full of enterprise, beyond the pale of civilization, taking with him a young wife, who was soon called upon, far from any human habitation, to bury him with her own hands, and return alone over the long waste to her eastern home. As years went on, and children were married, or were called away, silence and loneliness came to this house of Uncle Caleb's that so long had echoed the ringing voices of so many happy friends and children. And so it was that Aunt Caleb, a widow now, left the dear old home, and built a small cottage in which, with fewer cares, to pass the remainder of her days. Here her old friends did not forget to visit her, always richly entertained by her originality of thought and expression, retaining to the last, as she did, all those characteristics which marked her earlier years. The angel of death had visited this family circle many times; but, whatever sickness or affliction came, this strong-minded woman's faith in the goodness and mercy of God was never for a moment shaken; she seemed prepared for all the vicissitudes of life, calm and self-possessed under all circumstances. I shall ever retain the memory of my last visit to her; she spoke tenderly of my mother, recalling some incidents in her early life, and assuring me of the affection and esteem in which she had always held her. She was, at that time, suffering with a serious trouble in one of her eyes, which gradually grew worse, and eventually proved the cause of her death.

CHAPTER XXXVI.

SINCE I laid down my pen, another picture of the old times comes to me; so I will go back from where I last was wandering, and turn to this. It was the morning after an evening party, given for the entertainment of some strangers who were visiting in Walpole, that I heard my Aunt Louisa inquire of her brother Abel, with whom she was conversing, if he was aware of the sensation, when their brother Thomas brought in his wife, leading her to the hostess, who presented her to these strangers. He replied, that was nothing unusual; she was always the cynosure of all eyes, when entering a room where many persons were present. Her tall, elegant figure moved with queenly grace, her face beaming with all the sweetness and gentleness of her nature. Her costume always seemed a part of herself. It was a common saying, that Mrs. Maj. Tom, as she was usually distinguished from others of the name, could not array herself in anything that was not especially becoming; her personal charms were wholly independent of dress or adornment. I have never, in my long life, seen but one who could compare with her for regal beauty and elegance, when in full dress. I can, at the present moment, recall many comments I have heard after a party, but more especially when a ball was given in honor of some distinguished guest; for, at that period, it should be recorded, this grand old town paid the old-time courtesy to strangers, never failing to give honor to whom honor was due; and on such occasions, and they occurred often, it can easily be supposed she was a star of the first magnitude. There was always a thrill of expectancy apparent in the whole assembly when Maj. Thomas appeared with the one upon his arm that all were looking for. And then such a buzz of admiration, with here and there an audible exclamation of, "How superbly she walks!" and nothing could be more true, for she moved with an air and grace that no one could imitate.

All this was in the fresh bloom of her young beauty, before any of life's sorrows or misfortunes had come to her, and her sweetness and affability to all were her shield from envy or jealousy from any source. Her first great sorrow was occasioned by the loss of her only child, a little girl of six years, to whom she had given much of her own beauty and loveliness. This was a terrible blow both to the father and mother; and it was only when another little daughter, two or three years after, was placed in her loving arms, that she partially recovered her cheerful ways; but the old playful manner, so delightful to her friends, was lost forever.

To this little one was given the name of her mother. I used to think, it should have been Solace instead of Sarah; for she was like the balm of Gilead to that mother's wounded heart. Her babyhood was lovely, but still more so her childhood. To her remarkable intelligence was added a passionate love of music; and, at the age of four years, she would sing little songs with her father; but more especially I remember the beautiful hymn, commencing, "So fades the lovely blooming flower."

This hymn was sung at the funeral, when the dear

little sister was laid away forever from mortal sight; and, during the few years her father lived after her death, this was the sacred song of the household. The mother unfortunately had no ear for music, but her soul was full of sentiment; and, when my uncle and little Sarah were singing this, she could not restrain herself from joining them, and it can well be supposed it was not always in perfect chord; but, putting his arm about her, with sometimes a tear glistening in his eye, he would say, "Dear little mother, you may sing with us; it is sweet and lovely to me." She would then look tenderly and gratefully into his face, saying, "O, Tom! how good you are!"

Soon after this little daughter had reached the age of five years, her father was taken suddenly ill, and died within two days. I can never forget that scene. The agonies of a lifetime seemed concentrated in those few hours! Many feared this terrible blow would forever deprive this sufferer of her reason, but it showed how much can be suffered, and yet we cannot die.

And now this little daughter, always so precious to this loving mother, became the one object for which she seemingly cared to live; and there are a few still left who witnessed the devotion of this mother's life to her child. She had imparted to her something of her own loveliness, but in form and feature she resembled her father more. How well I remember her babyhood and her most interesting childhood, made peculiarly so by that charming mother bestowing such a wealth of love, in her own vocabulary of endearments. And nothing was lost upon her; for, with such enthusiasm as we seldom find in childhood, she reciprocated all this loving tenderness; and this beautiful intercourse of mother and daughter ever remained the same, in womanhood as in childhood, for their lives were inseparably woven together. A kind Providence so ordered, that, when this daughter's marriage took place, instead of losing her child, a son was added to this pleasant household. As I now look back upon that home, of which I have so many treasured memories, I see again that form, which more than seventy years had no power to rob of its native grace, and that fair face beaming with kindness, as she gave you a cordial welcome in her own sweet, silvery tones! And how distinctly I recall every lineament of that brilliant daughter's face, and especially her ardent and impulsive nature, leading her sometimes into the wildest exuberance of feeling! At such times, one appealing look from her mother was sufficient to restrain this seemingly irrepressible vivacity, in which her husband, if present, was always ready to join; for no one could enjoy it more than he. And, when the scene became still more enlivened by his quaint humor, her mother would remind them of the old saying, that "Our happiness and misery are measured to us in the same basket," and hoped their great mirthfulness would not be followed by the same measure of sorrow.

But this pleasant and attractive home had its allotted share of afflictions. Twice the angel of death visited this household, bearing away, each time, a bud of beauty and promise, leaving only two of the four little ones to comfort the bereaved parents. And now a sad misfortune came, which all who knew her deeply felt. The dear grandmother, one morning, in playing with her little grandson, fell and broke her hip, making her a cripple the remaining years of her life. The sweet patience and fortitude with which she bore this calamity was a lesson to us all; and, when she was able to occupy the chair in which she could transport herself about the room, loving friends and acquaintances were nearly always in attendance upon her, which was seemingly considered by them as a peculiar privilege.

There was one window in her sitting-room, looking out upon the sidewalk, beside which her chair was always placed; it was her favorite seat. Well do I recall that sweet smile and bow of recognition, we always looked for when passing there. As I think of the number of years she was in that spot, and of that look of sweet resignation while sitting there through the long weary days, it has often occurred to me, how beautiful, if that could have been made a memorial window.

As this mother and daughter were inseparable on earth, it seemed an especial interposition of Providence that death should not break this sacred bond. When the dark messenger came for her whose care was now so necessary to this mother who was fatally ill with pneumonia, the whole community was shocked by this unexpected blow. And now the question arose, who can tell her that the daughter who was bending lovingly over her pillow but a few hours ago is dead? It will kill her! But they were mistaken; she received the intelligence calmly, as if her spirit was already in another world with the one just gone, although her body was still lingering here. It need not be told how tenderly it was cared for, while it was permitted to remain.

As soon as possible, after receiving the sad intelligence, one hastened to her bedside from afar upon whom she had bestowed a mother's love from babyhood, and had ever kept enshrined in her heart as a daughter. It was a great joy to her to hear once more in her own loving terms the sacred name of mother, and receive again from her lips the caressing kisses of her childhood. But oh, what a mingling of joy and sorrow, to meet thus after years of absence! She had come to take the last look upon the face that ever wore a smile for her, and bid the last adieu to her with whom she had been in infancy intrusted by that mother in heaven.

As this daughter left her own family ill, she was soon summoned home, leaving to other, but not less tender hands the duties she had assumed, but which were not long needed after her departure.

No one, perhaps, ever left this community whose loss was more deeply mourned than she whom her friends and acquaintances always distinguished by the endearing name of Aunt Sarah.

CHAPTER XXXVII.

It has been said that the Bellows race had no natural taste for literature. My observation leads me to a different conclusion. There are as many, proportionately, in this family who love books as in any family I have ever known. Perhaps we can number as many by this name or of this descent who have attained honor in the professions as of any family in New England. The college catalogues of Harvard, Yale, and Hanover contain the names of some twenty or more of the descendants of the old colonel,—all of them, almost without exception, sound and thorough scholars, and entering the learned professions. And to-day, as I write, it happens that three of these are Professors or Instructors at Harvard College, Cambridge: one, a distinguished Professor in the Law School; the second, a Professor of Chemistry, who is quoted as authority in Germany, as well as in America; the third, as Instructor in that branch of the college called the Lawrence Scientific School. Several others, at this very time, are at the head of well-known private institutions of learning; while many more are engaged successfully in teaching. And with these last two classes may fitly be included the names of several of the daughters of the family,—women whose scholarship and success as teachers are marked and acknowledged: one, having established and now conducting what is perhaps the most popular and admirable school for young ladies in

Boston; another was one of the first graduates with highest honors, of "The Annex," at Cambridge: she is now, as I learn, a Professor of Languages in a Female College. And of those who are not teachers, but were marked for their literary attainments, I need but mention two or three. Rev. Dr. Bellows, who was not only a pulpit orator, but an original, bold, and brilliant writer,— the author of several valuable published volumes. A discriminating critic, speaking of him, says: " Dr. Bellows' literary productions were marked by lucidity, ease, richness of imagination, beauty and force of diction. He was an artist who painted rapidly, but imparted with every stroke a degree of finish." With Dr. Bellows as a writer and author, we may name also his elder brother John, whose contributions to various magazines were always marked by grace, freshness, and an earnest tone of humanity; nor must we omit in this list Judge Henry Adams Bellows, noted for his terse, forcible, and classical style.

Judge H. A. BELLOWS.

CHAPTER XXXVIII.

As I write the name of Judge Bellows,— Cousin Harry, we always called him,— I am led to turn again to my recollections of him, which are most vivid, as connected with his boyhood and early manhood.

When old enough to attend school, his father, Maj. Joseph Bellows, was living upon the great Rockingham farm, six miles from Walpole, just above Bellows Falls, and the school there was too distant for the frail little fellow to attend during the winter season: so he was brought, with his sister Eliza and brother George, who were several years older than he, to our Uncle Abel's, who lived a short distance from the old brick schoolhouse, where so many of us received our first lessons. At this time, also, there were here two of our Uncle John's sons,— John and Hamilton,— making altogether a pretty lively household. Dear old grandmother, she could never have had such control as she secured over those wild spirits, if she had not become thoroughly versed in the ways of boyhood when bringing up her own ten sons; and we had no reason to doubt her ability to preside over this bachelor home, full as it was of boys, although she was approaching her eightieth year.

At this time, Harry, as he was called in his boyhood, was ten years of age. I can distinctly recall the little fellow, at this moment, sitting astride a long cricket that was always placed on one side of the large fireplace. He found this convenient to hold his books as well as himself; and this also was grandmother's corner, and she liked his company. He was not fidgety, but absorbed in his book, which seemed to afford him more pleasure than any play ever did. His elder brother George, who had a very different temperament, would sometimes call him lazy, when he refused to join in the frolics that were usually going on between supper and bedtime; but his gentle nature and sweet, expressive face were his shield against any serious persecution, and beside, he was sure of a powerful ally in his grandmother. It was seldom, however, that any appeal to her became necessary, for he was a favorite with all the cousins, as well as with Becky, the cook. His turnover was seldom forgotten, when she made pies; and, when she fried pancakes, it was Harry she would call to come and get the crimps. This was a name he adopted for the scrawls that would break off and fry up crispy, which he particularly liked; and, as I also had a taste for them, a lively scramble would sometimes take place for the greater share; the scene being made still more lively with Becky's shouts, who was in an agony of fear lest her floor would get spotted by the crumbs. The kitchen floor was of white oak, and her especial pride. Nothing could surpass it in whiteness, after one of her scrubbings; and woe to any child who made a track, or was so unfortunate as to spill anything upon it! such an one was sure to receive the whole vocabulary of her anathemas.

Whenever the boys wanted some indulgence that was granted only occasionally, it was always Harry who must seek permission of their uncle; they knew it was seldom he was refused, for he was as much a favorite with his uncle as with themselves; and it was only once, as far as I can remember, that he was ever rebuked. Our uncle, at that time, was suffering greatly with dyspepsia, and, after a hearty supper and a sleepless night, trifling things even would disturb his equanimity in the morning. Cyrus, the colored man, had lived there long enough to understand his duties under all circumstances; and, when he heard the early footstep overhead which had so much significance to him, he would open the sitting-room door, and say, " Boys, has the fire got a good blaze?" And then, coming in with an air of importance, to assure himself, he would add, " You know Mr. Bellows must have a good fire this cold morning, special." It was on one of these mornings that Cyrus left the fire blazing after his own idea of perfection, when Harry thought he would lay on one more dry stick, to make it still brighter; but, unfortunately, he took a green one from the wood-box, laying it on just long enough before his uncle opened the door to nearly extinguish all the brightness of the fire. Cyrus was called, to give an account of negligence; but that was more than Harry could bear; his native sense of honor and justice gave him courage, and he told his uncle that Cyrus had a good fire and that it was he who had put it out, explaining how he had done it. He was told, rather spicily, not to meddle again with Cyrus' work. After waiting a moment, the little fellow said, with all the simplicity of a child, " Uncle Abel, did your supper hurt you, last night?" It was very apparent the inquiry was perfectly understood.

It was very evident, at an early age, that Harry had no taste for life on a farm; and his father, while he lived, gave him all the opportunities possible for acquiring an education; but, before he had reached his twentieth year, his father died, materially changing the condition of the family. Harry entered the Law office of Mr. William Bradley, in Westminster, with whom he was a great favorite from childhood.

I distinctly remember the first suit he conducted, which took place before he was admitted to the bar. Somebody killed somebody's dog, and damages were demanded for the outrage. Mr. Bradley undoubtedly took the case, and gave it to Harry for the purpose of calling out his rare wit and humor. It was long before the plea of this boy-lawyer was forgotten by those who heard it, and none had a more hearty laugh than Doctor Morse and Uncle Abel when reading Thomas Fessenden's report of it, in the Bellows Falls paper.

My memories of this cousin are of his early years, before either of us had reached mature life; after which our paths widely diverged, and I was permitted to see him but once after he was crowned with the honors he so nobly won.

He had a right by inheritance to the rare qualities which he possessed. Of his father, Maj. Joseph Bellows, I have already spoken; he was not merely an accomplished military officer, but a man of force and of character, and of charming social instincts. Harry's mother was Mary Adams, of Lunenburg, daughter of old Parson Adams, who was a cousin of John Quincy Adams. She was a woman of great originality and brightness of intellect, with a peculiarly quaint way of expressing herself. Wherever Aunt Mary appeared, there were sure to be scintillations of wit, which gave flashes of light through the room. Cousin Harry, as we have mentioned, married a daughter of Uncle Si, and he preserved the old family names, by giving them to his children,— Stella, Fanny Ann, Josiah, and John; the last filling an important position in Portland, Me., as a Unitarian minister.

I cannot give a more adequate idea of the estimation in which our cousin Harry was held than the following, taken from one of the many tributes paid to him at the time of his death.

"Judge Bellows was in his seventieth year, and had been on the Supreme Bench many years, and Chief Justice the last five years.

"His death, though sudden and unexpected, could hardly have been happier, or under more propitious circumstances. It is difficult to speak with moderation of virtues as great and numerous as his. Of a calm, mild, and balanced temperament, endowed with an understanding of sound, serious, and staple strength, a heart sweet, kind, and tender, and a will firm, patient, and unwavering, he had lived a life of untiring industry, persistent devotion to duty, and unselfish discharge of all domestic, personal, and public obligation.

"Excellent as his intellectual powers were, his moral faculties were still more marked. He had the judicial qualities in perfection,— a simple sense of justice, an absolute freedom from self-seeking, a thorough candor, and a perfect fairness of spirit. Clothed in unaffected dignity, free from arrogance or pride in person and in bearing, he drew the confidence and commanded the reverence of all who knew him.

"He was as simple in life, and as ascetic in taste and habits, as if he had belonged to the earliest days of the Republic.

"Profoundly religious, and interested in liberal Christianity and in public worship, he set an example of the most unaffected devoutness, and showed the sincerity of his faith by a life of unspotted purity and exalted moral fidelity. At a time when personal nobleness does not always accompany even judicial rank, his example is of pre-eminent worth.

"Of the mingled love and reverence in which he was held by his children and personal friends, we dare not speak as our heart prompts. Suffice it to say, that no father ever left a more fragrant heritage of saintly virtues to his children, and no long life that has fallen under our observation could be truly said to be of more consistent and perfect Christian proportions." So ends this tribute to one who to the author of it was Judge Bellows, but to all the kindred was "Cousin Harry."

CHAPTER XXXIX.

THERE was another member of that family to whom we are indebted for contributing his share of honor to the name he bore. Dr. George Bellows was worthy a place by the side of his distinguished half-brother, Chief Justice Bellows. He was his senior by a number of years, and, at the commencement of his practice, he won such fame as would have honored a much older practitioner. Those who knew him best prophesied he would soon stand among the first in his profession; but the hopes of his friends and the community in which he settled were soon ended, by his sudden death, caused by hemorrhage of the lungs, brought on by exposure and overwork.

It is more than half a century since he left his earthly home, and more than sixty years have passed since I saw him; and yet, should he stand suddenly before me in the same habiliments, and all the freshness and vigor of his young life, I should need no introduction, but say, as I did on that memorable morning, "George Bellows, where did you come from? You must have dropped from above," so clearly is his image stamped on my memory. He had been attending a course of medical lectures, at Harvard College, and had just returned.

As I look upon this name, I realize that I am the only one left of all his kindred who can have any knowledge whatever of his childhood, so let me recall it. I can distinctly remember the time when we were receiving our first lessons together at school, and when we got our new Webster's "Spelling Book." How sweet the fragrance of its damp, fresh leaves, as we turned back the bright blue cover, revealing to our eyes those mystic characters printed on its first page in two straight lines, the length of the book! How often, as we trudged along hand in hand, we stopped to regale ourselves with one more sniff of the lovely odor, getting much more out of the book in this way that we could appreciate and enjoy than we did in the struggle that followed, when trying to inhale or absorb its contents.

At that period, it was not unusual to send children to school as early as three years of age. I was hardly that, and George was between four and five when he was deemed competent to take me to and from school which was but a short distance from our two homes. It was a few years later, when Uncle Joseph left Walpole and went to reside on the Rockingham farm, as I have already stated, that he brought the children — George, Eliza, and Harry — to their old home, to attend the winter school. This privilege, however, was not long granted them. Their father was taken suddenly ill and died; leaving his hopes of a happy and successful future unfulfilled, and but limited means for the education of his sons. It can easily be imagined with what difficulties these two, George and Harry, made progress in what became their chosen pursuits; but they fully verified the old adage, that where there is a will, there is a way; and the effort through which they reached such eminence as they both attained adds another laurel to their wreath of fame.

When the account of the Family Gathering, in 1854,

was printed, there were added to it a few pages, entitled "Our Recent Graves"; written, as was understood, by our Uncle Knapp. From that I make the following extract concerning the one of whom I have just been speaking: "Few family circles have in one generation more of worth, promise, and beauty to deplore than our own. Who of us can forget the scientific attainments, the natural qualifications for his profession, the charming personal attributes, the early fame, and the large promise that were prematurely buried in the grave of Dr. George Bellows, son of Joseph? Had he lived, he would have been one of the most distinguished ornaments of the medical profession, as he was already the idol of the neighborhood, and the pride of his family. His last sickness, ministered to by the love of friends, who hurried from Walpole to his bedside, cast a gloom over a wide circle of kindred, with whom his memory is still green, though nearly thirty winters have beaten on his grave. The sweet voices of his sisters, Eliza and Fanny Ann, the last of whom died in early womanhood, are also hushed, but continue to sing on in the ears that loved their heart-music."

CHAPTER XL.

In connection with this mention of Judge Bellows and of Dr. George Bellows, his brother, I may also fitly set forth more fully something which I only briefly referred to, when speaking about the character and peculiar services of our Cousin Henry, Rev. Dr. Bellows; and it is something which ought not to be omitted.

It is concerning what he did for his country and for humanity as the originator, the organizer, and the President of the United States Sanitary Commission, during the War of the Rebellion. By many persons, it is regarded as the great work of his life, beneficent and noble as had been his labors in his own profession.

I have been furnished with an account of what the commission was, by our cousin, Mr. Frederick N. Knapp, who was associated with Dr. Bellows in this work during the entire four years of the war. He says, "The plan, which Dr. Bellows designed, and so successfully carried out, was not merely a humane work, it was conceived in the spirit of patriotism and broad statesmanship. The design was, that through an organization of citizens, indorsed by Government, the arm of war should be strengthened, by protecting the soldiers from disease, and caring for the sick and wounded, through the voluntary aid and contributions of the people, additional to what Government itself might do. It aimed not to supplant, but to develop and support, the regular medical and military authorities and methods ; to stimulate the departments having the charge of food transportation, camp equipage, and drainage ; and incite them by wholesome criticism and counsel and by force of public opinion to do their utmost for the prevention of disease and needless exposure of every kind. How to accomplish this without interfering with existing machinery was the problem first to be solved.

Dr. Bellows saw the need, and thus the opportunity ; and he seized upon it without an hour's delay, and with a strong hand. Hardly had the first gun been fired at Sumter, when he summoned for council several of the leading men of New York, and laid his plan before them. He advised that they at once repair to Washington, to inform themselves, from correct sources, of what the Government could do and would do, and what might be allowed to citizens to undertake. They were convinced that, in this moment of National emergency, the provisions for meeting the relief work of a great army were entirely inadequate.

A draft was made of powers to be asked for from the Government, and on June 9, 1861, the United States Sanitary Commission was ordered by the Secretary of War, and approved by President Lincoln. They promptly elected Dr. Bellows as President of the Commission ; secured as their General Secretary and chief executive officer, Fred Law Olmsted,* acknowledged to be one of the ablest organizers, probably, in the coun-

* Dr. Bellows himself thus acknowledges his large indebtedness to Mr. Olmsted. He says: "The burden of the labor fell upon the general secretary at the head of the central office at Washington. Mr. Fred Law Olmsted occupied this post for the first two years; and it is not too much to say, that he impressed his genius upon the Commission, which had originated with others, in such a way as to make it doubtful whether without his fine power of organization, his influence with subordinates, his experience in great undertakings, and his extraordinary powers of concentrated attention upon what he undertakes, the Sanitary Commission would have survived its youth."

try; issued their appeal to the people; started their Aid Societies all over the country; engaged their corps of assistants, and then entered upon their four years' campaign.

All this was the work of but a few days, such was the impulse given it by the one who conceived and started it. Money and supplies flowed in from every town and hamlet. Dr. Bellows went to many of the great cities, far and near, East and West, month after month, and year after year, and by his eloquent appeals enlisted the masses. And, while arousing their sympathies for the soldiers, he also kindled their patriotic ardor, and nerved them for the sacrifices necessary for the continuance of the war. The value of his service in this last direction is of a kind that can never be estimated. Wherever he had been, uttering his words all afire with patriotism, the recruits for the army were more ready, and even eager, to enroll their names. Thus through his agency was the fighting force itself strengthened.

So wise and comprehensive was the plan of this Sanitary Commission, with Dr. Bellows at its head, and at its heart too, and so thorough and efficient in its working, that it secured at once the co-operation of millions of the loyal citizens at home, and reached out its help to every regiment, every hospital, and every battlefield, during the entire war. It carried succor to more than a hundred and fifty thousand sick or wounded soldiers, often finding them before the more cumbrous machinery of Government, controlled by strict, but perhaps necessary, army regulations, could be brought into service; and in numberless classes of cases of need or suffering calling for aid, for whose relief Government had made no provision. By its presence and its demands, the Sanitary Commission stimulated Government itself to care for its soldiers, and to provide for its hospitals, as otherwise it never would have done. It was an organization such as never existed before in any nation, and could exist only in a Republic. It was the hand of the citizens at home reached out to the citizen soldier in the field; or, as some one expressed it, it was "the great artery, bearing the people's love to the people's army."

And, moreover, what was of vast significance, it served to stimulate the idea of nationality, in distinction from local or State interests. It was a "United States" work; it refused to recognize any narrower lines. Whatever was placed in its hands must be for all soldiers alike, wherever there was need. Its seven thousand aid societies, representing at least seven hundred thousand earnest workers, poured in their gifts to a common storehouse; and those seven hundred thousand hearts were cemented, and the very base of the Union made more firm.

And so it is recorded by one who has written of the war with rare discrimination pointing to the time when Dr. Bellows and his associates secured the organization of the Sanitary Commission: "The wisdom and devotion of one man gained on that day, for suffering humanity, the greatest relief ever perhaps wrought out by any human organization."

Rev. Mr. Stowell, in his commemorative sermon, entitled "The Beloved High Priest," preached soon after the death of Dr. Bellows, makes special reference to his connection with the war and his work for the soldiers and for the nation. After speaking of Dr. Bel-

lows' power as a preacher, and his potent influence in
the cause of liberal Christianity, and also of his wonderful conversational powers and his unfailing cheerfulness of heart, Mr. Stowell goes on to say, " Great solid
rifts of New England granite lay beneath that playful,
sunny, and luxuriant exterior. By his splendid gifts,
he took care of the temple, that it should not fall, and
built it from the foundation to the double height. But
not for this did he neglect the buttresses of Jerusalem,
nor for this did he remain idle when armies thundered
at the gates of his beloved country. Can we who
were present ever forget the Sunday when was brought
to him the message that the firing on Sumter had
begun, and that vast congregation rose with streaming
eyes to sing our National Hymn? We remember, too,
how from week to week, as the tide of battle rolled
uncertain between the conflicting hosts, he would hurry
back to us from the field, the hospital, or camp, or
from solemn councils at Washington, with tidings of
re-assurance to our doubting hearts. Omnipresent, unremitting in toil, zealous, practical, and hopeful, then
did he reveal the fundamental stratum of his character, the ability to suffer and to do. The vast scheme
of the Sanitary Commission, inspired and organized by
him, gaining in a few months, by the skill and efficiency
of its management the unbounded confidence of the
wives and mothers whose heroes it protected; relying
upon no official patronage for support; out of the voluntary contributions of the people distributing in the
course of its existence the enormous sum of five millions in money, and fifteen millions in supplies, with no
check or serious embarrassment in its thousand-fold
operations, here is the grandest monument to his mem-

ory! Every detail and ramification of its complex machinery was familiar to him: now remonstrating with the prejudices of a conservative medical staff; now inspecting the sanitary arrangements of hospital and camp; now forwarding supplies to a proper destination; and ever and anon sending out his thrilling appeals for aid.

What an hour was that in which he returned from the Golden State of California, with her patriotic offering of over a million of dollars in his hand, which his eloquent appeals had called forth!"

On June 2, 1886, there was unveiled, with appropriate ceremonies, a bas-relief statue of Dr. Bellows, erected in All Souls' Church, New York.* It is said to be the most beautiful work of art, of this sort, in America. The unveiling was by the hands of Dr. Bellows' two little sons, Henry Whitney and Robert Peabody Bellows. This bas-relief is by Mr. Augustus St. Gaudens, acknowledged by common consent to be an artist of rarest genius. In *The American Architect*, in an article on "The Growth of Decorative Art in America," there is a description of this statue, which I propose to copy here, as it has so much which cannot fail to be of interest to all of our kindred:—

"The Unitarian congregation which worship in Dr. Bellows' former church, on Fourth Avenue, has recently proved its desire to possess a work of true art. When a memorial to its former pastor, Dr. Bellows, was proposed, it was felt that a mere inscribed tablet would be insufficient; and Mr. St. Gaudens was commissioned to design and execute something that would do all that American art could do to honor one who was not only

---

* The impression of the bas-relief which accompanies this is furnished by the courtesy of "The Century Company" of New York, in whose magazine (November, 1887) it originally appeared.

a great preacher, but a public-spirited and most happily influential citizen. In this monument, unveiled some months ago, we have, I think, the finest ecclesiastic work that one of our sculptors has yet produced, and a work which may, without fear, stand comparison with the best in any other land or of any age.

"Fine and beautiful as are Mr. St. Gaudens' works in the round, his works in relief seem to me still more remarkable and still more individual! Nowhere else is so fully shown his power over linear beauty, the charm, the supreme distinction, the grace combined with strength, the refinement and the purity of his manner. Such a bas-relief as this of Dr. Bellows is to be counted not only one of the best in quality among modern works of sculpture, but one of the rarest in kind.

"It impresses us, first of all, as a complete and beautiful work of art,— one which would excite interest and command admiration, even though we knew not whom it represented. And this is to say that, although it is a faithful, simple, and thoroughly modern-seeming piece of portraiture, it is a spiritualized, ennobled, idealistic portrait, too. I am speaking without personal memory of Dr. Bellows' features, and therefore without knowledge as to whether or no they have been reproduced with entire exactness. But it really matters very little whether they have or not. What is wanted in a work of this sort — the portrait of a public man which is to preserve his memory green with the public of coming years — is less an accurate reproduction of his features than a clearly expressed, vital conception of his character and presence,— one which will agreeably, faithfully, and effectively supplement and explain to eyes which never saw him the general portrait left in tradition and in print. And this, I am very sure, is what Mr. St. Gaudens has given us,— probably a faithful likeness in detail, certainly a faithful, typical, interesting and ennobling conception of the nature of the man.

"The figure is rather larger than life, appearing, now that it is in place on the wall, but just about life-size. The inscription and the cross upon the bronze refer to Dr. Bellows' valuable public services as President of the Sanitary Commission during the war ; and the longer inscription on the marble below bears tribute to his work within his church and to his qualities as a man.

"The architectural accessories add greatly to the beauty of the result."

The inscription beneath the statue is as follows : —

HENRY WHITNEY BELLOWS,

BORN IN BOSTON, JUNE 11, 1814; DIED IN NEW YORK, JAN. 30, 1882.

FORTY-THREE YEARS MINISTER OF THIS CHURCH,
TO WHICH HE GAVE THE NAME ALL SOULS.

A PREACHER, STRONG, FERVENT, UPLIFTING ;
A COURAGEOUS THINKER,
A PERSUASIVE ORATOR.

A PATRIOT, LOVING FREEDOM, INDIGNANT AT WRONG,
A LIFELONG PHILANTHROPIST.

PRESIDENT OF THE
UNITED STATES SANITARY COMMISSION, 1861–1878.

AN ARDENT, GENEROUS FRIEND; JOYOUS WITH THE
JOYFUL, TENDER WITH THE SORROWFUL.
A DEVOUT CHRISTIAN; TRUSTING IN GOD,
AND HOPING ALL THINGS OF MEN.

CHAPTER XLI.

AND there is another page in the nature of a supplement, which I must add. I find, on turning back, that in what I have said of General Ben, I have given but little idea of his military services, excepting by incidental reference. But I now realize that some more full account of the general as a military man would not merely show what he was, but would also illustrate the state of the town and of the country at that time, before the revolution.

I, therefore, collect here, from whatever sources I may, such records as seem reliable upon this point: some of them, and the most valuable, I find in Dr. Bellows' address, some in Aldrich's *Town History* ;* some are from private documents.

First, in regard to Col. Bellows, the founder. We are to bear in mind the fact, that at the time of the settlement of Walpole, the second French war was going on, covering nearly twenty years of Col. Benjamin Bellows' life,— 1744 to 1763, eleven of his first years in Walpole; consequently, as a leading military man, his services were constantly called into requisition. It may be mentioned, that, although New Hampshire was so sparsely settled, she furnished, according to the muster rolls, five hundred, or one-eighth of the entire land force, in that most successful expedition against the city and fortress of Cape Breton, the capture of which is said to have filled America with joy and Europe with

* *Walpole as it was, and as it is.* By George Aldrich. 1880.

astonishment. And the records also show, that, whenever soldiers were to be enrolled, Walpole was always prompt, under Col. Bellows' leadership and his son Benjamin's, to respond with her full quota of men.

And now in regard to Gen. Benjamin. In a book called *Sketches of the History of New Hampshire*, by Whiton, mention is made of Gen. Bellows, of Walpole, among "the distinguished patriots of the Revolution, and those who had influence in the public counsels of the State."

Next, let us bear in mind the fact, which Dr. Bellows emphasizes in his address, that Gen. Bellows, before and through the Revolutionary war, rose from the lowest office in the militia of the State to be a brigadier general, through his actual services to the State and country.

Although not in the field for a very considerable portion of the time, he was largely engaged in raising troops for the regular United States service, and was counted on by the General and the State Government as a dependable, prompt, and efficient man, whenever any military steps were to be taken.

Twice he marched his own regiment to Ticonderoga, first in October, 1776, for a service of twenty-five days; and again, June 28, 1777, to reinforce the garrison there when besieged by the enemy. Finally, he carried his regiment, Sept. 21, 1777, to reinforce the Northern Continental army at Saratoga, under the command of Gen. Gates, at the time when Burgoyne surrendered.

The historian says, after a battle "severe and bloody," the "victory of the Americans was complete." Gen. Gates detached strong bodies of his troops in various directions, to cut off the retreat of the enemy. Burgoyne retired by Saratoga Creek to the Hudson, at which point he was met by the New Hampshire militia, under the command of Cols. Webster, Bellows, and Morey. At this place the enemy halted, and Burgoyne observed that "it was vain to contend with the owners of the soil." Therefore he and his army laid down their arms, and surrendered themselves prisoners of war.

Some of the old soldiers from Walpole, who went with the general, used to say that the regiment captured one hundred and fifty Indians the first day of their service. Munn Hall, of Walpole, is reported to have said to Burgoyne at the surrender, "We've got you for breakfast, and we'll have Lord Cornwallis for dinner."

Gen. Gates highly complimented the regiments from Cheshire County, under Col. Ashley and Col. Bellows, for their services on this occasion. His letter runs thus : —

TICONDEROGA, Nov. 9, 1776.

Gentlemen, I return you and the officers and soldiers of the regiments under your command my thanks for the spirit and expedition both you and they have shown in marching, upon the first alarm, upwards of one hundred miles, to the support of this important pass, when threatened with an immediate attack from the enemy's army. I now dismiss you with the honor you have so well deserved. I further certify, that neither you nor any under your command have received any pay or reward from me, for your services on this occasion; that I leave to be settled by the General Congress with the convention of your State.

With great respect, I am, gentlemen,

Your most obedient, humble servant,

HORATIO GATES.

To Col. Ashley and Col. Bellows, Commanders the Regiments of Militia from the County of Cheshire, in the State of New Hampshire.

Whenever men were to be raised for the war, in any part of the North, New Hampshire, and especially Walpole, was always ready; and Gen. Bellows was the agent through whom all recruits were furnished and all payments were made.

But some consider that, in its final issues, the best military service which Gen. Bellows ever rendered was much nearer home, at Westminster, Vt., on the fourteenth of March, 1775, when he was a simple captain. And this will call to our minds what we are all now so apt entirely to forget, namely, the violent internal struggles which were going on at the very time when we had to meet foreign invasion; and the consequent value of a service of any one who could by his authority or persuasion settle any of these internal strifes.

New York claimed jurisdiction over the whole territory now called Vermont, under the charter of Charles II. Vermont resisted this jurisdiction.

Some of the people of Vermont, however, sympathized with the New York or royal claim, and of course the country was filled with civil feuds. The owners of the lands, who had bought and paid for them, were of course not willing to have the authority under which they held their titles questioned; while New York naturally relinquished very slowly the control of so fair and promising a district of country. After a great deal of exasperation and controversy, the people determined that the New York Royal Court should not be held at Westminster, at its approaching session; and, accordingly, after peaceably attempting to dissuade the judges from holding the court, and obtaining only some equivocal promises, they seized the court house (though without arms) on the afternoon of the day when the court was to be holden. The royal authorities determined to enforce their rights by arms; and, in the short struggle which ensued, William French, a young man twenty-two years of age, was shot in the court house at eleven o'clock at night, and dragged by the enraged authorities, whose blood was now up, out of the court house, with many oaths and indignities, and challenges to the people.* The Westminster folks, with their friends from neighboring towns, were terribly enraged at what they termed this massacre, and surrounded the court house all night, in serious doubt whether or not to burn it down with the whole court in it, as a fitting sacrifice to their vengeance. Gen. Bellows (then Captain) heard of the terrible excitement, hastened from across the river at Walpole, at the head of his company, to the ground, and mingling in the crowd, as the professed friend and aider of the popular cause against this royal oppression, soon so far got possession of the confidence of the mob as to convert their threatened lynch law into regular legal action. He persuaded the maddened people, who might otherwise have gone to the extremity of a general butchery of the royalists, to seize the principal men, and carry them, under his military escort, to Northampton, where the

---

* Mr. French's epitaph still stands in the burial-ground at Westminster, and runs thus:

" In memory of WILLIAM FRENCH, son to Mr. Nathaniel French, who was shot at Westminster, March ye 13th, 1775, by the hands of cruel ministerial tools of Georg ye 3d, in the corthouse, at a 11 a clock at night, in the 22d year of his age.

Here William French his body lies.
For murder his blood for vengeance cries.
King Georg the third, his Tory crew,
Tha with a bawl his head shot threw.
For Liberty and his country's Good
He lost his Life, his Dearest blood."

From Slade's Vermont State Papers.

only strong jail could be found, outside of disputed territory. This was done; and although the interference of New York procured afterwards the liberation of the prisoners, yet time was gained, and a bloody and most disastrous result averted. It has been said that the news of the massacre at Westminster, with its consequences, reaching Gen. Gage at Boston, exasperated him, as an indication of the spirit of our people, and prompted him to march to Lexington and inflict the blow which introduced the Revolutionary War and the Declaration of Independence. No event, at any rate in Gen. Bellows' life, was more important or more honorable than his pacific influence at the Westminster massacre, joined to his exercise of military authority.

The moment the news of the battle of Lexington, 19th of April, 1775, reached Walpole, Gen. Bellows, with his next brother, Col. John, hastened to the scene of action, followed by a party of thirty-five volunteers.

The town itself was among the foremost in manifesting its interest in the Revolution. The town records contain a set of spirited and patriotic instructions to Capt. Webber, sent as a representative to Exeter, in 1776. In 1778, the town voted to assume the care of the men engaged in the Continental service. It may be here mentioned, though not a military record, that Gen. Bellows was chosen President of the College of Electors in this State, for the choice of the first President of the United States, Jan. 7, 1789.

And now, before this record of Gen. Benjamin is concluded, let me give an account of his generalship, in averting what threatened to be a very serious crisis.

Early in the history of the State, in 1781, there was an active *Secession* movement, not quite equalling that of the Southern States, in 1861, but still of vital importance to the State of New Hampshire. It was Gen. Bellows, who by his wise counsel, and efficient management, was foremost, as we shall see, in crushing out this spirit of rebellion. Serious difficulty had arisen between New Hampshire and Vermont, in regard to the question of boundary. Vermont claimed jurisdiction on the east side of the river, and in some way found means to induce several of the river towns into a desertion of New Hampshire: they were either to be absorbed by Vermont, or to join with towns of eastern Vermont, and form a new "Confederacy." And Vermont went so far as to hold her courts in Charlestown just above, and Chesterfield just below, Walpole. And what was still worse, Walpole itself, after a while, seemed likely to indorse this desertion of the flag, and to be ready to go over to the enemy; thirty-four towns in all, on the New Hampshire side, joining in the movement. We can imagine the mingled grief and indignation of the general, in seeing this town of his pride, with its rich meadows and prosperous village, about to demean itself by this act! It was too much for his loyal spirit. His letters to the Governor of the State speak in guarded, yet almost wrathful language of the audacity of the Vermont authorities; and he advises and demands prompt and decisive resistance. One who has carefully read these letters, still on file, says that they are full of judgment, of mingled energy and moderation, and show the general to have been both a skilful diplomatist and a resolute and loyal man; not disposed to yield to mere majorities without protest, where right and public duty were concerned.

The present generation has no idea of the troubled state of political affairs which existed at that day, and which these early settlers had to meet, at the same time that they were struggling with all the difficulties of a frontier life. In order to show how serious was the impending danger, I will give a condensed account of one or two incidents connected with this secession movement. The official records are quite full.

In several places, people who were loyal to New Hampshire, and spoke their minds freely, but living in towns where the majority were secessionists,— in favor of going over to Vermont,— were obliged to flee from their houses, and leave their families and business, and seek shelter in neighboring towns.

In one of the seceding towns, Chesterfield, certain loyal men resisted the authority of a constable who held his commission under the Vermont government; they were arrested and lodged in jail at Charlestown (No. 4), where Vermont, as I have stated, had established a court and appointed sheriffs. Col. Enoch Hale, the sheriff of Cheshire County, loyal to New Hampshire, was sent to release these men from prison. He attempted it, but was himself arrested, and imprisoned. He obtained a parole, in order to visit Gen. Bellows at Walpole. Gen. Bellows immediately addressed a letter to President Weare, deploring the humiliating position of New Hampshire, advising him to raise a force outside of Cheshire County sufficient to maintain her authority in the western part of the State. President Weare, on the receipt of Gen. Bellows' letter, called the Committee of Safety together. They immediately issued orders to the brigadier generals of the State to call out the militia under their commands for the release of Col. Hale and others confined in Charlestown jail.

The sheriff of Vermont took measures to call out the militia of Vermont, in order to resist the New Hampshire forces. Finally, New Hampshire decided to raise an armed force of a thousand men, to be sent into Cheshire County to support civil authority. And the government issued a proclamation, requiring the revolted towns to return to their allegiance, and to subscribe within forty days an acknowledgment of the jurisdiction of the State of New Hampshire. This determined action, added to the move of New Hampshire to refer the matter to Congress, doubtless led Vermont to withdraw from her position, and the seceding towns to take the oath of allegiance. The steps which led to this result are largely to be traced to the action taken and the influence exerted by Gen. Bellows. Thus was secession put down, and Walpole and all the other towns along the Connecticut River remained in the New Hampshire union.

I shall now add to this account a copy of one of Gen. Bellows' letters, written at this time to Meshech Weare, Provincial President of the State of New Hampshire, because I think it will help us realize still more fully what troublous times those were in which that first generation — the children of the old colonel — lived.

The letter is as follows : —

"WALPOLE, Jan. 2, 1782.

Benjamin Bellows to Pres. Weare :

Sir,— I have often troubled you with a narrative of our distresses and difficulties in this part of the State. Notwithstanding, I presume you, and the rest of your Honorable Committee of Safety, will exercise your wonted indulgence, while I give account of some new difficulties, arising upon the officers attempting to convey one Samuel King, of Chesterfield, to Exeter: which rescue you will have an account of before this reaches you. Upon the return of the mob, after proper refreshments at said King's, they sought for all those persons who were in any way concerned in assisting the aforesaid officer; some of whom they got into their hands, and have abused them in a shameful and barbarous manner, by striking and kicking, and all the indignities which such a hellish pack can be guilty of; obliging them to promise and engage never to appear against the new State again. And that is not all: they swear they will extirpate all the adherents of New Hampshire, threatening to kill, burn, and destroy, the persons and property of all who oppose them. The friends of this State cannot continue at said Chesterfield with their families, but are obliged to seek an asylum in other towns, among the Hampshire people. I have two respectable inhabitants of said Chesterfield now sheltering themselves under my roof, who, I have the greatest reason to think, would be treated by them in a barbarous manner, were they in their power, as they have stove in doors and broken up houses in search of them. I am credibly informed, that there is in said Chesterfield about one hundred persons who support said King, and say they (New Hampshire) can do nothing but in a mean and underhanded way; in short, they defy all the authority and force of the State, and are determined to support and maintain their usurped authority, maugre all attempts that have or shall be made to curb or restrain their usurpations. The wrath of man and the raging of the sea are in Scripture put together, and it is He alone who can rule the latter and restrain the former.

I hope and trust the Author of Wisdom will direct the Honorable Committee to such measures as will ultimately tend to the peace and happiness of this part of the State, and especially those adherents of New Hampshire who are in a sense suffering for righteousness' sake.

    I am, with all esteem and respect,
     Your most obedient and humble servant,
       BENJAMIN BELLOWS."

CHAPTER XLII.

Just here, where I have been referring to military affairs, and the early calls to meet dangers, I may fitly insert, what I ought to have brought forward long ago, something about the exposures of the early settlers of Walpole. In order to convey an idea of the terrible apprehension under which, for many years, they lived in fear of the Indians, I will append a short letter of Col. Benjamin Bellows, written in 1754; and also the account, as it has come down to us, of the Indian fight near the fort.

The letter is addressed to Col. Bellows' brother-in-law, Col. Joseph Blanchard, who had active command of a regiment of soldiers somewhere lower down the river. It is written from Westmoreland, the town next below Walpole, where Col. Bellows had been recruiting men for the defence of the settlements, as apparently the whole country round looked to him for protection. Here is the letter.

Sir,— We have the news from Charlestown, that on Thursday morning, the 29th of this instant, the Indians came to the house of James Johnson, and broke in and took sd Johnson, his wife and three children, and a maid, and one Ebenr. Farnsworth and one Labbaree, and they suppose they have carried them all off; they have not found any of them killed. The people are in great distress all down the river, and at Keene and at Swanzey, and the few men sent will not more than supply one town, and the people can not secure their grain, nor hardly keep their garrison, etc.

BENJ. BELLOWS.

WESTMORELAND, *Aug.* 31, 1754.

P.S.— I have got no further than Westmoreland, when I wrote this; I got all the men safe there. B. B.

This foray of the savages into Charlestown, with the captivity of Mrs. Johnson — the day but one before the date of this letter — gave rise to one of the most celebrated memoirs of Indian cruelty and heroic endurance on the part of its victim, ever furnished from that sort of annals.

Col. Bellows' apprehensions were destined to be very shortly realized. Two men, by name Daniel Twichel, and Mr. Flynt, in the summer of 1755, had gone back to the hills, about a mile and a half northeast of the Fort, on what is now the Drewsville road, to procure some timber for oars. Here they were shot by the Indians; one of them was scalped, the other cut open, his heart taken out and laid in pieces upon his breast. This was the first Christian blood spilt in Walpole. The bodies were buried on the spot, which is accurately pointed out at this day.

Shortly before this, an Indian by the name of Philip had visited Kilburn's house in a friendly way, pretending to be in want of provisions. He was supplied with flints, flour, etc., and dismissed. Soon after, it was ascertained that this same Indian had visited all the settlements on the river, doubtless to procure information of the state of their defences. Gov. Shirley about this time sent information to all the forts in this region, that five hundred Indians were collecting in Canada, whose aim was the butchery and extinction of the whole white population on the river. Greatly alarmed, the sparse population, unwilling to abandon their crops, had strengthened their feeble garrisons, and bravely determined to stand by their rude, but promising homes.

Col. Benjamin Bellows had at this time about thirty men at his fort, about half a mile south of Kilburn's house, but too distant from it to give him prompt aid. About noon, on the 17th of August, 1755, Kilburn and his son John, in his eighteenth year, a man by the name of Peak and his son, were returning home to dinner from the field, when one of them discovered the red legs of the Indians among the alders, "as thick as grasshoppers." They instantly made for the house, fastened the door, and prepared for an obstinate defence. Kilburn's wife Ruth and his daughter Hetty were already in the house. In about fifteen minutes, the savages were seen crawling up the bank east of the house, and as they crossed a foot-path, one by one, one hundred and ninety-seven were counted; about the same number, it afterwards proved, had remained in ambush, near the mouth of Cold River, but joined the attacking party soon.

The savages appeared to have learned that Col. Bellows and his men were at work at his mill, about a mile east (on what is called the Blanchard Brook, near where it is crossed by the Drewsville road, it being built at that distance from the fort on account of the convenience of a water-fall), and they intended to waylay and murder them before attacking Kilburn's house. Col. Bellows and his men were now returning home, each with a bag of meal on his back, when the dogs began to growl and betray the neighborhood of an enemy. The colonel, knowing the language of the dogs and the wiles of the Indians, instantly adopted his policy. He directed his men, throwing off the meal, to crawl carefully to the rise of the land, and, on reaching the top of the bank, to spring together to their feet, give one whoop, and instantly drop into the sweet fern. This manœuvre had the desired effect to draw the Indians from their ambush. At the sound of the whoop, fancying themselves discovered, the whole body of the savages arose from the bushes in a semi-circle round the path Col. Bellows was to have followed. His men improved instantly the excellent opportunity for a shot offered by the enemy; who were so disconcerted, that, without firing a gun, they darted into the bushes and disappeared. The colonel, sensible of his unequal force, hurried his men off by the shortest cut to the fort, and prepared for its defence.

The cowardly savages had, however, no intention of coming again into the range of his guns. They determined to take their vengeance out of a weaker party, and soon after appeared on the eminence east of Kilburn's house. Here the same treacherous Philip, who had visited him and partaken his hospitality so short a time before, came forward under shelter of a tree, and summoned the little garrison to surrender. "Old John, Young John," was his cry, "I know ye; come out here. We give you good quarter." "Quarter!" vociferated old Kilburn, in a voice of thunder. "You black rascals, begone, or we'll *quarter* you!" It was a brave reply for four men to make to four hundred! Philip returned, and after a short consultation, the war-whoop rang out, as if, to use the language of an ear-witness, "all the devils in hell had been let loose." Kilburn was lucky and prudent enough to get the first fire, before the smoke of the battle perplexed his aim, and was confident he saw Philip himself fall. The fire from the little garrison was returned by a shower of balls from the savages, who rushed forward to the attack. The roof was a perfect "riddle-sieve." Some of the Indians fell at once to butchering the cattle, others to a wanton destruction of the grain, while the larger part kept up an incessant fire at the house. Meanwhile, Kilburn and his men — aye, and his women — were all busily at work. Their powder they poured into their hats for greater convenience; the women loaded the guns, of which they had several spare ones, all of them being kept hot by incessant use. As their stock of lead grew short, they suspended blankets over their heads to catch the balls of the enemy, which penetrated one side of the roof and fell short of the other. These were immediately run by these Spartan women into bullets, and, before they had time to cool, were sent back to the enemy, from whom they came. Several attempts were made to force the door, but the unerring aim of the marksmen within sent such certain death to these assailants that they soon desisted from their efforts. Most of the time the Indians kept behind logs and stumps, and avoided, as they best could, the fire of the little Gibraltar. The whole afternoon, even till sundown, the battle continued; until, as the sun set, the savages, unable to conquer so small a fortress, discouraged and baffled, forsook the ground, and, as was supposed, returned to Canada, abandoning the expedition on which they had set out. It is not unreasonable to suppose that their fatal experience here, through the matchless defence of those Walpole heroes and heroines, was instrumental in saving hundreds of the dwellers on the frontier from the horrors of an Indian massacre.

Seldom did it fall to the lot of our forefathers to win a more brilliant crown than John Kilburn earned in this glorious exploit. Peck got the only wound of his party, receiving a ball in the hip, from exposure at a port-hole, which unhappily, for lack of surgical care, caused his death on the fifth day. The Indians never again appeared in Walpole, although the war did not terminate until eight years afterwards.

I am going to insert here a story, which is found in Arnold's *History of Alstead*, because it brings before us so vividly the trials of those early settlers, and the perseverance and tender-heartedness of Gen. Bellows. It shows us how this necessity for mutual help rallied, in times of trouble, not neighbors only of the same village or hamlet, but even from all the adjoining towns; calling out thereby the best affections, and making these scattered communities into brotherhoods, such as we rarely see at the present day.

The story is as follows:. "In 1770, Jacob Cady, a child two-and-a-half years old, son of Isaac Cady, was one day missing." This was in Alstead, a town north of and adjoining Walpole, some eight or ten miles distant. "The region around was one vast wilderness, and thickly inhabited by beasts of prey. Jacob, peculiarly dear to his mother, left her one afternoon to go to his father, who was chopping in the woods at a very little distance. But, when the father returned at night, the child was missing. The anxious parents flew immediately in search of their little boy, and the more they hunted and called, as the thick darkness of night gathered around them, the more their anxiety increased and their hopes desponded. The night was spent in anxious search and awful suspense. But all their care and toil were vain. The light of morning returned, and yet their child was lost. But the day was now before them, and parental affection does not easily relinquish its object. The neighbors, though distant and few, were friendly and kind. Some immediately joined with the afflicted parents in ranging the woods, and others carried information to the neighboring towns. But the day declined, and the hopes which were for a time enkindled sunk in despondency as the darkness closed upon the light. Fires were kindled at distances from each other, suited to direct their search and attract the attention of the child, and numbers spent the night in fruitless attempts for his recovery.

"As the light of another day gilded the horizon, and invited their renewed exertions, multitudes were collected from Charlestown, Walpole, Marlow, Keene, and all the neighboring towns,— four hundred or five hundred persons in all,— to lend their assistance to make one united effort, and if possible to relieve the anxiety of these bereaved parents. Hope was again revived, and earnest expectations were entertained as the bands went forth to scour the woods, with critical and careful attention to every nook, and to every circumstance that might show signs of the lost child. In their faithful searches among the rocks, and forest trees, and fallen timber, they discovered the tracks of a child and also those of a bear, or of some wild beast very near them. Eager and trembling were the pursuers. Soon, however, all indications of discovery disappeared, and as the second day began to decline, they relinquished their object as hopeless, and many returned to the house of Mr. Cady. 'Alas!' said the mother, under the burthen of fatigue, a want of sleep, and a spirit sinking in despair, 'if I could know that the child was relieved from suffering, even by the devouring beasts, I could be still. Could I even see a fragment of his torn limbs, I would say no more. But how can I lie down to rest, not knowing but my little Jacob is wandering and starving in yonder gloom? Think of this terrible deep forest! Can a parent forget her child, or cease to look for the little wanderer? Even the sleep of night would be disturbed by the dreams of his suffering state, and the seeming cries for a mother's aid.'

"Such artless eloquence as this could not fail to move those generous feelings and noble sentiments which our fathers inherited. It was sufficient to put in lively exercise that compassion and benevolence, that spirit of enterprise and perseverance, for which they were so much distinguished.

"Gen. Benjamin Bellows and Capt. Jennison of Walpole, Capt. John Burroughs of this town,— Alstead,— Mr. Abner Bingham of Marlow, and a few others who had not left the house, immediately determined to renew the search. And even the prospect of a dark night only served to hasten their steps and nerve their weary limbs. They agreed on the following signal, and set off in the pursuit. If they should discover any signs of the child, *one gun* was to be discharged; if he should be found dead, or to have been destroyed, *two guns* were to be discharged; and, if he should be found alive, the discharge of *three* would give notice. With anxious, though enfeebled solicitude did the parents and those at the house listen to catch the first sound that might burst upon the ear from the still expanse of the south. No sooner had their eager attention begun to subside than the first signal was heard. Every countenance instantly glowed with a fluctuating crimson, which told the emotions of joy and fear that struggled alternately within. But these emotions soon gave way to deadly paleness and fearful apprehensions when the second discharge was heard. Is the child dead? was the secret inquiry of every look. Now all were breathless to hear, and were afraid they should not. But soon the third discharge broke the dreadful suspense, and burst the veil of uncertainty that hung over the scene. The change that so quickly succeeded, the joy that kindled in every breast, glowed in every countenance, and sparkled in every eye, can be more easily imagined than described. The child was found asleep east or south east of Warren's pond, and restored with peculiar satisfaction and joyful triumph to the embrace of its delighted parents by Gen. Bellows of Walpole."

CHAPTER XLIII.

WHEN looking over some relics, a day or two ago, I discovered a printed sermon, preached by Parson Fessenden, on the fourth of July, 1802. This memorable day came on the Sabbath, and he improved the opportunity to set forth his patriotic views; telling his congregation, in the language which was customary to use in that far off time, how the nation was born, raising its people to the grandeur of freedom and independence; also the importance of marking the day in some special manner that would arouse the enthusiasm of the populace, and make them understand its significance, "Ring your bells, fire your cannons, illumine your houses, display your battle-flags, that led our noble sons to victory!" There seems to have been a call for just such a sermon, for Walpole had never, up to that time, made any public demonstration on the Fourth, and I have reason to think the good parson's advice was not thrown away. I was two years old when this sermon was preached and printed, and among my earliest recollections that follow, two or three years afterward, is a table spread upon the common sufficiently long to give a place to every individual, man, woman, and child, in town. It was embowered with green branches and decorated with flowers, which served to impress it upon my memory. I could not have been quite five years old at that time, but what interested me most was my Uncle Joseph,— Maj. Jo. He was riding about with a plumed hat upon his head, and a long white roll in his hand, and wearing the badge of a colonel; other officers, his aids, were riding with him; but I think he must have been the chief marshal of the day, as his brilliant costume denoted him a superior officer. Those gilded trappings which I beheld for the first time, had so metamorphosed, my uncle that I could not be quite sure it was he, until he smiled up at the window, where I was standing with my grandmother, looking out upon the scene. These horsemen headed a long procession, a mile long it seemed to me, composed of the citizens who had listened to an oration delivered by somebody in a grove somewhere, probably the Oak Grove, which is now our cemetery; for they were marching from that direction, escorted by a military company, the band played our national air, which at that time was Hail Columbia. Yankee Doodle must have been born some time later, I think. A sumptuous dinner had been prepared, where, as I have said, ladies as well as gentlemen had seats at the table. And we have a right to suppose it was conducted in the good, old-fashioned manner of that time, when louder enthusiasm over the toasts was permissible in the presence of ladies. I think the toasts must have been an important feature on this occasion; for the story of one of them has survived all the individuals who had the opportunity of hearing it.

There was a man, then living in Walpole, by the name of Casper. He was a German; and, although he had been a resident many years, he had not learned the English language so as to speak it intelligibly. I remember he was an inexhaustible source of amusement to all who knew him. He was invariably called upon for a speech on town-meeting days, and many persons would go to hear Casper's speech who would not go to vote. His vague ideas of our institutions, and misconceptions of things in general, were simply ridiculous, and made more so by the flowery language in which he attempted to express them: and, when given in a mixture of English and German, nothing could be more laughable. His toasts, however, quite surpassed his speeches; and no opportunity was lost, when it was possible to call for one. At this dinner, on the glorious Fourth, it was said he quite outdid himself. He toasted the American Eagle that soared aloft, and everything in America that the Eagle looked down upon, or was likely to look down upon in the future of the Republic: but his imagination soared higher than the bird, poised awhile in mid-air, and then met an Icarian fall. As this toast was given mostly in his native language, the wits, who were not a few at that time, translated it to suit themselves, in varied forms of both prose and verse. And so poor Casper's toast outlived himself and all those who heard it.

This appears to have been the first public celebration of the Fourth of July, with procession, oration, and dinner, which gathered around those long tables those old worthies and sainted mothers and fair daughters of whom I have been writing.

CHAPTER XLIV.

For many years, there was but one religious society in Walpole, and Parson Leavitt was the first minister settled here; but his pastorate was of short duration. When our grandfather, Col. Benjamin Bellows, heard that Parson Leavitt had brought his slave-girl home on foot, leading her tied with a rope to his saddle, he was roused to indignation, and said, that, as he had settled that man, it now became his business to unsettle him ; and unsettle him he did, never allowing him again to enter that pulpit.

The old colonel was a man who could not tolerate tyranny or cruelty in any form, especially, as we can readily conceive, at the hands of his spiritual teacher ; and Rev. Thomas Fessenden was soon installed in Parson Leavitt's place. But whence he came I cannot tell; I only know that he spent a long life here, for he was settled in 1767, and he occupied the pulpit with a colleague when I was a child. I have heard him spoken of as an excellent scholar, a graduate of Harvard College, and far superior to the ordinary class of country ministers at that time, and decidedly in advance of the age, exhibiting a liberal and progressive spirit, entirely in accord, as we may believe, with the spirit and views of our ancestors. Many of his sermons were printed, and his volume entitled *The Science of Sanctity* was as original as its title, and quite out of the line of the writings of that period;

and, as I was recently told, it is still referred to in some theological institutions as a rich source of suggestive thought.

During his long pastorate, Parson Fessenden occupied the house standing opposite the old burying-ground. He had sons and daughters, of whom I have no knowledge save two,— Patty, and Thomas. Patty was very diminutive in size, and her features so exceedingly plain that she became a proverb. The following story was told of her, in my childhood.

There were tramps then as now, but probably not as many of them. There was one called "old Grimes," who made his periodical appearance in this town; but the people were not so much afraid of his seriously harming them as of the absurd jokes he was sure to play upon them. At one time, he went to Rev. Mr. Fessenden's, and entered a room where Patty was sitting alone. He stood gazing at her for a few moments, and then suddenly caught her up in his arms, and ran out of the house, saying he was going to bury her, for she was too handsome to live. Her screams soon brought her father from his study, and the rest of the household, who all gave hot pursuit; until, when nearly reaching the burying-ground, Grimes dropped his burden, and ran, calling to them to finish the noble work he had attempted for the benefit of the human race; for such beauties should not be permitted to transmit their features to posterity. This story was often told when I was young, but it is quite possible I am the only one now living who ever heard it. Thomas Fessenden, the son, who was also a graduate of Harvard College, was noted for his wit and humor. His paper, published at Bellows Falls, as I have already stated, was eagerly sought every week, especially by the young people, who were anxious to know what more he would find to set everybody laughing. He was not, however, distinguished for these traits alone; he inherited a clear intellect and much good sense from his father, and knew how to use it for his own advantage.

When following the course of our noble senator in Congress, bearing this same name, I have often speculated on the probability of his being a descendant of this brilliant editor, from whom, or from the father before him, he may have inherited his inspiration.

I think that I only very briefly referred to the fact, that in the early days of Parson Fessenden, and when Judge Vose, who married Col. John's eldest daughter, was in his prime, Walpole was noted as a literary centre, as well as a place of large hospitality and good-fellowship. Dr. Bellows emphasizes this fact, and makes it prominent in his account of Walpole, in which he says: A little knot of wits, then living here, attracted the gay and witty society of the whole region round: Joe Denny, Jerry Mason, Roger Vose, resided in Walpole; Royal Tyler, afterward Chief Justice of Vermont, full of wit, came from Brattleboro to join this circle, as did other noted men from Keene, on the one side, and Charlestown, N.H., on the other. Walpole lay on the main road of travel up the river; and not only were the military men led to stop here, where there were so many brother officers — as almost every Bellows was a colonel or major or captain or general — but the lawyers on their circuits made it their aim to spend at least one night at Maj. Bullard's hotel, where a rich assembly would be quickly summoned of congenial spirits. Joe Denny, before referred to, wrote here in

Walpole his "Lay Preacher," afterward appearing in the *Portfolio*, which he edited in Philadelphia. Dr. Bellows says of him, "He wrote in a style of elegance unexampled in his day, and which fully entitled him to the name of the American Addison."

CHAPTER XLV.

PARSON FESSENDEN died in 1812, when Mr. Dickinson, who had been his assistant for some years, became his successor; and his pastorate, also, ended with his life.

It would be difficult to follow the changes that have taken place in the houses of worship since that time.

A new Orthodox Church and Society was formed in 1832; and that which has since been the Unitarian Society was left in possession of the old meeting-house, which had been moved from the hill-top in 1824, where for so many years the villagers climbed the hill of difficulty to get the bread of life. When that building was moved, it took some time and a good deal of talking to decide upon its new location. The common at last received the sacred edifice; and it was used a few years longer for public worship, and then converted into a town-house, remaining as such to the present time.* May those who shall hereafter gather beneath its sheltering roof, in council for the public good, ever hear from out its venerable walls an echo of the past, when the words of wisdom, peace, and love were listened to within that sanctuary, uttered by lips that have long been silent in the grave!

In connection with the mention of the old meeting-house, I will say a word more about the early provision that was made by Col. Benjamin and his fellow-townsmen for public worship. Col. Bellows, from the very

* See Appendix; " Re-dedication of the Town Hall."

first, manifested his care of all that concerned the religious and educational interests of the new settlement.

While there were as yet only some ten or fifteen dwellings in the town, and most of these log houses, a meeting-house was commenced. But, before that time, Sunday services were held in the fort, or in its protecting shadows. At a town-meeting, it was voted that each settler be taxed seven shillings sterling, to pay for preaching; and a vote was passed, "to meet at the Fort, or near by, on the Lord's day." It was voted at the same meeting, "that Col. Bellows provide seats and other conveniences for said purpose."

It was before any meeting-house was built that the first minister, Rev. Jonathan Leavitt, was called and ordained; and one, Mr. Israel Calkins, was "voted and paid two dollars for his services in going for the ministers to attend Mr. Leavitt's ordination." In 1762, ten years after the date of the charter of the town, it was voted, " That each settler or inhabitant work four days each, or pay twelve shillings, toward setting up a frame for a meeting-house fifty-six feet in length and forty-six feet in breadth, and that Benjamin Bellows make up the rest!" This meeting-house was on Uncle Si's Hill nearly on the spot where his dwelling-house has since stood. It may be worth while to copy here, as found in the town records, the terms of Parson Leavitt's settlement, which were considered very liberal for those times, and for this small community. First, seventy-five pounds was voted as an "endowment," to start with; then "£37.10s. regular salary for the first year, to rise annually £31.5s. until it amounts to £60; there to stand until there be eighty polls; then rise 15 shillings per poll, until it amounts to £75, and there to stand so long as he shall remain pastor of the town." Benjamin Bellows was to make up whatever the town could not raise toward Mr. Leavitt's endowment and support.

In 1767, when Rev. Mr. Fessenden was settled in the place of Mr. Leavitt, whose hasty relief from duty I have mentioned, his salary was fifty pounds the first year, "half the salary to be in wheat at 4s. per bushel; rye 3s. and Indian corn at 2s.: good beef, at 2 pence per pound, and good pork at 3 pence per pound, the pork being hogs that weigh 8 score." Parson Fessenden remonstrated successfully against this form of payment, "as it would compel him to turn merchant, and divert him from his proper duties."

There are two or three items connected with the Hill Meeting-House not of much importance, but which might be of interest. The records show that there were repeated town-meetings, and warm debates as to the location, and then as to the style of the proposed new meeting-house; especially whether to have seats or square pews on the broad aisle, and whether the building should have a dome or a steeple. The records show that when the town was called upon to decide upon the color, they had the good taste, even at that early day, to paint the outside straw color. Col. John and Gen. Ben. seem to have been the forces, in the way of will and of liberal contributions, which pushed this large undertaking to completion. In the warrant for town-meeting, in 1791, is a curious article, "To see if the town will come to any method to prevent sheep lying round the new meeting-house;" and, at the same meeting, the town voted "with most ferocious unanimity," as Dr. Bellows puts it, "That Asa Gage and Nicanor Townsley take care and keep the dogs out of the meeting-house on Sabbath days, and KILL THEM!"

In connection with reference to the meeting-house, we may recall the fact, that as early as March, 1768, sixteen years only after the charter, the town voted to support three winter schools. And, in 1775, at the same time when the town voted "to pay its proportion of charge for the meeting of the Provincial Congress," it also voted to look up a lot of land for the establishment of a Grammar school. Thus, as we see, provision for the church and the school had been the old colonel's first care. He was ready to bear the whole burden himself, as is evident from the repeated votes of the town, prior to 1777, that " Col. Bellows do the rest;" but his open hand wisely waited until the self-respect of all the citizens had been secured, by demanding of them such payments, in the form of taxes, as their means would allow.

This illustrates the fact, which Mr. George Aldrich so well states in his History of Walpole. He says, "The influence of the Bellows family in the town was the natural outgrowth of their wealth and higher attainments, and was in perfect harmony with the principles of human nature. No instance is known where an abuse of the family's influence was felt."

CHAPTER XLVI.

PASSING from the old "Hill Meeting-House,"— built in 1786, with its immense timbers of white oak, some of them thirty feet long, and square hewn, fourteen inches on a side, as sound to-day as when those hardy settlers cut and framed them with such toilsome labor, — passing from this building, let us turn our eyes to some of the dwelling-houses of that day.

Of the houses built and occupied by the first generation, or their children, several are still standing firm and sound, good for another hundred years; and many of these are occupied by the direct descendants of the original owners. Thus the large house, built in 1762, by the old colonel near the fort, is held by Thomas Bellows, grandson of the settler. It stands there, as of old, with its broad acres, on an elevation which commands the rich meadows up and down the river.

The house built by Col. John, and for years filled with sons and daughters, was for the lifetime of another generation occupied by the colonel's son, Hubbard Bellows; while for many years past, until recently, it has been owned and occupied by Rev. Dr. Bellows, as his summer home, where he retreated from the city's din for rest. It is now in possession of his son, Rev. Russell N. Bellows; and, on its broad piazzas, it welcomes its guests as of old times, where they can look upon the village beneath them and the hills and mountains far away.

"UNCLE ... BELLOWS' HOUSE."

Just across the street from Col. John's house is that built by him in 1812 for his son Josiah, Si, 2d. For some fifty years after Josiah gave it up, it was owned and occupied by our Uncle and Aunt Knapp,— she a grand-daughter of the founder,— and is to-day held by their oldest son, Francis Bellows Knapp.

On the opposite hill, the old mansion house built by Uncle Si, youngest son of Col. Benjamin, is held by his grandson, John W. Hayward, who is interested in preserving the memory and transmitting the virtues of his ancestors.

On the same hill-side, looking southward, is the spacious house where Uncle Si's son, Josiah, lived; it is held still by one who bears the same name, with the well-earned title of judge prefixed.

In the centre of the village, between these houses on the hills, stands as it stood in old Parson Fessenden's day, Aunt Richardson's house, with its look of oldtime comfort; this, too, is still in the family, owned and occupied by her who was Martha Bellows, and her son Thomas Bellows Peck, named for his honored grandsire, Uncle Squire.

And here, separated only by a garden from Aunt Richardson's house, we see still standing the house of Uncle Abel Bellows, to which I have so often referred, and in which I saw so much of joy and hospitality, away back some three-quarters of a century ago. Directly across the street is the spacious dwelling where Gen. Benjamin Bellows lived; the house stanch in its timbers as the man himself was in his moral build.

The house that was owned by Col. Caleb Bellows has indeed passed into other hands; but of these grand old mansions, some of them built over a hundred years ago, six still remain, as we see, in the possession of direct descendants. These houses were all built with the idea of space and comfort and endurance, with solid masonry and heavy timbers. They had large windows for the sunlight to come in, and great, welcoming open fireplaces, and the traditional long entry, wide and high, running through the middle of the house; in some of them a similar great entry also on the second floor. The carpenter work and finish of these houses show, as has been suggested, that the mechanics employed were masters of their trade, and had the English thoroughness and patience, and the English model of building before their eyes. The immense amount of panel wainscoting in some of these old mansions tells of the time and money expended in their building.

We may mention, too, that these seven houses had each originally that ancient square roof, running up from each side toward the centre, sometimes finished with a heavy balustrade around the roof, and a large square centre section raised vertically above the rest of the roof, with small windows in it, and a balustrade finishing this also.

Such was the original style of roof; but the difficulty of keeping so many ridges in repair, and the spirit of modern improvement, (?) have removed from several of these old mansions these attractive square roofs, and substituted the barn-like roof, with its staring gable. Photograph pictures of these houses, as they now stand, I hope to be able to obtain, to be bound in with these pages. They will show, in a measure, to the present generation what the home of their grandparents were in outward appearance, though they can never tell to them, what they do to me, of the life and sunshine, the large hospitality and good cheer, the beauty, refinement, and loving hearts, the joys and the sorrows, that in times long gone found place beneath those sheltering roofs.

At the last moment it has been suggested to me to bind in with these pages pictures of such of the kindred, now gone, as had their likenesses preserved. Of these I have obtained only a few,—those nearest at hand. Had time allowed, I should gladly have inserted more. Taken as these pictures are from crayons or miniatures, they unavoidably lack the vivacity of life; but to some of us, at least, they will help to recall features with which of old we were familiar, and voices that were dear.

CHAPTER XLVII.

IN my own rambling way, by narratives, anecdotes, trivial incidents, and pictures of every-day life, as I promised to do in the beginning, have I told you, scattered along through these pages, of our founder and of his immediate descendants, and of my own impression of them. And I wish it were in my power to follow out in the various lines all the descendants,— both those who have gone, and those now living,— and thus show how rich an inheritance, in the form of true men and strong, virtuous women, those noble ancestors of ours bequeathed to the world. But this is not in my power. And if I have omitted the mention, as I doubtless have done, of individuals whom their descendants or near relatives feel ought surely to have been brought forward, I can only say, I have written of those I really knew about, or could readily obtain knowledge of. I presume I shall myself, after these pages have gone out of my hands, recall memories of others whom I shall regret not having thought of earlier. But so it is.*

---

* Even now, since I wrote that sentence, some interesting information has come in to me from the far West about one branch of the family of which I had lost all trace,— descendants of Sophia Bellows, who was a grand-daughter of that honored and much-loved man, Col. John Bellows. She married Joel H. Tracy, civil engineer; who after holding many positions of trust and honor, though advanced in years, enlisted with two of his sons at his side during the war; one of whom, Edward by name, a captain and staff-officer with Gen. Newton, fell mortally wounded in the battle of St. Marks, Florida. By the same mail, also, came to me information from Canada about certain descendants of Uncle Ben. But it is too late for me to insert all this, as all my previous pages, where these things belong, are in the hands of the printer.

I now propose, as furnishing the best possible indorsement of my estimates of the characters and the characteristics of the earliest generation, to quote for you the series of regular toasts which were prepared with discriminating care by our Uncle Knapp, referring to the ten children of the old colonel; presenting the names of the sons and daughters in the order of birth, — toasts read and responded to at the time of the family gathering, in 1854.

I. The toast-master read as follows: "Having honored the trunk, we will now call your attention to the ten principal branches of the tree.

"Abigail, the first child, the fondling of her father's heart, was beautiful and lovely, of sweet temper and engaging manners, intelligent and good.

"When at school, at Northampton, in the twentieth year of her age, she left this earthly scene and took her upward flight.

"The memory of Abigail, the first child of the founder of this town, the fairest, earliest-blown flower in Walpole, was consecrated an offering to heaven."

"II. The second child was of small size, but of a bright mind and keen wit. He loved social intercourse, and was the life of it. Abounding in humor and ingenious repartee, he delighted the young, and made the aged throw off their gravity. The spirit of avarice never got hold of him, and its meanness never degraded him. Tranquillity and freedom from care were his ruling passion."

"The memory of Peter, the first son:

"Some place their bliss in action, some in ease;
Those call it pleasure, and contentment these:"

"III. The second son commanded great respect by his personal appearance, even where the weight of his character was not known, an unaffected suavity and politeness conciliated esteem and affection. His integrity and veracity were unimpeachable. Avarice never approached him. He found greater pleasure in giving than in accumulating. His hospitality, like that of his father, was limited only by the opportunities of exercising it. His friendship was lasting. The purity of his character defied suspicion. His political views were formed under Washington influences. He was a nobleman, with republican principles. He had wisdom to aid in the councils of his country, and courage and skill to fight her battles.

"The memory of Gen. Benjamin Bellows: Nature stamped him with her imperial signet, 'to give the world assurance of a man.'"

"IV. The third son had a manly and commanding bearing. His countenance had no commonplace expression. He had a quickness of perception, soundness of judgment, and a penetrating foresight. Shrewd and calculating, his success in business was conspicuous. He accumulated safely, and in his family expended liberally. He was punctual and exact in the fulfilment of his promises, and brought others up to the same standard. The careless, lazy, or slack found with him neither sympathy nor indulgence. His determined energy was felt in whatever he engaged. His virtues and talents gained esteem, and commanded respect.

"The memory of Col. John Bellows, the third son: 'The hand of the diligent maketh rich.' 'He who causes two spears of grass to grow where only one grew before is a benefactor to mankind.'"

"V. The fourth son was a man of commanding person and dignified manners; of enlarged benevolence and humanity; much loved and confided in for his rectitude, and often referred to for the soundness of his judgment and the weight of his character. As a Revolutionary patriot, he was ardent and active. He was a faithful and tender husband, and an affectionate father. 'The elements were so kindly mixed in him' that neither malice, envy, nor ill-nature ever found even a transient entrance into his heart. He was of that sensitive temperament which belongs to a poetic love of the beauty and harmony of nature, and of great susceptibility to what is intellectually and morally sublime. It was because of this sensitive temperament that he received so great a shock from misfortune as to bring a lasting cloud over his intellectual vision.

"The memory of Col. Joseph Bellows: 'The pure in heart shall see God.'"

"VI. The second daughter was a lady of great worth. When young, she was the observed of all observers, and 'cynosure of neighboring eyes.' She was a woman of quick perceptions and clear judgment; of great cheerfulness of temper and playful wit; a thorough and practical housewife, and a delightful companion to the old and the young: for although she lived to be more than eighty years of age, her heart never lost any of its warmth or freshness. From natural temperament and religious influence, she was social, kind, benevolent, charitable in her opinions, compassionate and forgiving.

"The memory of Abigail Richardson: It lies embalmed in the hearts of all who knew her."

"VII. The fifth son was of great stature, and remarkable strength, and of an easy and kind temper. The restless spirit of ambition never possessed him, or involved him in its complicated intrigues. He never entered the list of competitors for wealth or glory.

"The memory of Theodore Bellows: The Samson of the family, who never had his locks shorn by a Delilah, or had any quarrel with Philistines, or was compelled to grind in a prison."

"VIII. The sixth son was a person extensively known, and, wherever known, loved and respected. Much employed in offices of private trust, his honesty was proverbial, his veracity was unquestionable, his judgment was never blinded nor perverted by strong passions. He was, in all matters referred to him, just as Aristides. His patriotism was not ephemeral, but a permanent principle and an unchangeable feeling. His integrity, like that of Fabricius, was incorruptible, by offers of wealth or power. As a lover of improvements, his purse was opened liberally. A friend of good institutions, he was always generous in support of them. In public offices, he commanded confidence and respect. Popularity followed him. Benevolence was the most striking trait in his character. With him, it was not only a principle, but an innate warmth of heart. The needy never carried away an empty bag from his granary. He was the friend of humanity, and the benefactor of the destitute.

"The memory of Thomas Bellows: Always a useful, exemplary, and honorable man. 'The memory of the just is blessed.'"

"IX. The third daughter was a lady of commanding person and dignified manners. Her mind had great strength and clearness. Her conversation was marked by argument and seriousness. Her courage was heroic.

She never set up new theories on the rights of women, but with readiness and fidelity performed all the duties which God and nature taught her belonged to the good wife, tender mother, and to an exemplary member of society. She lived and died an earnest and devout Christian.

"The memory of Mary Kinsley: 'Blessed are the dead that die in the Lord.'"

"X. The seventh son was a man of strong mind and inflexible integrity, liberal and just. His promise was a bond which was never forfeited. When intrusted with a secret, no one could find the key or pick the lock which secured it. He despised flippery and ostentation; was firm in his resolves, and persevering in his purposes. His house offered a generous board and a hearty welcome. The love of notoriety never allured him. Political office he never sought or desired. He lived and died a private, a useful, intelligent citizen.

"The memory of Josiah Bellows, youngest son of the Founder of Walpole: His tombstone may say,—

'What few vain marbles can:
Here lies an honest man.'"

CHAPTER XLVIII.

From time to time, in this narrative, I have referred to the Family Meeting, and made several extracts from the records and addresses. An account of that gathering obviously claims a place in my pages; and, as I cannot possibly put it into a more compact form than as it stands in the Bellows Book, so-called, I copy from that, and place it in an appendix. In the appendix will be found also the circular referred to in the account which I now give. I append that circular, because it indicates the nature of the appeal to which so many of the kindred cordially responded.

As these memories of the past were commenced with a glimpse into the dear old home of our great-grandparents, when many years of life were apparently before them, which were evidently lived in a most generous and hospitable manner, I have thought it might be interesting to his descendants to know something of the old colonel's provision for the close of his life, and for those who were to come after him. Consequently, in the Appendix, I shall make a copy of his will; and I give it to our kindred as a relic worthy of being kept in the family archives.

It is my hope to append to these narratives a genealogical table of the Bellows family. In the preparation of this, I am dependent upon the skill and kindness of our kinsman, Henry Gassett Wheelock, of New York, a grandson of Uncle Si Bellows. He is familiar as no one else is with the subject. Whether he will find time to prepare the table, I do not know ; but, if it does not appear appended to this volume, we will hope that it may soon be perfected by him, and issued on a separate sheet for those of the kindred who may apply for it.

In conclusion : Fully realizing what my readers will find in this book that may seem to them trivial, or that they do not deem essential, and how much they will fail to find which they might desire and expect to meet, I will adopt the words which a friend recently pointed out to me, as perhaps meeting my case, when I told him how I had collected my materials, and what I felt to be the defects of these pages of "Narratives." He referred, he said, to the words which formed the concluding sentence of a magazine article that he had just been reading, entitled "The Tories and Loyalists of America."

The writer declares, "On a final reading of this contribution of mine, it suggests to me some resemblance to a trunk, hastily packed for a journey, with an opportunity for selecting from a sufficiently large wardrobe, indeed ; but, when the trunk is resorted to, it is found to contain some articles far better fitted for the seclusion of a private apartment than for use in public ! and to lack many others more adaptable, but unfortunately left behind."

[APPENDIX A.]

THE CHARTER OF WALPOLE.

THE charter under which Col. Bellows obtained Walpole is as follows: —

"George II., by advice of Benning Wentworth, Governor, granted unto his loving subjects, inhabitants of New-Hampshire, and his majesty's other governments, in equal shares, whose names are entered on his grant, to be divided among them in sixty-seven equal shares, all that tract of land in said province of New-Hampshire described, etc., etc. And the same is incorporated as Walpole, and inhabitants thereof are enfranchised and declared entitled to the privileges of other towns in said province, and as soon as there shall be fifty families resident there, shall have the liberty of holding two fairs annually, and shall also have a market opened and kept one or more days in each week, as may be thought advantageous. The first meeting of said town shall be held third Wednesday of March next, (1752,) and Benj. Bellows is appointed moderator of such meeting, and to call the same.

"To hold said land upon these conditions, namely, every grantee shall, within five years, cultivate five acres of land for every fifty acres of his share, and shall continue to improve and settle the same by additional cultivation, on penalty of forfeiture of his share.

"That all white and other pine trees, fit for our royal navy, be preserved for use, and none be cut or felled without his majesty's special license, upon same forfeiture and punishment of any acts of parliament now or hereafter enacted.

"That before division of land, a tract or centre of township shall be marked in town-lots, one of which shall be allotted to each grantee, of the contents of one acre, yielding and paying therefor to us, etc., for ten years, one ear of Indian corn, annually, on first day of January, if lawfully demanded.

"Every proprietor, settler, or inhabitant shall yield and pay us, etc., yearly, after the expiration of ten years, one shilling, proclamation money, for every hundred acres he so owns, settles, or possesses, and so in proportion for greater or less tracts, which said money shall be paid to our council-chamber, or to officers appointed to receive it.

(Signed by)
"BENNING WENTWORTH.

"In testimony, etc., Feb. 13, 1752, and twenty-fifth year of George's reign. Recorded by THEODORE ATKINSON, Sec."

A plan of the town accompanies the original charter. Nine years afterward, the following entry is made (Lib. 1, Charter Records, fol. 229): "The grantees having represented that, by reason of Indian wars, it has become impracticable to comply with the conditions of the grant; the time is lengthened one year, and one year thereafter annually, until our plenary instructions shall be received. Dated March 12, 1761. First year of George III."

[APPENDIX B.]

CONCERNING "THE BELLOWS COAT OF ARMS."

The coat of arms, of which we give an engraving, is thus described: "The field or ground of the escutcheon is black, the bars interlaced are of a gold color, the chevron is blue, and bears three lions' heads (erased of the second) in gold. The crest is an arm embowed, habited, the hand proper grasping a chalice pouring water (belle eau) into a basin: Motto, Tout d'en haut."

The sentiment of this coat of arms was seized upon with rare felicity by Dr. Bellows, at the time of the dedication of the monument; and I copy here his closing paragraph, as a fitting explanation of the significance of these emblems:—

"Yonder marble monument is a fitting tribute to the worth which created from the forest so fair and rich a scene as this, — which originated a race such as has gathered around it. But a righteous Providence was beforehand with us, and had anticipated the fitting memorial of our honored ancestor. The Falls themselves,— Bellows Falls,— they are the everlasting memorial of him who chose their neighborhood for his home, and the home of his race. Everlasting,— because, while their waters continue to be replenished from the snows of distant mountains and the contributions of a thousand streams, their name is embodied in the topography and history of our country and the world. They bear his name as far as the sound of the English language is known, and will hand it down as long as it lasts. Bursting through mountain walls, and falling on rocks, they fitly typify his resolute spirit, which no obstacles could hinder, no hardships break. Beautiful waters, we have seen, is the etymological purport of our family fame. The Falls do but repeat their own praise in taking the name of their founder.

"The old crest, an arm raised to pour water from a chalice into a basin, anticipated the ornament of our Walpole Home, and the natural feature with which our family name is alone publicly associated,— Bellows Falls. Let us make that crest universal and honorable, symbolical and Christian. 'Whoso giveth a cup of cold water only, in the name of a disciple, shall in no wise lose his reward.' Type of purity, of truth, of abundance, we adopt the cup of water, taken from our Founder's Falls, as the family crest, and with it that beautiful motto, so pious and so expressive:—

'All from on high.'
(Tout d'en haut.)

"'Every good and perfect gift cometh down from above.'" God gave us our fathers; and, while the waters pour over the Great Fall of our river, we will not forget them, or Him.

[APPENDIX C.]

COPY OF THE LAST WILL OF COL. BENJAMIN BELLOWS.

In the Name of God, Amen:

I, BENJAMIN BELLOWS, of Walpole, in the County of Cheshire and State of New Hampshire, Esq., being of health of body, and of perfect mind and memory, thanks be given to God therefor, and calling to mind the mortality of my body, and knowing that it is appointed for all men once to die, do make and ordain this my last will and testament; that is to say, principally and first of all, I do give and recommend my soul into the hands of Almighty God that gave it; and my body I recommend to the earth, to be buried in a decent Christian manner, at the discretion of my executor, nothing doubting, but at the general resurrection I shall receive the same again by the mighty power of God; and as touching such worldly estate wherewith it has pleased God to bless me with in this life, I give and devise and dispose of the same in the following manner and form: and, first of all, I give and bequeath to my beloved wife, Mary Bellows, the improvement of the one third part of my now dwelling-house, and the third part of my now improved lands in Walpole, with the improvement of my barn on the east side of the road, so long as she, the said Mary, shall continue my widow. I also give to my said wife one yoke of oxen, three cows, and one horse, which she shall please to choose out of my stock; also a cart, plough, yoke, and chain, all which she is to have the improvement of during her life, these then to be returned, or the like stock, to my children; and I further give to my said wife one third part of all my household furniture, to be set off to her to dispose of as she shall think fit amongst my children as she shall see cause. I also give her a side-saddle and bridle, and fifty pounds lawful money, to be paid her when she shall call for the same; and if my said wife shall see cause to marry, then the improvement of my house and lands to return to my children, that is, willed to her, she has done with them, and in lieu thereof, to have a hundred dollars per year, paid her by my children, to be equally divided, that is, about eleven dollars each per year.

Imprimis. I give to my well-beloved son, Peter Bellows, and his children, two whole rights of land in Rockingham, in the County of Cumberland and State of New-York, containing about seven hundred acres, and is No. two and No. three in the twentieth range of lots in said town, and lies altogether as by the plan may appear, and is the rights drawn to the names of Benjamin French and Peter Bellows. I also give to him and his children six hundred acres of land in Walpole, and *lyeth* above the Great Falls on Connecticut River; said land *lyeth* in Walpole, and bounds west on said river; north on land called the Governor's farm; east on my own land, and south on land of Col. Atkinson. Also the ninth parts of all the lands I shall leave in Rockingham undisposed of, which, together with the lands I have given him by deed in Charlestown, to be the full part and portion out of my estate, with one yoke of oxen, two cows, and a horse, and one hundred pounds in cash, to be laid out to finish his house, and fifty pounds to cloathe his family.

Impr. I give and bequeath to my well-beloved son, Benjamin Bellows, four hundred acres of land in Walpole; bounded south on the town line; west on land sold to one Burt and one Fisk; north on land sold to William Smeed; east on land of Booth, Nicholas, and Maj'r Richardson, and the ninth part of what land I shall leave undisposed of in Rockingham, which, together with what I have given him by deed, and the fourth part of all my estate which may be left, not disposed of after my estate is settled and paid out all legacies ; also I give him one hundred pounds for his trouble in settling my estate ; and I further give him one yoke of oxen, two cows, and a horse.

Impr. I give to my well-beloved son, John Bellows, a certain piece of land in Walpole aforesaid, and contains about four hundred acres, be the same more or less; and it begins at the north-east corner of a hundred acre lot given him by deed, and to run north ten degrees ; east till it comes to the south line of Col. Atkinson's land ; then runs west on Col. Atkinson's land till it comes to what he has a deed of, till it comes to Connecticut River; and I further give him four hundred acres of land east of the line given heretofore, to *lye* in a square form, where he shall pitch the same, and this, with the ninth part of what land I shall leave unsold in Rockingham, with what I have heretofore given him deed of, to be his full part and share in my estate, except one yoke of oxen, two cows, and a horse, which is to be given out of my stock.

Impr. I give to my well-beloved son, Joseph Bellows, all my lands which I have in Luningburgh, that he has not heretofore a deed of ; as also what land I have in a town in New-Hampshire, called Mason, being half of a right drawn to the name of John Butterfield ; also all the land I have in the township of Rindge, which was about five hundred acres, but part of it is sold to pay taxes; also two hundred acres in the township of Fitzwilliam, as may appear drawn to me, and I further give him the ninth part of what land I shall leave undisposed of in the township of Rockingham, which, together with what he has a deed of, to be his part of my estate, except one yoke of oxen, two cows, and a horse, which I further give him out of my stock.

Impr. I give to my well-beloved daughter, Abigail Bellows, my house and land I bought of Moses Brown, on the east side of the road to Westmoreland ; as also fifty acres of the lot Denison lives on, on the south side, and about twenty-three acres adjoining, called " Mepas " lot, which land I give to her and heirs of her body for ever, not to be disposed of out of the family. Said lands contain about one hundred and thirty acres, the house, and the house Doctor Ashley lives in. I do also give to my said daughter Abigail the one third part of all my household furniture after my decease, to be kept for her till she comes to the age of twenty-one or marries; the improvement of said lands be for her use improved by my executor, till she comes to age; and I further give her the sixth part of all my personal estate that shall be left after my estate is settled; and I give her the ninth part of all my lands that I shall not dispose of in Rockingham; and I further give my daughter forty acres of land, being the land Daniel Bixby lives on, which I give to her and her heirs for ever, bounded north on land of Aaron Hodgskins; west on land of Delano; south on lands of Hinds; east on Bundy. I also give her one yoke of oxen, two cows, and a horse, and one hundred pounds in money, which is her portion of my estate.

Impr. I give to well-beloved son, Theodore Bellows, about eighty acres of meadow land and about two hundred acres of upland, lying adjoining to the land given to John Bellows, and south of his land, beginning at an oak stump in the corner of John Bellows's land fence, and runs north, as the fence runs to the river, about twenty-six rods; then runs down by the river about one hundred and fifty rods to a walnut tree, marked near the end of the ditch; then runs on the ditch; goes through the meadow to the end of the ditch; then to run east by the needle about four hundred rods to the line of John Bellows's land to a white oak tree, marked for a corner; then to run north on John Bellows's land, as the same is marked to a corner, being a white oak; then to run west on his land to the first-mentioned stump. And I also give about two hundred and forty acres to my said son Theodore, called my great pasture, bounded west on land of Col. Atkinson; south on land of Jona'n Hall; east partly on land of Babcock and the road as it is now fenced; and north on land of John Bellows; and I further give my son Theodore three hundred pounds in money, to be paid him by my executors, to help build him a house and barn, to be laid out for that use by my executors; as also the ninth part of what lands I shall leave undisposed of in Rockingham, and the fourth part of what estate shall be left, both real and personal, in Walpole, and part of my live stock, namely, one yoke of oxen, two cows, and one horse, also a cart, yoke, and chain.

Impr. I give to my beloved son, Thomas Bellows, about three hundred and fifty acres of land and meadow in Walpole aforesaid, with all the buildings thereon, being the house and land I now live on and improve, reserving to his mother the part I heretofore willed her. Said land begins at the walnut tree marked, at the river at the end of the ditch being the south-west corner of Theodore's land, and runs down the river one hundred and twenty rods to a walnut stump, with a stake and some stones about it near the lower fence; then runs east through the meadow till it comes to the meadow fence; then runs south about twenty rods as the fence stands to a corner; then runs east to a great white pine, so as to take the spring, and so to continue east by the needle till it comes to the line of John Bellows's land; then runs northerly on said John's land, as the same is marked on trees, to the south-east corner of Theodore's land; then runs west by Theodore's land to the east end of the ditch, so on the ditch to the first-mentioned corner. And I further give to my said son Thomas three hundred acres of land on the east line of said town, to begin at Col. Atkinson's corner, and run south to the end of the lots laid out, being about two hundred and sixty rods; then to run west as the lot lyeth and on Col. Atkinson's till it makes three hundred acres; and I give him the ninth part of what land I leave unsold in Rockingham, and the fourth part of the estate I shall leave undisposed of in Walpole, and I give him one yoke of oxen, two cows, and a horse, also a cart, yoke, and chain.

Impr. I give to my well-beloved daughter, Molley Bellows, about two hundred and fifty acres of land and meadow in Westminster, in the County of Cumberland and New State, so called, adjoining to Connecticut River, being the nine first meadow lots in the Governour's meadow, so called, and four fifty acre lots, being No. twenty-two, twenty-three in the first range of fifty acre lots, and No. twenty-six in the second range of fifty acres, and another fifty acre lot I had of Bildad Andrews, with all the buildings thereon, which I give to my said daughter Molley and the heirs of her body forever, not to be disposed of from them. I also give to my said daughter the one third part of all my household furniture, which I shall leave to be set off to her, and kept safe by my executors for her till she comes to the age of twenty-one or marries, and the improvement of said lands to be for her use to bring her up at the discretion of my executors, and I further give her the ninth part of all my land that I shall not dispose of in Rockingham, and one yoke of oxen, two cows, and a horse, and one hundred pounds in money, which is her part of my estate.

Impr. I give to my well-beloved son, Josiah Bellows, about four hundred acres of land and meadow in Walpole, and beginning at a walnut stump and stake and stones, being the south-west corner of Thomas Bellows's land, and runs south on the river till it comes to land of Doctr. Chase; then east on said Chase's land and runeth to the meeting-house land; thence on that and land of Mr. Sparhawk and Mr. Fessenden to the north end of his land; then runs east by said Fessenden's land to land Trotts; then on land of John Kilburn; then on land till it comes to Moses Stearns; then on land of Stearns about north-west to a road; then on said road till it comes to Thomas Bellows; then west on his land to the first mentioned corner by the river. Also a lot of land, called Jonathan Jennison's lot, being about one hundred acres, and bounded south on land of Mr. Sparhawk, west on Kilbourn's, and north on Hartwell, east on Bordman. And I give him about thirty-three acres of land in Westminster, being a house lot and three meadow lots where my potash house is. And I also give him the ninth part of what land I shall leave in Rockingham, and three hundred pounds in money, to help build him a house and barn; and I further give him the fourth part of all my lands which is not here willed, and the fourth part of my personal estate not disposed of, and one yoke of oxen, two cows, and a horse, and a cart yoke and chain.

Impr. I give to the town of Walpole one hundred acres of land in Walpole for the use of a Grammar School to be kept at the School house near where the meeting house now stands, provided the town will clear and put under improvement sixty acres of the land in six years, which improvement is to be let for the use of said school and no other use made thereof; said land to be laid out by a committee, where it is not heretofore disposed of.

Impr. I give to my daughter in law, Mary Willard, a seventy acre lot in Keene, on the east line of the town, according as the same is laid out; and I give it to her and her children born of her.

Impr. I give to my son in law, John Jennison, fifty acres of land in Walpole, north of the road to Alstead, in a good form, to be laid where he shall pitch the same between the road and Col. Atkinson's land, not before disposed of, for one of his sons.

Impr. I give to my son in law, Jonathan Jennison, a cow and heifer two years old, and what money he owes to me, to be discharged by my executors.

And my will further is, that all my lands and personal estate, if any be found after that my debts and charges be paid, be equally divided among my nine children, and the will further is, if it should please God to take any of my children out of the world before they have children of their own, then the estate I give them be equally divided between the rest of my surviving children. And I do hereby appoint my well-beloved wife, Mary Bellows, and my son, Benjamin Bellows, to be my executors to this my last will and testament. And I hereby give my executors full power to give deed to any and all persons that I have contracted with for lands; they fulfilling their contracts *precisely* and paying the same fully up, according to their bargains. And I do hereby utterly disallow and revoke and disannul all and every other former wills and testaments by me heretofore made, in any way before. Ratifying and confirming this to be my last will and testament.

In witness whereof I have hereunto set my hand and seal this twenty-third day of June, Anno Domini 1777.

Signed, pronounced and declared this my last will and testament in presence of Elisha Harding.

MARTIN ASHLEY,   B. BELLOWS. [Seal.]
JOSEPH DOUGLAS.

The foregoing will was proved in the usual form by

    THOS. SPARHAWK, J. Probate.

Recorded by ICHABOD FISHER, Redgr. Probate.

[APPENDIX D.]

CIRCULAR ADDRESSED TO THE DESCENDANTS OF COL. BENJAMIN BELLOWS.

To ———:   WALPOLE, N.H., 1853.

DEAR COUSIN,— Many of the descendants of Col. Benjamin Bellows, deeply impressed with their obligations to the father of their family, and the founder of the beautiful town, Walpole, have for many years contemplated the pleasure and duty of erecting, in connection with their relatives absent from the homestead, a monument to his worthy name, near the spot where his ashes repose. The recent consecration of the cemetery (an enlargement of the graveyard) has revived the interest of the whole town in the memories of its dead, and brought the indefinite project of a monument to its founder to a direct point in the intentions of his descendants.

At a recent meeting, held at the village-inn, where several branches of the family were represented, after a full comparison of views, a committee was appointed to procure an appropriate design, with an estimate of the expense, and to report upon the best method of obtaining the co-operation of all Col. Bellows's descendants, in the proposed tribute to his memory. The present circular embodies the results, and completes the suggestions of this committee.

A table of all the living descendants has been made; and, in reviewing their number and character, we have experienced an honest pride which every member of the race is entitled to share and to express; an honest pride which the united family, we trust, will eagerly join to make public, permanent, and inspiring, by a monumental tribute to its father and head, Col. Benjamin Bellows, who, a little more than a hundred years ago, obtained a grant of a township of land, and founded Walpole; and, for many years, struggled with eminent prudence and success with the hardships of a frontier settlement, aggravated by the fierce border-conflicts of the French and Indian wars, during which he frequently displayed the personal heroism of the distinguished partisan, and the prudent skill of a veteran commander; detecting by his sagacity the stratagems of the wily savages, and by his commanding presence and cool courage exciting their fears and defeating their attacks.

An extensive block-house on a rich meadow of the Connecticut was his fortress and dwelling, and gave to the passing stranger protection, a bountiful board, and a hearty welcome, prompted by a hospitality inborn and generous, but unostentatious.

His great and enduring energy and sound judgment enabled him to overcome every obstacle; and, by his efforts and fostering care, the infant settlement grew and flourished; and, by his example of industry, integrity, and love of good government, he implanted in it the vital principles of continued growth. He has bequeathed to his posterity an unsullied name, and a bright example of integrity, truth, and duty.

In this contemplated monument we aim at two objects,— gratitude to our ancestor, and justice to our future descendants. The character of the man forbids alike meanness and ostentation in his memorial; and we have sought to avoid both these extremes in our plan. We have no desire to present him as a national benefactor, nor our family as one of notoriety; but self-respect and an affectionate veneration for our ancestor justify and require a dignified memorial.

The design exhibits an obelisk of Italian marble, twenty feet in height, with inscriptions and emblems on the four sides, symbolical of Col. Bellows's history as a pioneer and founder. The estimated cost, including an iron fence, is fifteen hundred dollars.

It is manifestly desirable to extend the opportunity of contributing to this monument — as a privilege too sacred to be withheld — to each and every descendant of our founder. This circular is therefore sent to every known descendant of Col. Bellows. We ask a hearty, immediate response from every man, woman, and child, in the form of a contribution to the monument-fund, larger or smaller, as ability or feeling shall warrant or demand. We shall be sadly mistaken in the public-spirit, generous enterprise, and family feeling, if any apathy or difficulty is met with in securing the means for so honorable a purpose.

Any surplus in the fund may be appropriated by those present at the consecration of the monument, at which time it is proposed to have a general family gathering at the home of our ancestors.

In bonds of blood and hereditary affection,
We subscribe ourselves,
Your friends and kinsmen,

BENJAMIN BELLOWS GRANT,
A. HERBERT BELLOWS,
FREDERICK VOSE,
DAVID BUFFUM,
ISAAC F. BELLOWS,
PHILIP PECK,
FREDERICK N. KNAPP.

[APPENDIX E.]

AN ACCOUNT OF THE FAMILY MEETING.

OCT. 11, 1854.

The descendants of Col. Benjamin Bellows, the founder of Walpole, wishing to erect in the New Cemetery a monument to the virtues of their ancestor, issued, by their committee, a circular address to all the known members of the family, stating the object, and requesting their co-operation. The invitation was accepted with cheerful promptitude. The sum of $1,500 was raised. Early in October, the monument, made of Italian marble, twenty feet in height, with appropriate inscriptions, and with figures emblematic of the frontier life, beautifully sculptured, was erected by Bowker, Torrey & Co., of Boston.

On the 11th of October, the descendants came from the north, south, east, and far west, to join in consecrating, with filial veneration, this monumental memorial to their ancestor. They met in the cemetery, at the foot of the monument. The weather was delightful. The design of the meeting was announced by Benjamin Bellows Grant, Esq., the judicious, energetic, and indefatigable chairman of the committee, superintendent of the work and of subsequent arrangements.

The exercises were commenced with a devout and strikingly appropriate prayer, by the Rev. John N. Bellows, of Wilton. A short address was then made by the Rev. Dr. Henry W. Bellows, of New York; an original hymn followed; and the exercises at the cemetery were closed with an earnest prayer and benediction by the Rev. Mr. Tilden, of Walpole. The meeting then moved to the town hall, where many had already assembled. Expectation sat with ready ears and excited anticipations for the speaker, Dr. Bellows, to begin his address. He held the audience in riveted attention for three hours. The address was replete with local history, biographical sketches, amusing anecdotes, humorous allusions, and just remarks. It was delivered with those various modulations of voice, occasional playful expressions of countenance, ease and elegance for which he is distinguished.

The relatives and invited guests then passed into the lower hall, a spacious room, which was tastefully decorated with evergreens. A collation had been prepared by a committee of ladies, with skill and elegance, and with a profusion worthy of the olden days of Walpole, when its hills and meadows flowed with milk and honey. After fasting from breakfast until four o'clock, a blessing being asked, the company, with no doubtful appetites, performed their parts in a manner worthy the example of their healthy ancestors.

When the repast was finished, sentiments, speeches, and odes followed, and were continued into the evening.

From the collation, many of the company, by an invitation given to all, spent the remaining part of the evening at the house of Dr. Bellows. His spacious rooms were filled. Friends met there who had not seen one another for years. Mutual congratulations, pleasant recognitions, agreeable introductions to new connections, affectionate inquiries, and interesting reminiscences were crowded into a few hours. Some returned to their homes on the following morning. Those who remained spent the day in social calls, and in visiting the spots endeared to them by recollections of their childhood, or in hunting up the old fort and the battle-grounds of Indian warfare. Some went to view Bellows Falls; others, the old burying-ground, to find the graves of relatives and friends, and to read the tombstone annals of the early settlers,—

"Men to fortune and to fame unknown."

"Oft did the harvest to their sickle yield;
Their furrow oft the stubborn glebe has broke.
How jocund did they drive their team a-field!
How bowed the woods beneath their sturdy stroke!"

On Friday morning, nearly all those remaining from abroad left for home, much gratified with the warm welcome which they had received, and that they had visited the spot consecrated by so many tender recollections.

[APPENDIX F.]

CONCERNING "THE OLD HILL-MEETING-HOUSE."

Since writing what I did about Walpole, as it was in former days, the old meeting-house — built more than a century ago, and moved from the hill on to the common in 1820, and in which so many hundred of our family have met for worship — has been reconstructed as a town house, furnishing now one of the most admirable and spacious town halls in the State. This has been done at a cost of some ten thousand dollars, and with excellent taste and judgment; thus, as we trust, preserving those immense oak timbers for centuries to come. A short time since, nearly a thousand of the citizens were gathered to listen to the Address of Dedication by Rev. Frederick N. Knapp, which followed the Introductory Address by Josiah G. Bellows, Chairman of the Committee of Arrangements, each of these individuals being a great-grandson of Col. Bellows, the first settler. The poem written for the occasion was from the pen of Rev. Dr. Hill, whose wife was daughter of Uncle Josiah Bellows, youngest son of the old colonel.

This poem of Dr. Hill's I am going to insert here, as it expresses the feeling with which we all think of the old church, now converted into the new town hall. And I am going to make, also, a short extract from Mr. Knapp's address, where he refers to two of the ministers whom I have had occasion so often to name, Mr. Fessenden and Mr. Dickinson. The picture of them which he draws in these few lines will, I think, agree with the portraits of them which I have painted.

He says: "While thinking of the ministers who have preached in this house, one can hardly help wondering what old Parson Fessenden, settled here just 110 years ago, and Rev. Pliny Dickinson, his successor, would say, if they were to look in here to-night, and see the transformation of this building (in which together they preached for nearly three-quarters of a century), and were to listen to some of the views now advanced; and be told, too, that the dedicating service was to be closed with a grand ball and lively music! Parson Fessenden, the little man in black, arrayed in his full wig, with short-clothes neatly buckled, or else 'straight-laced' at the knee; he the man of inexhaustible wit and wisdom: Rev. Pliny Dickinson, the scholar and theologian, in more modern garb, but himself tied up in a somewhat strait-laced theology,— we cannot help wondering what they would say.

"I am a little puzzled, I confess, to know just how they would take it; but from what I have been informed of the characteristics of those two worthies, I am inclined to think that Mr. Dickinson, after a little wise, evangelical hesitation, would say, frankly and generously, 'I am glad, my friends, that the world is moving, even if, in its progress, it has left me, and my theology, a little in the rear.' And as to Parson Fessenden, I think that in his open-hearted, old-fashioned, cordial manner, and with that keen, merry twinkle of the eye, for which he was noted, he would say, 'Friends, all! I rejoice in these exercises, and in this day; and if you'll excuse my short clothes, I'll lead out a partner, and join in the dance!'

"I am not sure, you know, that he would say this; but I think he would."

POEM

WRITTEN FOR THE DEDICATION OF THE TOWN HALL AT WALPOLE, N.H., FEBRUARY, 1887, BY REV. THOMAS HILL, D.D., OF PORTLAND, ME.

"'Tis sixty years since!" Thus the wizard wrote,
   Whose magic pen entranced the human race;
'Tis sixty years since, faithful history writes,
   Since these firm timbers found this resting-place.*

Ah! could some magic touch call back the sounds
   Which, first and last, have made their fibres thrill,
With what a rapt attention we should hear,
   What mingled feelings would our bosoms thrill!

Come fancy's microphone, assist our sense;
   No old Cremona in a master's hand
Waits more obedient to pour forth its tones
   Than now these timbers wait for thy command.

Hark! first a woodland melody begins,
   Of branches rustling in a summer breeze,
While squirrels chatter, and the insects chirp,
   And birds are singing in the leafy trees.

* Built 1787. Removed to present site in 1826.

And next the woodman with remorseless axe
    Cuts short this harmony of grateful sound;
Before his sturdier blows, the sturdy oaks
    Soon yield, and, crashing, fall upon the ground.

Then what a medley of confusing noise!
    Of axe and saw; of mallet, chisel, plane;
Of nails that sink beneath the hammer's blow;
    Till in new form the timbers stand again.

Now hearken to the sound of holy psalm,
    Of fervent prayer, of argument and plea,
Made in the Master's name, that men in chains
    Of sin should look to him to set them free.

*Richly, among those pleas, re-echoes one
    Made when this house to other use was turned.
Hark! What a solemn hush came o'er the throng!
    Within their hearts what holy fervor burned.

"Praise ye the Lord!" the theme the preacher chose,
    Praise him, by loving man whom he has made!
With wondrous power upon that theme he spoke,
    At his own will his hearers' hearts he swayed.

Laughter and tears alternate filled the hall;
    With shame and high resolve each bosom swelled.
The coldest, sternest hearts were melted there;
    The giddiest mind to close attention held.

Never again such eloquence as that
    The fibres of this oaken frame may thrill;
Nor such a mingled tide of holy thought
    And holy feelings every bosom fill.

But oft hereafter, as in decades past,
    May words of kindness, words of friendly cheer,
Words of wise counsel, words of love and truth,
    Be heard within these walls for many a year!

---

* Reference is here made to an eloquent and touching sermon preached by Father Taylor, the seaman's friend, in the old Town Meeting-house, some forty-five years ago.

[APPENDIX G.]

CONCERNING THE GENEALOGICAL TABLE OF THE BELLOWS FAMILY.

The printing of the Genealogical Table, which I thought might possibly accompany this volume of "Narratives," is, to my great regret, unavoidably omitted. It is my hope, however, that it will be seen before long.

For two reasons was its printing postponed. First, the subscriptions to the book have been too limited (not yet enough to cover the cost of publication) to allow me to incur this additional expense, as this Genealogical Table would add some forty pages to the book. Secondly, although so much devoted and gratuitous labor has been given by Mr. Wheelock to the preparation of this table, the record of several branches of the family is still incomplete, persons applied to for information having failed to respond; and a full record is so desirable that, in consultation with friends, it has been thought best, before issuing it, to make a further attempt to fill the gaps. To this end, proof-sheets or copies of so much of the record as pertains to each branch of the family will be sent to representatives of that branch, with an earnest request that they exert themselves to complete their part of the family genealogy *at the earliest day possible.* If our friends could at all realize the tediousness and perplexity of the work of making out with accuracy such a table, involving even months of labor in making corrections and additions, they would, I am sure, promptly co-operate with our cousin, Mr. Wheelock. When thus filled out, the records should be mailed to Henry G. Wheelock, 66 Wall Street, New York City.

Each person wishing a copy of the pamphlet containing the completed Genealogical Table will please at once notify Mr. George H. Ellis, publisher, 141 Franklin Street, Boston, Mass. The price per copy will not exceed one dollar. It will be merely the cost of printing and issuing.

E. R. B.

www.ingramcontent.com/pod-product-compliance
Lightning Source LLC
Chambersburg PA
CBHW022115290426

44112CB00008B/678